PREEMPTIVE STRIKE

THE SECRET PLAN THAT WOULD HAVE PREVENTED THE ATTACK ON PEARL HARBOR

Alan Armstrong

Foreword by Colonel Walter J. Boyne, USAF (Ret.)

The Lyons Press
Guilford, Connecticut
An imprint of The Globe Pequot Press

To Marlene and Sarah

The Lyons Press is an imprint of The Globe Pequot Press.

10 9 8 7 6 5 4 3 2 1

Printed in the United States of America.

Library of Congress Cataloging-in-Publication Data

Armstrong, Alan, 1950–
    Preemptive strike / Alan Armstrong.
        p. cm.
    Includes bibliographical references and index.
    ISBN-13: 978-1-59228-913-4 (alk. paper)
    ISBN-10: 1-59228-913-4 (alk. paper)
1. World War, 1939–1945—United States. 2. Military planning—United States—History—20th century. 3. World War, 1939–1945—Japan. 4. Preemptive attack (Military science) 5. World War, 1939–1945—Campaigns—Pacific Area. 6. Strategy. 7. United States—History, Military—20th century. I. Title.
D769.2.A87 2006
940.54'25—dc22

These, in the day when heaven was falling,
The hour when earth's foundations fled,
Followed their mercenary calling
And took their wages and are dead.

Their shoulders held the sky suspended;
They stood, and earth's foundations stay;
What God abandoned, these defended,
And saved the sum of things for pay.

—A. E. Housman, "Epitaph on an Army of Mercenaries"

(Author's note: According to legend, A. E. Housman's poem played a role in America's decision to sponsor the covert formation of a guerrilla air corps for service in China, complete with American warplanes, pilots, and support personnel.)

208

To Jonathan
Gruber, with
best wishes,

Alan Armstrong

OCT. 18, 2006

CONTENTS

FOREWORD

It is very rare when a book offers not one but two views on the world. Alan Armstrong's book *Preemptive Strike* is a delight to read because it not only illustrates how often history repeats itself but also underlines the fact that great events are always driven by great personalities.

The events Armstrong describes in this fast-moving account occurred prior to the entrance of the United States into World War II. Throughout, he raises the question of whether or not the war might have been avoided by a preemptive strike on the Japanese homeland.

Such an act would seem impossible to anyone who lived through those days, when conservatives were of the same stripe as Idaho's Senator William E. Borah, or Montana's Representative Jeannette Rankin. Borah opposed everything that threatened to move the United States away from isolationism. He opposed intervention anywhere in the world and even fought the revision of the Neutrality Act in 1939, the narrow avenue through which aid was to be rendered to the Allies. Rankin was the first woman elected to the House of Representatives, and has the distinction, however dubious, of casting the sole votes against entering World Wars I and II. Such stories of politicians blindly putting their personal or party interests above those of the nation are perennial.

Fortunately for the United States, there were hard-working, ill-paid people prior to our entrance into World War II who saw what was coming and who worked hard to help save an America apparently determined not to defend itself. One significant group, whose work is foreshadowed in this book, included the four men who determined with great exactitude the amount of effort and the amount of sacrifice that would be required by the United States to triumph in what was already known as World War II. Those four men—Lieutenant Colonels Harold George, Kenneth Walker, and Haywood S. Hansel and Major Laurence Kuter—carved out a war plan indicating that the United States would have to increase its aircraft production from about 3,000 planes per year to 100,000 per year—and were believed.

The people of the United States have always understood the rationale of preemptive warfare, even though the United States refrained from undertaking such action until the modern era. The Japanese attack at Pearl Harbor was much maligned for its infamy, but many practical people in the military and in the public arena knew that a sucker punch is a useful tool, whether in a bar-room brawl or in war. They may have resented the impertinence of the Japanese in launching an attack against America, but they also saw that such an attack was the only way Japan could hope to win.

Armstrong also reveals that there were people of courage within and without the government who had the foresight and the daring to plan a military attack unlike any the United States had ever conducted. Had they succeeded, all of our lives might have been very different.

These courageous people represented a large and important section of both the American and the Nationalist Chinese governments. And they were insightful enough to see that the success of any really unusual military attack would depend upon those chosen to command it. Under any ordinary circumstance, the person selected to command this highly unusual military operation would not have been selected for the task: Claire Chennault had endured a difficult career in the military, loving the flying, but hating the mindset imposed upon the Army Air Corps by the "bomber boys." Ever since Billy Mitchell, the bomber had been regarded as the supreme Air Corps instrument of war—and most of the money from the ridiculously small military budget for the Air Corps had been devoted to bombers.

That being the case, there is no little irony in the fact that the leaders in Washington and in China both felt that Chennault was the man to undertake what might have been America's most important mission in World War II—a covert attack on Japan by American bombing planes flying under the Chinese flag. Had Chennault been given free rein, he might well have assembled a bombing force that could have made night attacks on the Japanese mainland. A "leaflet attack" had already been made on Japan by Chinese Martin bombers (which were similar to the American B-10B) in May of 1938.

If American leaders had possessed the courage, wisdom, and foresight to equip Chennault with the airplanes, crews, fuel, and bombs that he needed, he could certainly have launched a series of attacks that would force the Japanese militarists to recognize how basically defenseless their country was.

But it was not to be. Politics intervened, and Chennault was left to make history with the one hundred P-40s assigned to what became the American Volunteer Group—the famous Flying Tigers.

America has already forfeited one chance to learn from the mistake made by not providing Chennault with the equipment necessary for a preemptive strike. That chance was immediately available after September 11, 2001, when a preemptive strike against terrorist training bases all over the world would have been prudent and welcome. Now a second situation is looming that calls more than ever for a preemptive strike, and this is the threat of rogue states gaining and using nuclear arms. Fortunately, today the United States does not have to resort to subterfuge; it does not need a surrogate, as China would have been, to cloak its execution of a needed military task. It has instead a brilliant military organization, one that could execute a preemptive strike with skill and daring. There might be some in the world who would grumble, but there would be no one to question whether the United States meant business.

There are powerful lessons to be learned in Armstrong's book, and the most important of these is the cost of not exercising the capability to strike in advance of need. Had things eventuated as Armstrong suggests they might, all the casualties of Pearl Harbor, Wake, Guam, the Philippines, Guadalcanal, and elsewhere might have been avoided by a chastened, awakened Japan. America must recognize that at no time before or during World War II could Japan or Germany hurt the United States as much as terrorists and rogue states are now capable of doing. To avoid the catastrophic consequences of a terrorist or rogue-state nuclear attack, the United States should call on its current leaders to strike as soon and as powerfully as necessary. You can be sure that both Franklin Delano Roosevelt and Claire Chennault would approve.

—Colonel Walter J. Boyne , USAF (Ret.)
Ashburn, Virginia
April 11, 2006

PREFACE

The Japanese attack on Pearl Harbor, America's most humiliating military defeat, need not have happened. America's defeat in the Philippines and the Bataan Death March need not have happened. The American surrender at Wake Island need not have happened. With respect to the outbreak of the war between America and Japan, America's historical memory maintained that while America was at peace with Japan, Japan suddenly and deliberately attacked America at Pearl Harbor, without warning.

In reality, on July 23, 1941, President Roosevelt endorsed a Joint Board Plan that called for a campaign of air warfare against Japan, which included as its fourth strategic objective the "[d]estruction of Japanese factories in order to cripple production of munitions and essential articles for maintenance of economic structure in Japan." America's timely implementation and execution of Joint Army/Navy Board 355, Serial 691 ("the Joint Board Plan" or "the Plan") would have preempted Japanese aggression in Southeast Asia and the Pacific, and changed the course of history.

The first strategic objective of the Plan was to "Force diversion of considerable portion of available Japanese air force to defense of Japanese establishments on south China coast and in Japan to counter offensive operations in interior of China." The authors of the Plan correctly theorized that if Japan were occupied with a more powerful China, complete with an American "guerrilla air force," Japan would lack the military resources to initiate operations against American facilities, like those in the Philippines, on Wake and Midway Islands, and at Pearl Harbor, in Hawaii. An American guerrilla air force engaged in bombing Japanese interests would have forced Japan to "make necessary heavy reinforcement of Japanese troops in China," the second strategic objective of the Plan.

Finally, with the imposition of an American trade embargo on the sale of aviation fuel to Japan—following a Japanese initiative that forced the closure of the Yunnan railway on July 16, 1940—American war planners considered it likely that Japan would strike southward, to the oil-rich Dutch East Indies. This explains the third strategic objective, which called for the "[d]estruction of Japanese supplies and supply ships in order to handicap operations of an expeditionary force to the south of Indo-China." If large numbers of Japanese troops were to be assembled in China for a southern expedition into Malaya, the Dutch East Indies, and the Philippines, then an American guerrilla air force operating bombers in China would have bombed the troopships before they left port. For these reasons, the Joint Board Plan was intended to *preempt* Japanese military initiatives in Southeast Asia and the Pacific.

America's historical memory about the events that led up to the attack on Pearl Harbor ignores the Chinese-American bombing initiative sponsored by the Roosevelt administration. It further overlooks the fact that a plan was in place to prevent America's humiliating defeats at Pearl Harbor and in the Philippines.

In early February 1941, Rear Admiral Takijiro Onishi had asked Japanese commander Minoru Genda to formulate a plan for a preemptive strike against the American Pacific Fleet anchored at Pearl Harbor. Onishi's initiative resulted from a request by Admiral Isoroku Yamamoto, commander of the Japanese Combined Fleet, for a plan to deal a preemptive blow to the American Pacific Fleet anchored at Pearl Harbor. Genda was the perfect officer for the assignment. He had served as a Japanese naval attaché in London when antiquated Royal Air Force biplanes, flying from a British aircraft carrier, sank three Italian battleships in the shallow waters of Taranto Harbor. In fact, Genda had traveled to Taranto specifically to study how the British had conducted their surprise air attack. Genda's planning and preparations culminated in the catastrophic destruction of ships, planes, and military installations, with the resulting substantial loss of American lives, on Sunday morning, December 7, 1941.

However, Japan was not the only country that had been evaluating the feasibility of a preemptive strike prior to the attack on Pearl Harbor. Before Genda was asked to formulate his plan, members of President Roosevelt's cabinet were entertaining a proposal to launch bombing raids on Japanese military installations, ships, and the Japanese home islands. The architect of the American plan was not a member of the United States Armed Forces. He was a retired Air Corps captain in the employ of a foreign warlord, Generalissimo Chiang Kai-shek. His name was Claire Lee Chennault.

President Roosevelt, members of his cabinet and the American military, and the government of China had been discussing air attacks on Japanese interests since November of 1940.[1] These discussions involved a request from the Chinese government for the provision by America of B-17 Flying Fortresses and American crews that would operate from secret air bases in eastern China, positioned to bomb the Japanese home islands. Although initially tabled at the request of General George C. Marshall, the plan was resurrected in the spring of 1941, long before the Japanese attack on Pearl Harbor in Hawaii.

This book will explore the actions and circumstances of the individuals participating in these activities. The planning of this "preemptive strike" illustrates American democracy at work. It also demonstrates how public opinion often constrains the actions of the American government, with both positive and negative results. Finally, the administration's efforts to curtail Japanese aggression in China reveal the humanity of those who served in positions of public trust. They tried to make correct moral choices at a time when the mood of America was, to a considerable degree, isolationist.

How did the American government become involved in the formation of a mercenary air force in China?

How did Chennault develop his plan to mount bombing raids on Japanese interests, using American planes and airmen—ostensibly as agents of the government of China?

What were the legal and political impediments to the implementation of Chennault's plan?

Who supported the plan, and who opposed it?

How much did the Japanese know about American ambitions to bomb Japan before the attack on Pearl Harbor?

How did the formation of the American Volunteer Group, training in Burma for combat in China, and the American initiative to bomb Japan from bases in southeastern China and the Philippines ultimately prompt the Japanese attack on Pearl Harbor?

What lessons can America learn from her failure to mount preemptive bombing raids on Japan before the attack on Pearl Harbor and other U.S. military installations?

How has American foreign policy changed in the decades following the attack on Pearl Harbor?

This book will answer these and other questions surrounding the activities of the American government, Claire Chennault, and his confederates, who were officially called the "American Volunteer Group" (or AVG), but are better known in the annals of history as the "Flying Tigers."

These rugged aviators, individualists, and adventurers provided America with a ray of light during the darkest months of World War II, when they inflicted substantial losses on Japanese air units in aerial combat over Burma, Thailand, and China, with minimal losses to their own unit. Their exploits are woven into the fabric of American folklore and hearken back to a time when men did "the right thing" to save a nation in distress, despite a host of laws and regulations designed to obstruct and deter such unorthodox and controversial initiatives. Most of those warriors are gone now. This text may present the reader with some insights into Chennault and the Flying Tigers that have not appeared elsewhere. A review and discussion of the murky political origins of the Flying Tigers should in no way detract from the heroic acts of these soldiers of fortune and their leader. Rather, these and other facts revealed in this text should make their story all the more compelling.

The author has attempted to uncover and illuminate the truth about the Joint Board Plan, an obscure and overlooked chapter in American history. Readers with a keen interest in the historical documents and records supporting the facts and conclusions contained in this book may consult the appendices and bibliography that follow the text.

ACKNOWLEDGMENTS

The author wishes to express appreciation to persons and organizations that provided materials or assistance needed in the preparation of this work. Thanks are in order to Tom McCarthy and Holly Rubino at The Lyons Press, for their interest and assistance in bringing my manuscript to publication. A word of thanks is also in order to Richard L. Dunn, Lt. Colonel, USAF (Ret.); Thomas B. "Skipper" Steely; Stanley F. Bloyer, Captain, U.S. Navy (Ret.); Rick Wolf (son of AVG pilot, Fritz Wolf); B. J. (Bernie) Dvorscak (former test pilot for Lockheed-Georgia Company); Robert Ormsby Jr. (former president of Lockheed-Georgia Company); and AVG Crew Chief Frank Losonsky, who reviewed and commented on my manuscript. Richard L. Dunn unselfishly provided Japanese radio intercepts, information on the provision of American combat aircraft to China, reports of the American Naval Attaché and Assistant Naval Attaché for Air concerning the American Mission to China in May and June of 1941, data concerning aviation fuel supplies in China, Chinese airfield construction, and a host of other materials relevant to the American, Chinese, and British bombing initiative directed toward Japan. Thomas B. "Skipper" Steely graciously reviewed and made suggestions for the improvement of the manuscript.

Robert Parks, historian at the Roosevelt Presidential Library, provided invaluable assistance in locating materials essential to this work. Hill Goodspeed, historian at the National Museum of Naval Aviation, provided the U.S. Navy American Volunteer Group Papers (the "Pensacola Papers") on a CD-ROM, the information having been collected by Jackie Bowles, who passed away before this book was published. The U.S. Air Force Historical Research Agency provided a copy of General Claire Chennault's thesis, The Role of Defensive Pursuit. The Hoover Institution provided a copy of the American Volunteer Group Official War Diary (December 17, 1941, through July 19, 1942). Thomas Kimmel (grandson of Admiral Husband E. Kimmel) provided decoded intercepts of Japanese diplomatic (Purple Code) messages.

James W. Zobel, archivist at the General Douglas MacArthur Foundation, provided a copy of the memorandum from British General Headquarters in the Far East dated September 19, 1941, entitled: "The Problem of Defeating Japan—Review of the Situation." Peggy Dillard, assistant archivist at the George C. Marshall Foundation, provided a copy of General Marshall's letter to Hanson Baldwin, military correspondent for the *New York Times*, dated September 21, 1949.

Tab Lewis, archivist at the National Archives and Records Administration, provided minutes from the April 1941 meeting of the Steering Committee of the Export Control Commodity Division of the U.S. Department of Commerce, when the group discussed bombing of targets in Japan.

Ronald M. Bulatoff, archival specialist at the Hoover Institution, provided copies of correspondence between Claire Chennault and Dr. Lauchlin Currie. He also provided evidence that the Air Ministry of Great Britain, in conjunction with William Pawley, was developing a program to send volunteers from the United Kingdom to fly and fight for China. Finally, Mr. Bulatoff provided correspondence of Stanley K. Hornbeck in the U.S. State Department dealing with reports from the Korean underground of Japan's plans to attack Pearl Harbor.

AVG pilot, David Lee "Tex" Hill, General, USAF (Ret.), Mrs. Rosemary Chennault Simrall (General Chennault's daughter), Robert Ormsby Jr., and Daniel Fischer provided telephone interviews. Bert Kinzey and Richard L. Dunn provided information on the production of Boeing B-17 bombers. Tom Pandolfi provided the author with the initial copies of the Pensacola Papers and also made his collection of AVG photographs available. Mrs. Edna Chennault, wife of the late Max Chennault (one of General Chennault's sons), allowed the author to copy the family album, which contained newspaper articles regarding Chennault's activities during the Sino-Japanese War as well as photographs of Chennault. The Flying Tigers Association graciously allowed the reproduction of its photographs in this work, as did Shiela Bishop Irwin (daughter of AVG Pilot Lewis Sherman Bishop). The provision of these photographs is greatly appreciated.

Air Classics, a division of Challenge Publications, Inc. allowed the author to publish the photograph of the first Curtiss-Wright Hawk Model 75H prototype sold to China and flown by Claire Lee Chennault.

Jeff Brein (screenwriter), Bill Wages (director and director of photography), Phillip Bellury (screenwriter), Corkey Fornof (motion picture pilot), Tony Bill (film producer and director), and Andrew Velcoff, Esq. (entertainment lawyer) have been supportive of my work on this project.

Mrs. Kathy Orr and Ms. Mary Severson have typed, edited, and revised this manuscript with devotion and diligence.

To the host of other people who have helped the author along the way in the development of this book, thank you all for your kind assistance with this project.

Chapter One

"LADIES AND GENTLEMEN— THE THREE MEN ON THE FLYING TRAPEZE!"

The 1935 All-American Air Races

> *The trio gave its final performance at the Miami All-American Air Races in December, 1935. Their "section roll" [where the planes revolved around the leader, while all three planes retained their relative positions] brought cheers from the crowd and won them the trophy for group acrobatic flying.*
>
> —Martha Byrd, *Chennault: Giving Wings to the Tiger* [2]

Above the clear blue sky in Miami, three P-12 pursuit aircraft cavorted over the airfield while the announcer introduced the next performance: "Ladies and gentlemen—the three men on the flying trapeze!" The center and lead aircraft in the three-ship formation was flown by Captain Claire Lee Chennault, an instructor in fighter tactics stationed at Maxwell Air Base, just outside of Montgomery, Alabama. On his left wing was Lieutenant Billy McDonald, and on his right wing was Lieutenant Luke Williamson. The open-cockpit fighter planes flew in precise formation, amazing the audience with their tricks. They performed loops, Immelman turns, snap rolls, and Cuban Eight maneuvers with a level of skill and precision unequaled by any other aerial exhibition team. Colonel Mow Pang Tsu of the Chinese Air Force was in the audience, as well as William Pawley, president of the Central Aircraft Manufacturing Company (CAMCO), a sales representative of

Curtiss-Wright Aircraft Corporation in Buffalo, New York. Colonel Mow's presence at the 1935 All-American Air Races at Miami was no accident. He was there to recruit instructors for the Chinese Air Force.[3]

Shifting to an echelon-right formation, the aircraft broke sharply to the left over the runway, making continuous descending left turns and touching down with minimum airspeed, right at the airfield's threshold. The aircraft taxied in, in unison. The wingmen stopped their planes' engines on Chennault's signal. Chennault, McDonald, and Williamson exited their aircraft to enthusiastic applause. The spectators at this renowned event were dazzled by the performance of these three dashing airmen. The pilots made their way to the announcer's podium, where they received the trophy for group acrobatic flying. More than two and a half feet tall, the trophy featured an airplane mounted atop a globe, and was, effectively, a going-away present to the Air Corps demonstration team, since this was its last performance. Standing about five-foot-nine with a muscular build and leathery complexion, Chennault was an imposing figure in spite of his soft Louisiana drawl.[4] In contrast to Chennault's quiet intensity, his wingmen appeared more affable in their demeanor during the ceremony.

Following the presentation of the trophy, the three fliers were approached by Colonel Mow. When he invited them to join him on William Pawley's yacht, anchored in Miami Harbor, Chennault and his wingmen accepted.

That evening, Colonel Mow talked to Chennault, Williamson, and McDonald about China's plight. Manchuria had been occupied by the Japanese for over four years. The head of the Nationalist government, Generalissimo Chiang Kai-shek, was convinced Japan had designs to the south and would move to occupy Chinese coastal cities, including Shanghai. Colonel Mow explained that the Chinese Air Force (CAF) was still in its infancy, Chinese pilots having received their training beginning in 1932. Retired Air Corps colonel Jack Jouett was in charge of their instruction, assisted by a cadre of American flight instructors, including Harvey Greenlaw. Despite having graduated from West Point, Greenlaw had a fairly undistinguished career in the Air Corps, where he had served with Chennault prior to his retirement.

Pressing to make his point, Colonel Mow promised Chennault and his wingmen that as instructors in the CAF, they would earn salaries substantially higher than anything they could ever have expected to earn in the

Air Corps. For example, while Chennault may have earned $250 to $350 per month in the Air Corps, he could expect a salary of $1,000 per month from the Chinese.

McDonald and Williamson were receptive to the solicitation. Although they were allowed to wear the insignia of a lieutenant, in fact, both men held the permanent rank of sergeant. Their repeated requests for commissions in the Air Corps had been denied. Chennault had recognized their value to the Air Corps, but his requests for commissions for these fine fliers had also been ignored.

McDonald and Williamson were not the only Air Corps pilots who were dissatisfied with their careers. Although publicly applauded for his achievements in leading the aerial demonstration team, Chennault was derided by his contemporaries at the Air Corps Tactical School (ACTS) because of his belief in fighter planes. Chennault, a pragmatist and independent thinker, had the temerity to reject an Air Corps orthodoxy that focused almost exclusively on "bomber supremacy" and the erroneous belief that bombers were virtually immune from fighter interception. However, in 1935, most of the Air Corps leadership believed in the dogma espoused by General Billy Mitchell, along with the Italian general, Giulio Douhet: Bombers, not fighter planes, would decide the outcome of future wars. It was believed that giant bomber planes, bristling with machine guns, could roam the skies, level entire cities in a single bombing mission, and somehow remain immune from fighter attacks while doing so.

In 1921, General Mitchell had participated in military exercises with the navy[5], which insisted that as Mitchell's bombers attacked the *Ostfriesland*, a captured German battleship, only one bomb should be dropped at a time. This would enable them to evaluate the damage inflicted by each bomb. However, as Mitchell's bombers appeared overhead, sixty-seven 2,000-pound bombs were dropped in rapid succession, contrary to Mitchell's agreement with the navy. There were sixteen direct hits and three near misses. After the ship sank, the American press declared the "death of the dreadnoughts."[6] At the time, "dreadnought" was the fashionable name for battleship; the press had correctly concluded the destructive power of airplanes signaled the end of the battleship as the principal weapon to project power abroad. Airplanes, not battleships, would determine the course of future wars. It appears Mitchell saw nothing wrong with bending the rules if the result would advance his theories on the supremacy of airpower, as well as his own career.

Later, Mitchell would accuse army and navy leaders of "almost trea-sonable administration of the national defense."[7] He was court-martialed for insubordination and subsequently resigned from the army in 1926. However, Mitchell's protégé, Henry H. ("Hap") Arnold, later rose to power as chief of the Army Air Corps. There can be no doubt that Arnold, like Mitchell, believed the heavy bomber was the weapon of choice with which to achieve victory in future wars. Regardless of Mitchell's ignoring the rules of the exercise in sinking the *Ostfriesland*, by 1935, Mitchell's dogma had become Air Corps doctrine, and anyone who did not subscribe to it was considered a heretic.

Chennault was thus branded. He was seen as a maverick, out of step with the conventional wisdom that dominated strategic thinking in the Air Corps. Chennault believed unescorted bombers were vulnerable to being intercepted and destroyed by defending fighters, especially if the fighter pilots knew the location of the bombers from radio reports or in-structions. Before the advent of radar, Chennault had experimented with a radio-telephone network which demonstrated his theories were sound. Chennault's theories and principles of air interception were generally ig-nored by the officers in charge of the Air Corps. He had studied the tac-tics that evolved from combat in the Great War and had read the writings of the great German ace, Oswald Boelcke. Boelcke, an ace and commander of an elite German fighter unit in the First World War, had written and formulated "Boelcke's Dicta," the first rules concerning fighter tactics. Chennault believed that fighter planes—equipped with radios that drew information from a spiderweb of ground communica-tion facilities—could be in a position to strike the bombers with a sur-prise attack, from a superior altitude. Chennault maintained that fast-climbing interceptors would carry the day, and ultimately deprive the bombers of access to their targets. Alternately, he theorized that even if the bombers *did* get through, the unescorted bomber formations would sustain substantial losses from enemy fighter planes, making day-light raids impractical.

Yes, Chennault was tempted by Colonel Mow's invitation. In fact, his immediate response to Colonel Mow's offer to serve the CAF was "yes."[8] Despite the public acclaim he received at air shows, his life in the Air Corps was not a happy one. He had argued for his beliefs—unsuccess-fully—for years. When General Hap Arnold heard of the arguments ad-vanced by Chennault in his thesis, The Role of Defensive Pursuit,[9]

Arnold rebuked Chennault and his theories with the pejorative remark: "Who is this damned fellow Chennault?"

Chennault had more to consider than just his abysmal career with the Air Corps. He had a wife and seven children who counted on him for support. Although he was an acting major, he held the retirement rank of captain and knew his prospects for advancement in the Air Corps were not bright. Ultimately, despite Mow's lucrative offer, Chennault could not bring himself to leave America and his family. The next day, Chennault regretfully told Mow he could not accept the offer. However, Mow, McDonald, and Williamson had struck a deal. Chennault's wingmen bought up their contracts with the Air Corps and made plans to sail for China aboard the *Empress of Russia* in the early summer of 1936, leaving Chennault behind.

After turning down Mow's offer, Chennault continued to work tirelessly at the Air Corps Tactical School, fighting to keep the course on pursuit aviation as part of the curriculum even as the bomber proponents advocated that it be dropped.[10] In fact, between 1935 and 1936, he wrote three articles warning of the need to confront impending danger based on: 1) the Italian invasion of Ethiopia; 2) the Spanish Civil War, where he felt the Luftwaffe (the German air force) and the Russian air force were engaged in a dress rehearsal for World War II; and 3) Japan's military exploits in Manchuria.[11]

Following his final air show performance in December of 1935, Chennault suffered from flu, bronchitis, and low blood pressure.[12] At age forty-seven, he was exhausted and depressed. He had come to realize that the system would continue to demand that he take orders from men who knew far less than he did about fighter tactics. This angered him, and he began to consider retirement. The only problem was, he did not know what he would do next. Chennault had worked as a farmer after World War I, before Congress had appropriated additional funding for the military. He had discovered this was not to his liking, and felt fortunate when he was able to return to the Air Corps. The prospect of going back to his farm in Louisiana and once again grubbing cotton did not appeal to Chennault.

On July 20, 1936, the Chinese Commission on Aeronautical Affairs provided a more appealing opportunity for Chennault when they offered him complete control of advanced pursuit training in the CAF. His would be the deciding vote when choosing what kind of fighter planes would be purchased by the CAF. He would draw up the training manuals and tactical directives concerning the operation of the CAF. He would enjoy the cooperation of the Chinese government in developing an aircraft warning system. His transportation expenses to and from China would be paid, and he would receive $12,000 per year as air defense advisor to the Chinese Aeronautical Commission. China had upped the ante with the new offer to Chennault. Service in China might well afford him the very thing the Air Corps had refused, an environment in which to prove the validity of his theories on air combat.

Nominally, his employer would be the Bank of China, to preclude any violation of the American Neutrality Law. Dr. T. V. Soong, brother of Madame Chiang, was in charge of the bank and other Chinese interests, such as the Universal Trading Corporation (UTC), which used American credit to buy supplies in the United States. (Dr. Soong—and his lobbying efforts as a special envoy from China—will be explored later in Chapter 3 of this text.) In the event of his death in the service of China, Chennault's family would receive one year's salary.[13] China also offered Chennault an option to develop and train an air force in the event he was forced to retire from the Air Corps.

Chennault possessed an aggressive and ambitious character. He had been raised in the austere environment of Franklin Parish in Louisiana. A strong will to survive and prevail was one of the attributes he acquired from his father, who raised him after the death of his mother. Chennault had learned to be an effective fighter in physical confrontations with other men and had mastered the use of firearms. He had come to accept the inevitability of struggling for the things he desired in life. Even learning how to fly had been a struggle when an instructor tried to wash him out of flight training. Chennault's character was shaped by a harsh and adverse environment, both before and during his military career. One can only imagine the personal struggle Chennault grappled with as he weighed the option to prove his theories in China versus his family's interest in remaining in the States. However, if he were forced to leave the Air Corps, it seemed that employment in China would provide him with the best option to prove himself and his theories, something he must have longed for after years of criticism and rejection in the Air Corps.

Chennault had a lot to think about.

CHENNAULT'S DARKEST HOUR

Chennault had flown in open-cockpit airplanes for nearly two thousand hours over a period of twenty years, and by 1936, he was virtually deaf. The Air Corps had allowed him to fly on a medical waiver for years. During the summer of 1936, after the initial offer from Mow, he was reassigned from his position as an instructor at the Tactical School, becoming the executive officer of a fighter group at Barksdale Air Corps Base in Louisiana. It was during this time that China upped the ante with the more appealing offer.

However, by September of 1936, he had been sent to the General Hospital in Hot Springs, Arkansas. This was the first in a series of hospitalizations throughout the winter of 1936–37 for exhaustion and what might today be called a nervous breakdown. Finally, the retirement board met on February 25, 1937, when it was recommended that Chennault retire. The long years of stress from teaching, arguing, and flying had caught up with the old warrior. Accepting the board's recommendation, Chennault wrote to his brother: ". . . both the Army and Air Corps have unmistakably indicated that they each, jointly and severally, could muddle along without my advice and services. While I sincerely believe that the time may come when they will regret our separation, I feel that both pride and honor urge me to cooperate fully in assuring that separation at present."[14]

As Chennault accepted the reality that his military career was ending in America, he continued to consider the offer he'd received from China. As he grew closer to accepting, he recognized that running away was part of his motivation, along with a desire to prove his theories about fighter planes. Curtiss-Wright Aircraft Company had offered him a position as a demonstration pilot and salesman,[15] but demonstrating aircraft would not afford him the same opportunity to prove his theories. Only the China option fulfilled that need. Effectively, Chennault's environment in America (the Air Corps, in particular) had made him ill. China offered him the opportunity to function in an environment, superficially more harsh and demanding than that of the States. However, free of critical superior officers and offering a working situation where he, not Air Corps officers, would be in control of his destiny, China just might be the very place where Chennault could flourish and not be extinguished by forces larger than himself.

As the day for his retirement approached, Chennault moved his family to a house on Lake St. John, near Waterproof, Louisiana. While his wife Nell was opposed to his decision to leave for China, she nevertheless supported him. He arranged for his Air Corps retirement pension to be sent to Nell, who still had four young children to raise. The three elder children had already moved away from home, with John in the Air Corps, Max at Auburn, and Peggy having married. In addition to his retirement pay, Chennault made arrangements with the Chinese Embassy and the Chase Manhattan Bank in New York to send part of his new salary to Nell.[16]

On April 30, 1937, Chennault retired from the Army Air Corps. As he contemplated his journey to China, he wrote his brother William, "When an old, well-known road is blocked, a new path must be opened. Obedient to the universal law, I am now surveying the outlines of a new life—a life which will have little in common with anything I've known before."[17]

In his diary on May 8, 1937, Chennault wrote: "Sailed on the Great Adventure at 2:00 P.M. aboard *Pres. Garfield*."[18] Departing San Francisco, Chennault made his way to Kobe on the Japanese main island of Honshu.[19] Waiting for Chennault was Billy McDonald, his former wingman from the Air Corps acrobatic team. Williamson, meanwhile, was in China teaching Chinese pilots to fly. These two fliers traveled about Japan acting as amateur spies. As best we can tell, this was a spontaneous act and not something they had been directed to do by their Chinese superiors. Chennault was quick to notice the flimsy construction of the homes and factories[20] and became convinced that incendiary devices dropped from the skies could wreak havoc on the Japanese structures. Back on the *Garfield*, McDonald and Chennault made their way to Shanghai, a remarkable port city in eastern China that borders the Yangtze River. There were many concessions in Shanghai that operated under the jurisdiction of America, Britain, France, and Italy. These were the "treaty ports" that had been taken from China as a consequence of the application of military power by the occidental nations against the Chinese. China was a fractured country. In fact, at this time, it was more of a territory than a unified nation.[21] In effect, the Chinese, as evidence of their inability to project and protect their own sovereignty, had been forced to relinquish control of land in their country to Western powers. This made Shanghai remarkable because it was an international city with a pronounced European influence. On the other hand, Japan, an emerging power in the region, looked upon the presence of foreign interest in China with concern and disdain. Asia should be ruled by Asians, not Europeans and Americans. After all, in 1854, America, in a display of gunboat diplomacy, had forced Japan to engage in commerce with the Western powers with Commodore Perry's arrival in Japanese home waters as the commander of a flotilla of mighty American warships.

As Chennault and McDonald disembarked from the *President Garfield*, they were met by the other member of their trio, Luke Williamson. Chennault would be whisked off to the Metropole Hotel where the airmen partied into the night. As he attempted to adjust to his new environment, Chennault found much of the Chinese personality to be an enigma, especially their intense concern about "losing face." In Western culture, airmen learning to fly recognize that making mistakes—which are then corrected by the instructor pilot—is a part of the learning process. However, the Chinese emphasis on "face," or "pride," would prove to be an impediment—not only to training and directing Chinese pilots, but also in Chennault's daily interactions with military personnel and political figures.

The political figurehead and sponsor of the Chinese Air Force was Madame Chiang Kai-shek, formerly Soong Mei-ling. Madame Chiang was the second wife of Generalissimo Chiang Kai-shek. Chiang apparently reasoned that his prospects for dealing with the Westerners in his efforts to move China forward in the twentieth century would be improved with an American-educated wife. Madame Chiang spent her childhood years in Georgia and graduated from Wellesley College outside Boston in 1917. Her father had been educated at Vanderbilt University, and her brother, Dr. T. V. Soong (who had served as China's minister of finance), had been educated at Harvard. Madame Chiang's sister, Soong Ching-ling, was the widow of Dr. Sun Yat-sen, Chiang Kai-shek's predecessor as leader of the Kuomintang party.

In 1923, Sun had appointed Chiang as the military chief of staff. Upon Sun Yat-sen's death from cancer in 1925, Chiang was able to maneuver himself into position to fill the power vacuum in the Kuomintang party. He had been trained in military principles in Russia, and on December 1, 1927, he further strengthened his position when he married Soong Mei-ling, the third daughter of Charlie Soong, a prominent Christian leader in Shanghai.

While the generalissimo had training in military principles, he was not an authority on military aviation. Madame Chiang, with her appreciation for Western culture and technology, was put in charge of the Chinese Aeronautics Commission. Curious as it may seem, China had women practicing law and medicine and engaged in work outside the home in metropolitan areas during the 1930s.

While Chennault was settling down to business with his new job in China during 1937, Western nations were experimenting with the bombing principles espoused by Mitchell and Douhet during civil wars and wars of conquest. That year, German and Italian bombers killed over a thousand civilians in the bombing of Guernica, Spain, and dogfights between Republican and Nationalist fighter planes took place over the skies of Spain.[22]

The "experiments" in bombing in Spain must have been matters Chennault pondered as he awaited his meeting with Madame Chiang. Eventually, Chennault met the sponsor of his employment. He was introduced to her by fellow pilot, Roy Holbrook, and after the meeting, Chennault wrote in his diary that she would "hereafter be 'the princess' to me." Chennault's accounts indicate that he was captivated by Madame Chiang's beauty and charm.

Because Chennault was unable to speak Chinese, Major Po Yen Shu ("PY") was assigned to serve as his personal interpreter. PY accompanied Chennault to air bases in China in the cockpit of an open cockpit training plane as Chennault performed his inspections. Unfortunately, PY was prone to air sickness and paid the price of ill health in serving as Chennault's interpreter. Chennault discovered that most of the airfields in China were merely dirt, making them unsuitable for operations in rainy weather. Even though Chennault met five Chinese generals on the Aeronautical Commission as well as an Italian advisor, General Scaroni, his overall impression was there was no meaningful organization of the Chinese Air Force. As Chennault surveyed the Chinese Air Force and was allowed to fly Chinese airplanes, his need for flying was satisfied, while China's need for a tactical leader would soon be answered. Chennault's new role was first tested when, on July 7, 1937, a skirmish took place between Japanese and Chinese troops near the Marco Polo Bridge, ten miles outside of Peking. Clearly, there was trouble ahead. How would Chennault handle it—and was he ready?

CHENNAULT ASSUMES COMMAND

Upon learning of the outbreak of fighting between Japanese and Chinese troops at the Marco Polo Bridge, Chennault dispatched a telegram to the Chinese Aeronautical Commission offering his services, not merely as a military advisor inspecting the Chinese Air Force. Instead, he would, if allowed, take command of air operations against the Japanese following the outbreak of the "incident," as it was called, rather than a formal declaration of war between China and Japan. In his new role, Chennault was directed to take charge of combat training for an advanced flying school at Nanchang. This flight school was now under the command of Mow, the same gentleman who two years earlier had sought Chennault's aid as an instructor for the Chinese Air Force. However, Colonel Mow had since become General Mow, and his power and influence, as well as responsibility, over the Chinese Air Force were increasing.

On July 23, 1937, Chennault and General Mow reported to the generalissimo on the state of readiness of the Chinese Air Force. Fewer than two hundred combat-worthy aircraft were available to resist an attack by the Japanese. Enraged, the generalissimo threatened Mow with execution by firing squad. The aircraft—a collection from America, Germany, and Italy—included ten Boeing P-26 fighter planes, six German-built Heinkels, nine Martin B-10s, and six Savoia-Marchetti tri-motor bombers. Fortunately, China had purchased a number of Curtiss Hawk biplane fighters from William Pawley's company, CAMCO. These Hawk IIs and Hawk IIIs were rugged aircraft that could serve as both fighters and bombers. These would be the principal weapons employed by China in the upcoming air battles with Japan over the skies of eastern China.

As the Japanese assault fell upon Shanghai, Chennault and Billy Mc-Donald began planning on Friday, August 13, for an attack on the Japanese flagship, *Idzumo*.[23] The Chinese air attack was carried out the next day.

It was a disaster. The Chinese pilots ended up bombing their own people, due to their being forced to descend below the clouds and their subsequent failure to appreciate the effect this would have on the trajectory of their bombs. Chennault had flown above the scene of the bombing and been fired upon by a British ship flying the Union Jack.[24]

The situation soon improved, however. When twelve Japanese bombers departed the aircraft carrier *Kaga*, they were decimated by the best of the Chinese fighter pilots, all of whom had been picked by Chennault. Eleven of the bombers were destroyed.[25]

On August 15, Nanking, the capital of China, was attacked by sixteen Mitsubishi Type 96 (Model G3M) bombers. These bombers had departed Taiwan and flown a round-trip distance of over 1,200 miles, a feat the Chinese had not imagined possible. While Japan had historically purchased aircraft from other nations, the presence of the bombers over eastern China indicated an ability on the part of the Japanese to develop indigenous aircraft with remarkable performance for their day. In 1937, the only American bomber capable of performing such a feat was Boeing's legendary B-17 "Flying Fortress."

By early September, Chennault had set up a radio spiderweb in Nanking, with his command center located in an athletic stadium.[26] A Chinese radio operator, Lieutenant Lee, raced around the city in a command car that was equipped with a radio, conveying information to Chinese flight leaders to ensure the interception of Japanese airplanes.[27] Unhappily, the Mitsubishi Type 96 (Model A5M), a Navy fighter, made its combat debut over Nanking, and the new Japanese fighters—faster and more maneuverable—outperformed the Chinese Curtiss Hawks, with devastating results for the latter.

After Shanghai fell to the Japanese, the Chinese reverted to night bombing attacks on the Japanese vessels. The skill with which these Chinese aircraft were flown prompted Western observers to question whether or not the aircraft were flown by Chinese airmen. On September 14, six Japanese bombers were intercepted and destroyed by Chinese fighters during what Chennault called the Japanese "annual bombing maneuvers." Writing home to Haywood (Possum) Hansell Jr., one of his old wingmen in the aerial demonstration team, Chennault speculated about what might be achieved over the skies of China with one hundred good fighter planes and one hundred competent pilots to fly them.

THE RUSSIANS TAKE OVER

As the Japanese juggernaut ravaged China, panic began to set in during the fall of 1937. European and U.S. airmen who claimed to have combat experience made their way to China, lured by a salary of $500 a month and a "bonus" of $1,000 for each Japanese plane destroyed. The mercenary pilots constituted China's 14th International Volunteer Squadron, which was equipped with the Vultee V-11 attack plane. The International Squadron flew a number of bombing missions, attacking bridges and rail yards. When they were not flying, the pilots were not strangers to the brothels and bars of Hankow, filled with watchful Chinese who were acting as Japanese collaborators. While one might normally imagine all Chinese were loyal to Chiang Kai-shek's government, there were those who, for various reasons, would collaborate with the invading Japanese and provide information that would compromise the efforts of Chennault, the Chinese Air Force, and the Nationalist Government. When word got out of Chennault's plans to have this collection of mercenaries bomb a Japanese troop depot in Tsinan in Shantung province, Japanese planes destroyed the planes of the International Squadron on the evening before the bombing mission. With no planes remaining, the International Squadron was disbanded.

Between late 1937 and 1939 the number of flyable planes in the Chinese Air Force dwindled due to heavy losses either from combat or training accidents. Thus, the defense of China's skies fell to Russian volunteers who were nominally "instructors" flying Polikarpov I-15 biplanes and Tupolev SB-2 bombers. It was in Russia's best interest that China not fall to the invading Japanese. Besides, Russia had not forgotten that Japan had wrested control of Port Arthur in Manchuria following the surprise attack on elements of the Russian fleet in 1904. The air wars raging over China were an excuse for the Russian air force to give their pilots "combat experience." It appears that at this point in history, Chennault's power and influence over the Chinese Air Force ebbed as General Asanov of the Soviet Union took command of the Russian fighter pilots and their planes. In time, the Russian biplane fighters were supplanted with Polikarpov I-16 monoplane fighters, which were engaged in combat over the China skies with Nakajima Type 97 (Model Ki-27) fighter planes of the Japanese Army Air Force.

It is worth mentioning that while America was providing aircraft to the Chinese, Vought Aircraft Corporation, an American company, had sold one prototype—its beautiful monoplane fighter, the V-143—to the Japanese in 1937, complete with diagrams and drawings. According to aviation historian Warren M. Bodie, the Japanese acquisition of the Vought V-143 "was absolutely instrumental in forcing design redirection of the Mitsubishi A6M (Zero) fighter of the Japanese Navy and the Nakajima Ki-43 Hayabusa, later known by the Allied codename 'Oscar' of the Japanese Army."[28] Despite Japanese denials that the Vought V-143 influenced the design of the Zero or the Oscar, Bodie maintains that the Japanese timing in changing their design concepts refutes their official position on the matter.[29]

With Stalin's provision of Russian fighters and bombers flown by Russian pilots (who were officially "instructors"), much of the air defense of China now fell to Russian officers. Chennault served the cause of China by working as chief flight instructor at the Chinese flight school at Yunnan-yi, about one hundred miles west of Kunming (the terminus of the road from Burma). Chennault's new position was a substantial demotion from his previous de facto role as key strategist for the Chinese Air Force. While Chennault had planned, supervised, and flown combat missions at the beginning of the Sino-Japanese War, as the Chinese Air

Force suffered mounting losses in pilots and planes, Chennault's energies were focused on an effort to rebuild the air force.

By 1939, Chiang Kai-shek and his government had retreated westward to the town of Chungking. Located in the interior of China along the Yangtze River, Chungking was ensconced in mountainous terrain. Unhappily, the retreat of Chiang Kai-shek and his government into central China did not spare the Chinese people from the relentless bombing by the Japanese. On May 4, 1939, at least five thousand Chinese were killed in a bombing raid on Chungking.

While war materials and aircraft had poured into China by way of Hong Kong and Hanoi (in French Indochina), Chiang astutely developed the Burma Road, which was seven hundred miles of twisting roadway from Lashio, Burma, to Kunming, China. Goods brought by ship into the port city of Rangoon, Burma (a British colony), could make their way by rail from Rangoon to Lashio, and thence by road from Lashio to Kunming. William Pawley, always a shrewd businessman, had a branch of his CAMCO aircraft factory built in Loiwing in southwest China, just to the northeast of the border with Burma.

Among the aircraft being assembled by CAMCO was the Curtiss-Wright Hawk 75 (Model 75H), an export version of the Air Corps P-36 fighter plane. Dispensing with the feature of retractable landing gear, this monoplane fighter was powered by a Wright GR-1820-G3 radial engine (about 875 horsepower) and had a top speed of 280 miles per hour. It was considered to be a match for the Japanese fighters if flown by a skilled pilot. Even though these aircraft were in short supply, an American-built model was given to Chennault as a gift from Madame Chiang. Of course, recognizing Chennault's keen flying abilities and aggressive personality, it is not unreasonable to conclude that he did more than merely maintain flying proficiency in the aircraft. In fact, as reported in Jack Samson's *The Flying Tiger*, in 1951 following the death of Rolfe Watson, Chennault wrote his widow confirming Watson "kept the guns of my personal plane in the finest condition. My guns never failed to fire when I needed them." Additional evidence of Chennault's flying the Hawk 75 in combat is found on page 58 of his autobiography, *Way of a Fighter*, where he admitted: "The Hawk Special acquired some bullet holes much too close for comfort as I learned very, very early in the game that trying to turn with Jap fighters was non-habit forming." To this day, rumors circulate about Chennault's having supported his family back in the States from bounties paid by the Chinese government for shooting down Japanese planes. The suggestion has even been made that Chennault was the leading American ace who flew against Japanese pilots. While Chennault has been scrupulously silent, officially, about any Japanese planes he may have destroyed, his admissions clearly prove he had occasion to fire his guns in anger.

Chapter Two

"AN EFFICIENT GUERRILLA AIR CORPS"

Thus, the groundwork of an efficient guerrilla air corps is already laid and could be made an actuality simply by adding to the present personnel of the Intercontinent Corporation . . . It would not require more than fifty United States pilots . . . Japan would have no grounds to object to this procedure.

—Major Rodney A. Boone, USMC, Office of Naval Intelligence—
Far Eastern Section, January 17, 1940[30]

The Roosevelt Presidential Library in Hyde Park, New York, houses a folder entitled "J.B. No. 355 (serial 691) Aircraft Requirements of the Chinese Government." This folder is replete with documents relating to the provision of military aircraft to the Chinese government. It includes communications between President Roosevelt, Acting Secretary of War Robert P. Patterson, Navy Secretary Frank Knox, Dr. Lauchlin Currie, commanders of the American Armed Forces, including General Marshall (chairman of the Joint Chiefs of Staff), Admiral Harold R. "Betty" Stark (chief of Naval Operations), and General Hap Arnold (commanding general of the U.S. Army Air Corps).[31]

As one might expect, communications from the American Joint Aircraft Committee are also contained in this folder, which makes sense. The Joint Aircraft Committee was charged with making recommendations to the Joint Army/Navy Board (the "Joint Board") concerning the allocation of aircraft produced in the United States. In January of 1940, the concept was introduced to the American government of providing American planes and pilots to fly in combat for China. How did this come about, and who was behind this initiative?

Chennault's agreement with the Chinese afforded him one month of annual leave, so in late 1939 and early 1940, Chennault was making his way around the United States. He found himself in the company of two remarkable people: William Pawley, and Commander Bruce Leighton, a pilot and a retired naval officer. They flew together in Pawley's private plane touring aircraft manufacturing plants in California.

If anyone in America had significant business contacts in China in 1939, it was Pawley. Over the years he had held many positions, but by 1939, in addition to serving as president of CAMCO, he was president of Intercontinent Corporation. His was an interesting history and provides more insight into the American intrigues in China during the undeclared Sino-Japanese War beginning in 1937.

The American-owned China Airways was first granted the exclusive right to fly the mail between major cities in China in 1929. In order to appease the Nationalist government's reluctance to open China to foreign business interests, China Airways was reorganized in 1930 into China National Aviation Corporation (CNAC). Fifty-five percent of the stock in CNAC was held by Chinese interests, while the remainder was owned by Intercontinent Corporation, which actually controlled CNAC.

Three years after the arrangement between CNAC and Intercontinent Corporation, William Pawley visited China in May of 1930. Over time, Pawley gained the trust of officials in the Nationalist government. By May of 1939, Pawley had been approached by the Chinese government to use his power and influence in America with a view toward forming a "foreign legion" composed of American pilots and combat aircraft.

As we know from earlier passages in this text, CNAC was not Intercontinent's only business interest in China. Intercontinent's other concern in China was CAMCO, which sold aircraft to China and assembled, maintained, and repaired aircraft serving in the Chinese Air Force. By some accounts, Pawley was the sole stockholder; by others, CAMCO was a subsidiary of Intercontinent. Whatever the case may be, by 1939, Commander Bruce Leighton was CAMCO's vice president, and it appears he was also the vice president of Intercontinent.

Pawley had good reasons for bringing Leighton on board at CAMCO. A graduate of the Naval Academy, Leighton was trained as a naval aviator and had served in the Orient with then-commander, Richmond Kelly Turner. In time, Turner would rise to the rank of admiral and be in charge of navy war plans. In view of his military contacts and aeronautical experience, Leighton was a good man to have at Pawley's disposal. The extent to which Leighton was an asset—not only to Pawley, but to the Chinese government—would soon become apparent.

While Chennault admitted to touring aircraft factories in California with Pawley and Leighton in January 1940, he claimed to know nothing about a Chinese request for American military airplanes submitted to the Navy Department that same month.[32] Even if Chennault was unaware of Leighton's overtures to the Navy Department, it is clear that Leighton and Chennault were thinking along the same lines. Further, as related in his biography, based upon his experience flying a captured Japanese Nakajima Army Type 97 fighter, during his annual Stateside visit in 1939, Chennault briefed Air Corps personnel in the Munitions Building in Washington on his combat experienced in China. Chennault's briefings appear to have had no effect on Air Corps estimates of the Japanese air forces, nor was Chennault invited to return to the fold as an Air Corps instructor in fighter tactics. In early 1940, General H. H. "Hap" Arnold offered Chennault a position as an instructor at the coast artillery at Fortress Monroe.

In Chennault's 1949 autobiography, he explained his idea for a Chinese air force:

> My plan proposed to throw a small but well-equipped air force into China. Japan, like England, floated her lifeblood on the sea and could be defeated more easily by slashing her salty arteries than by stabbing for her heart. Air bases in Free China could put all of the vital Japanese supply lines and advanced staging areas under attack. Begun in time and delivered with sufficient weight, an air offensive from China could have smashed the Japanese southern offensive before it left its home ports and staging areas.[33]

Turning to the records of Joint Board 355, three telling documents relate to Leighton's efforts in January 1940 to enlist the aid of the United States government in providing fighter and bomber planes to China as part of a "commercial venture." The three documents are intriguing. First, there is a single typewritten page with no identifying data as to the author or the intended recipient, stamped CONFIDENTIAL. Second, there is a "Report of Interview with Lieutenant-Commander Bruce G. Leighton, USNR," dated January 17, 1940, authored by Major Rodney A. Boone, USMC. Boone served under Lieutenant Commander Arthur H. McCollum, head of the Far East Section of the Office of Naval Intelligence (ONI). Third, Rear Admiral Walter S. Anderson[34] wrote a "Memorandum for the Chief of Naval Operations" (Admiral Stark), dated January 17, 1940.

According to Major Boone's Report of Interview with Commander Leighton, the Intercontinent Corporation was established in the District of Columbia with Pawley as president and Leighton as vice president.[35] Intercontinent had been operating an aircraft factory in China since the outbreak of hostilities in 1937.[36] Initially, the factory was in Hanchow, but was later moved to Hankow, and subsequently "to Lowning [sic] on the Burma border in Hunan Province."[37] Intercontinent had fifteen American experts in key positions with 1,500 Chinese employees[38] and planned to expand to about 3,000 Chinese personnel and ten additional American experts.[39] Leighton claimed the factory could produce 200 planes per year.

According to Leighton, Intercontinent was the sales representative—with CAMCO serving as the actual representative—for Curtiss-Wright, along with Sperry Corporation and other aircraft component manufacturers. At the time of his interview, Leighton related that the factory was assembling "30 Curtiss-Hawk 3s [sic],"[40] the materials having been ordered three years earlier (in 1937). He also said that Intercontinent had an order from China for seventy-five single-engine Vultee bombers,[41] fifty P-36s,[42] and thirty Curtiss-Wright Interceptors.[43] Besides the factory in Loiwing, Intercontinent had a factory dug into the side of a mountain in Chungking, where materials were on hand to construct sixty Russian fighter planes.[44] Transportation facilities to the factory were somewhat poor, consisting of river steamers on the Irrawaddy River and unimproved roads. However, the Loiwing factory was in close proximity to the Burma Road. They had the capability to ship aircraft components via the Chekiang railroad, which bypassed Japanese-occupied Nanchang.

Commander Leighton claimed that China possessed between one and two hundred pursuit aircraft (a big difference) and between fifty and one hundred bombers (another substantial margin). He also related that the Chinese had 450 airplane engines "badly in need of overhaul, on which the factory is now working."[45] If the Chinese Air Force had 450 airplane engines badly in need of repair, it means these engines were "run out," and the Chinese lacked either the resources, man power, or both to get these war materials vital to China's defense back in an airworthy condition and installed on airplanes where they could be of some value. It suggests the factory was unable to service and repair these engines in a timely manner.

A COMMERCIAL VENTURE "WITHOUT ANY DIRECT PARTICIPATION BY THE UNITED STATES GOVERNMENT"

Intercontinent was able to secure any number of orders from the Chinese government for military airplanes. The problem was money. The Chinese Air Force was a "leveraged business venture," meaning that when the Chinese government placed an order for military aircraft, it made a 20 percent down payment. The balance of the money was paid over a period of three or four years (after the aircraft were probably no longer operational and would be of little value). The sales agent, Intercontinent, had to go to a bank and borrow enough money to pay the American manufacturers a 50 percent down payment, accompanied by a 50 percent letter of credit to ensure that the balance was paid upon delivery of the aircraft. To do so, Intercontinent was borrowing money from the Hong Kong-Shanghai Bank, with interest at 5 percent.

Boone's "Report of Interview of January 17, 1940" details his conversation with Commander Leighton: "The Hong Kong-Shanghai Bank, and also other foreign banks, according to Commander Leighton, consider this a good risk. The Chinese government has made their monthly payments completely."[46] In a strictly commercial context, this would not be considered a *good* risk. The collateral that would secure the loan would likely be worn out, or worse, destroyed in combat. The only real security for this financial venture would be the economic integrity of the Chinese government. Obviously, that is why Commander Leighton emphasized the fact that the monthly payments had always been made on time.

Boone also includes Leighton's explanation of the apparent significance of China in relation to the balance of power in the Pacific and Southeast Asia[47]: "[Leighton] argues that a small, efficient group of planes, consisting of fifty dive-bombers, fifty twin-engine bombers, fifty pursuits, and ten transports, could make the Japanese lines of communications untenable. This is because the Japanese lines are particularly vulnerable on the Yangtze and Pearl Rivers and at Nanning [sic]."[48]

Clearly, Leighton and Chennault were thinking the same thing, even if it was not expressed. It is hard to imagine that Chennault, Leighton, and Pawley were flying around California inspecting aircraft factories and not having some discussions concerning the needs of the Chinese Air Force. Reason would suggest that the three men were considering what a small, well-equipped air force could do in China to combat the Japanese in their war of aggression.

Returning to the concept of a "commercial venture," all America had to do to improve China's circumstance "without any direct participation by the United States Government"[49] were three things: First, the United States government was to influence the Import-Export Bank to guarantee loans to China of $25 million. The loans to finance the operation of the Chinese Air Force would need to be guaranteed by the Import-Export Bank because, according to Leighton, "The European situation has caused the Hong Kong-Shanghai Bank to get tight with its money."[50] Today, of course, we know that when political climates become unstable, lenders become more apprehensive and their criteria for making loans are more restrictive. Commander Leighton's comment is to be entirely expected in this context. Leighton emphasized the Import-Export Bank would only be *guaranteeing* the loan, not actually making it. The Hong Kong-Shanghai Bank merely wanted some additional resources to provide more comfort in this economic transaction.

The second element of this "commercial venture" was that the United States "interposed no objection to the hiring by Intercontinent Corporation of competent American Army, Navy, and Marine Corps Reserve flyers."[51] The employment concept evolved to the point where CAMCO (Intercontinent's subsidiary) would actually serve as the *putative employer* of the American pilots and technicians.

The third concept of Commander Leighton's plan was that "[t]he United States should make it easy for China to obtain the required number of planes and fuel for their operation."[52] This third component was addressed to the American Joint Aircraft Commission. Making it easy for China to get airplanes meant making it more difficult for Britain, the Army Air Corps, and the American navy to get their airplanes.

It was as simple as that. Get the loans guaranteed. Allow an American company to buy American aircraft, to be flown by American pilots in a combat zone. Divert allocations of American aircraft from Britain, the Army Air Corps, and the navy, so that they could be provided to China. Sounding more like a sales pitch than a military briefing, Boone summarized Leighton's remarks: "Thus, the groundwork of an efficient *guerrilla air force* [emphasis added] is already laid and could be made an actuality simply by adding to the present personnel of the Intercontinent Corporation."[53]

This proposed guerrilla air force in China could be maintained at a cost of only $5 million per month, and would only require about fifty United States pilots. Leighton emphasized "that Japan would have no grounds to object to this procedure."[54] Leighton's sales pitch concluded with a declaration that if China won the war with Japan, and if a strong China emerged, it would likely be friendly to the United States government.

Also found in the file of Joint Board 355 is Rear Admiral Anderson's confidential memorandum directed to Admiral Stark.[55] As chief of naval operations (CNO)—and as such, having direct contact with President Roosevelt—Admiral Stark was blamed by Admiral Husband E. Kimmel, the navy commander at Pearl Harbor on the date of the surprise attack, for not giving pertinent information as to Japanese intentions. Stark would be relieved of his duties as CNO a few months after the Japanese attack.[56] In that memorandum to Admiral Stark, the following was related:

> "Attached hereto is a memorandum prepared by Mr. Bruce G. Leighton, formerly of the United States Navy and now Vice-President of Intercontinent Corporation, which has been engaged in aircraft manufacturing and sales in China for the past ten years. His plan appears to offer a possibility of immediately so strengthening Chinese resistance to Japan at relatively little cost to the United States, as to eventually cause them to abandon her policy of armed aggression on the continent of Asia in open violation of treaties."[57]

Again, Leighton's memorandum contains absolutely *no identifying information*. It is not addressed to anyone; it is not from anyone. It has no date or signature. It has six numbered paragraphs and one unnumbered paragraph.[58] The details on economics and number of pilots are generally consistent between the Boone Report and the Leighton memorandum, except that in the written document Leighton gave the Naval Department, he requested one hundred bombers and one hundred pursuit aircraft as opposed to fifty dive-bombers, fifty twin-engine bombers, and fifty pursuit aircraft.[59]

After asserting that army and navy reserve pilots would "welcome an opportunity to engage in such a venture, provided they were not discouraged from doing so by the U.S. Government,"[60] Leighton's sales pitch continued: "I believe that the interest with which I am connected could arrange all the essentials of establishing bases, supplying equipment, training personnel, and organizing maintenance facilities, under *commercial contracts* [emphasis added] with the Chinese Government, *without any direct participation by the U.S. Government* [emphasis added]."[61]

To suggest that Major Boone would have been anything other than receptive to Leighton's sales pitch would appear to be misleading. After all, less than ten months after the meeting was held in mid-January 1940, Boone's boss, McCollum, would write an action memorandum suggesting eight initiatives to force Japan to commit an overt act of war against the United States. As Robert Stinnett writes in *Day of Deceit—The Truth About FDR and Pearl Harbor*, "Its eight actions called for virtually inciting a Japanese attack on American ground, air, and naval forces in Hawaii, as well as on British and Dutch colonial outposts in the Pacific region."[62]

According to Stinnett, McCollum was responsible for routing intelligence communications to Roosevelt from early 1940 through December 7, 1941.[63] It cannot be argued that Leighton's meeting with Boone produced no effect on American military or foreign policy, since the third initiative in McCollum's Memorandum for the Director (of Navy Intelligence) dated October 7, 1940, advocated: "Give all possible aid to the Chinese government of Chiang Kai-shek."[64]

A seed was planted with the Office of Naval Intelligence (and, quite likely, with President Roosevelt) when Leighton visited Boone in January of 1940. In time, it would blossom and mature into an American guerrilla air force serving the interests of a foreign warlord.

Chapter Three

THE CHINA LOBBY

In Washington I reported to shrewd, erudite Dr. T. V. Soong. From his mansion on Woodley Road, Dr. Soong was directing China's campaign to extract concrete aid from the United States.

—General Claire Lee Chennault[65]

China benefited from the influence-peddling and lobbying efforts of Pawley and Leighton. Pawley was in China during the opening months of the Sino-Japanese War and concluded "that China needed a fast interceptor with a high rate of climb and excellent maneuverability."[66] Pawley, at great expense to his companies, asked Curtiss-Wright Corporation to produce a lightweight monoplane fighter, the Curtiss Model 21 (or CW-21).

During the fall of 1940, Chennault was still employed as a civilian advisor to the secretary of the Chinese Commission for Aeronautical Affairs. While Chennault initially reported in June of 1937 to Madame Chiang in China, in December of 1940 he reported to her older brother, Dr. T. V. Soong in Washington. Chennault's service to China brought him back to America for one simple reason. China needed American planes and American pilots to fly them in an undeclared war with Japan.

After the Japanese invasion of Manchuria and the first air attack on Shanghai in 1931, Dr. Soong began organizing the central government's military airpower. It was at Soong's request that Colonel Jack Jouett went to China in 1932 with twenty Air Corps reserve officers, including Roy Holbrook, who would eventually serve as the generalissimo's personal pilot. Harvard-educated and influenced by Western values, Soong was criticized for introducing too many foreign advisors. Soong's chief antagonist was Dr. H. H. Kung, the generalissimo's brother. In 1934, when Jouett's American pilots refused to fly combat missions to suppress an uprising in Fukien province, Kung, who was vacationing in Italy, secured the service of Mussolini's pilots and planes—at no small expense to China. The outbreak of the Sino-Japanese War revealed the corrupt practices of the Italians, who carried aircraft on the air force inventory that had been destroyed or rendered un-airworthy.

By the fall of 1940, Soong was serving as China's foreign minister in Washington, D.C., and had become close personal friends with Treasury secretary Henry Morgenthau and Navy secretary Frank Knox. Well-educated and impeccably dressed, Soong was a powerful advocate for America's provision of airpower to China. Also that fall, Harvard-educated lawyer Thomas Corcoran, who had served as a speechwriter for President Roosevelt, would join in efforts to assist the Chinese. Corcoran's influence with members of the Senate and Congress ensured that plans for a "Special Air Unit" in China could be safely carried out by the Roosevelt administration, guaranteeing that no political ruckus would emerge from this shadowy activity.

Presidential aide Lauchlin Currie, PhD,[67] was another key member of the team, eventually assuming the duties of administering and supervising aid to China. Dr. Currie supported China and became a zealous advocate both for saving China from the Japanese and for using China as a device to attack the Japanese military and their war-making capability. Both Chinese and American interests would be served by this arrangement. China would have the warplanes it required to fight the invading Japanese; and America, though not an official belligerent in the Sino-Japanese War, could (hopefully) keep Japan bogged down in China, thereby reducing the risk of Japan's having the men and resources to attack American interests in Asia and the Pacific.

Unbeknownst to Roosevelt, the American military, or the American intelligence community, Currie was actually a Soviet spy.[68] Although Currie had not joined the Communist Party USA (CPUSA), he did provide personnel in the Russian embassy with classified information and, occasionally, secret documents. Currie's codename was "Page."[69] Apparently, part of Currie's enthusiasm for aiding China was a function of his desire to protect Russia from Japanese aggression. In his passionate work to protect China, Dr.

Currie clearly had divided loyalties. If, as some argue, Currie had loyalties or concerns directed toward Russia, he would have recognized the necessity for a strong defense in China against the expansionist ambitions of Japan. If Hitler's Nazi Germany was a threat to Russia's western flank, Russia certainly did not need China to become a Japanese puppet state to its south. A strong Japanese presence in China would not bode well for Russia's future.

"THE PLUS FOUR"

Mrs. Henry Stimson, wife of Secretary of War Stimson, had a special name for the inner circle of the Roosevelt cabinet; she called them "The Plus Four." Members included her husband, Henry; secretary of the Treasury, Henry Morgenthau Jr.; secretary of the Navy, Frank Knox; and secretary of state, Cordell Hull. One member in particular would play a key role in our story.

Much of what we know today about the secret plan between China and America—to establish a "Special Air Unit" to operate bombers from eastern China that would bomb Tokyo and other Japanese cities—comes from memoranda carefully dictated by Henry Morgenthau Jr. Morgenthau was the grandson of Lazarus Morgenthau, a German-Jewish immigrant who arrived in New York in 1866 on the verge of bankruptcy but overcame his financial difficulties, setting the stage for continued success in the family. Morgenthau's father, Henry Sr., graduated from Columbia Law School and rose to prominence in American politics, eventually serving as ambassador to Turkey from 1913 to 1916.

Henry Morgenthau Jr. attended Cornell University, but left without graduating. Instead, he bought one thousand acres of land in Duchess County, New York, with the intention of farming. The Morgenthaus were neighbors of the Roosevelt family, and when Franklin Roosevelt became governor of New York, Morgenthau was appointed chairman of an agricultural advisory commission. Later, when Roosevelt became president, Morgenthau became chairman of the Federal Farm Board and governor of the Farm Credit Administration. When secretary of the Treasury William H. Woodin became ill, Morgenthau took over this position. Although he did not have a doctorate in economics like Dr. Currie, Morgenthau still enjoyed the confidence and friendship of Roosevelt.

Speeches given by Morgenthau after the outbreak of the Second World War indicate that he had an intense personality, and he made no secret of his dislike for the Japanese government. Because Morgenthau had the foresight to record his recollections and conversations, we have access today to the origins of America's secret plan. His detailed notes allow us to explore how America decided to provide China with bombers with which to attack Japan as an American surrogate in Southeast Asia.

Furthermore, although Morgenthau's official position was secretary of the Treasury, there is no doubt he was a powerful force in the Roosevelt administration. Morgenthau frequently acted outside his portfolio, becoming involved in matters of foreign policy. It is not surprising that a careful review of Morgenthau's diary, obtained from the Roosevelt Presidential Library, discloses his extensive involvement in providing military (in addition to financial) aid to China during the Sino-Japanese War. Morgenthau dictated memoranda following meetings or conversations with foreign government officials, other cabinet members, and most especially, President Roosevelt. Every telephone conversation was transcribed. Morgenthau was a very meticulous record-keeper and developed an inventory that thoroughly detailed his activities.

Frank Knox, another member of the Plus Four, truly personified the Horatio Alger story. Born in Massachusetts in 1874, his father ran a grocery store. The family then moved to Michigan when Knox was seven. By age eleven, Knox was peddling newspapers. Before finishing high school, he left Michigan to support himself as a salesman. Losing his job in 1893, he returned to Michigan and enrolled in Alma College, where he earned high marks and became an outstanding football player. With the outbreak of the Spanish-American War, Knox enlisted in Teddy Roosevelt's Rough Riders. After that war, Knox returned to Michigan and married his college sweetheart, Annie Reid, and soon landed a job as the city editor of the *Grand Rapids Herald*. He was promoted to circulation manager and became active in Republican politics.

With the outbreak of the First World War, Knox, at the age of forty-three, again enlisted in the army. After the Armistice, Knox returned to the newspaper business and by 1927 had become the general manager of all twenty-seven of William Randolph Hearst's newspapers. Knox embodied Teddy Roosevelt's "Doctrine of the Strenuous Life." He believed in physical exercise and clean living. Knox made a career of exposing crooked politicians and criminals.

When Franklin Delano Roosevelt was elected president, Knox called his economic policies alien, un-American, and a complete flop. Knox's criticism must be put in perspective, however: First, he was a Republican. Second, by the standards of the time, most Republicans would have viewed Roosevelt's economic initiatives as socialistic and clearly inconsistent with free-market capitalism. By 1936, Knox was the vice-presidential running mate of Governor Alfred Landon of Kansas. As Knox became increasingly critical of Roosevelt's domestic policies, Roosevelt sought to neutralize the criticism by appointing Knox to a post in his administration. Only on Roosevelt's second attempt did Knox agree to become secretary of the navy.

Knox campaigned for the repeal of the American Neutrality Laws and a bipartisan cabinet. In 1941, when Knox suggested that the American navy be used to clear the Atlantic of Nazi submarines, isolationists were infuriated and demanded his resignation. By today's standards, Knox would be viewed as a man with a hawkish sensibility—which clarifies why he was so receptive to the idea of developing an American guerrilla air force in China to combat the Japanese.

The third member of the Plus Four, Cordell Hull, was a native of Tennessee. He was born on October 2, 1871, in a log cabin near Byrdstown, part of Pickett County, Tennessee. His mother was part Cherokee, and both parents were mountain people. Considered gifted, Hull was privately educated by tutors and later attended Montvale Academy in Celina and Bowling Green, Kentucky. Hull graduated from National Normal University in Lebanon, Ohio, and attended Cumberland in Lebanon, Tennessee. He was apprenticed to lawyers in Nashville and received his law degree in 1891 after less than one year's study.

Hull was elected chairman of the Clay County Democratic Party at the age of nineteen. At the age of twenty, he was elected to the Tennessee House of Representatives. He resigned from the Tennessee legislature to serve in the Spanish-American War as a captain of the volunteers stationed in Cuba. Following that war, he returned to Gainesboro, Tennessee, where he served as a judge in the Fifth Judicial Circuit, riding a ten-county circuit on horseback or by buggy.

By 1906, Hull was elected to the United States House of Representatives, where he served (with the exception of two terms) until 1931. While out of office, Hull served as the chairman of the Democratic Committee from 1921 to 1924. While Woodrow Wilson was president, Hull played a significant role in drafting legislation that would serve as the cornerstone of the federal income tax system. Hull also shared President

Wilson's belief in the value of the League of Nations. He was elected to the Senate in 1931. Over the objections of many senators who considered him unqualified, President Roosevelt appointed Hull secretary of state in 1933.

Although Hull believed economic nationalism was a major cause of war, when Adolf Hitler ordered German troops to occupy Czechoslovakia, Hull placed import duties on German goods. Similarly, although the United States and Japan had a trade agreement in place in 1911, Hull repudiated that agreement in 1939 in economic retaliation for Japan's undeclared war against China.

Between 1939 and 1941, Hull absorbed himself in negotiations in an attempt to effect a peace agreement between Japan and China. He also attempted to strengthen the position of moderates in the Japanese government and weaken the position of militarists. Hull came to develop a respect for Japanese ambassador Kichisaburō Nomura. However, when Japanese special envoy Saburo Kurusu was sent to Washington in November of 1941 to aid Nomura, this effectively relieved Nomura of his ambassadorial role.

Even with the outbreak of World War II, Hull could envision an eventual peace, and he was instrumental in drafting a document entitled "Charter of the United Nations." In fact, in 1945, Hull received the Nobel Peace Prize for his efforts in organizing the United Nations. A tireless worker, Hull frequently met with key government personnel at his residence on Sunday mornings, until his family doctor ordered him to quit.

Like Cordell Hull, Henry Stimson enjoyed a long and distinguished life in public service. Born in New York City on September 21, 1867, Stimson attended Phillips Andover Academy and graduated from Yale University in 1888. After studying at Harvard Law School, he became a lawyer and was associated with Elihu Root, a well-known lawyer and statesman, while practicing law in New York City.

From 1906 to 1909, Stimson served as a United States attorney for the southern district of New York. In 1910, he ran unsuccessfully for governor of New York. Between 1911 and 1913, Stimson served as secretary of war under President Taft. With the outbreak of World War I, Stimson served as a colonel in the 31st Field Artillery.

By 1927, Stimson had been dispatched by President Coolidge to serve as governor general of the Philippines. A staunch Republican, Stimson left public office with the election of Franklin D. Roosevelt in

1933. Stimson resumed his law practice but retained a strong interest in international affairs. He advocated a firm attitude toward the Axis powers. As Roosevelt had done with Frank Knox, Stimson was appointed secretary of war in 1940. At the time of his appointment, Stimson was seventy-three years of age. During his term as secretary of state under President Hoover, Stimson also served as the chairman of the American delegation to the London Naval Conference in 1930–31.

Clearly, he was well versed in the balance of power negotiated between the British, the Americans, and the Japanese in relation to combat vessels. With the invasion of Manchuria in 1932, Stimson (then secretary of state) issued a declaration that would come to be known as the Stimson Doctrine. In his declaration, Stimson maintained that the United States would no longer be required to recognize any situation or treaty that might impair American treaty rights, or that was brought about by means contrary to the Kellogg-Briand Pact—that is, by an act of aggression such as the Japanese invasion of Manchuria.

With the exception of Morgenthau, the members of the Plus Four had all served in the United States Army. The paths of the Plus Four would cross with those of Chennault, Soong, and Mow during the fall of 1940 and would lead to one of the most clandestine and bizarre military initiatives ever undertaken by the United States government. The United States, ostensibly neutral in the Sino-Japanese War, would seriously entertain the idea of a preemptive bombing initiative directed toward Japan employing China as America's proxy in this unorthodox scheme.

Chapter Four

LUNCH AT THE WHITE HOUSE

"It would be a nice thing if China bombed Japan."

—President Franklin D. Roosevelt, December 1940

These were the words President Roosevelt uttered to Morgenthau, in the fall of 1940—a year before Japan attacked Pearl Harbor.[70] Morgenthau and his wife had attended a luncheon with President Roosevelt on Sunday, December 8, 1940, together with Dr. Soong and Mrs. Soong. The luncheon with President Roosevelt followed the receipt of a secret memorandum from Generalissimo Chiang Kai-shek, delivered to Roosevelt in November 1940. In the memo, Chiang had requested that a Special Air Unit be formed in China, which would, among other things, bomb cities in Japan.[71] In light of this, it can hardly be imagined that there was no discussion of the generalissimo's appeal during the luncheon. In fact, Morgenthau's report of the post-luncheon conversation with Dr. Soong indicates that they discussed the provision of long-range American bombers to China. There can be little doubt that the luncheon conversation with President Roosevelt was focused on China's request for a Special Air Unit.[72]

The White House luncheon in December 1940 was not the only time these discussions took place. On October 20, 1940, Chennault and General Mow were directed by the generalissimo and Madame Chiang to report to Washington to meet with Dr. Soong, who was in charge of an organization called China Defense Supplies. They were to assist Soong in obtaining American planes and pilots for service in China.

Chennault and Mow arrived in Washington on November 1, 1940. Unfortunately, Chennault's and Soong's initial discussions were less than encouraging.[73] Moreover, Dr. Soong had taken Chennault to dinner with two distinguished journalists, Joseph Alsop Jr. of the *New York Tribune* and Edgar Mower of the *Chicago Daily*. Chennault sounded them out on the idea of an American guerrilla air corps flying in the service of China. The reporters noted that Germany, not Japan was the principal focus of concern in Washington. Their comments were less than encouraging to Chennault's ambitions. However, the reporters were dismayed to hear how well the Japanese Model Zero fighter was performing, since the expectation had been that older types of American planes would suffice for service in China. Similarly, Soong's initial discussions with Morgenthau suggested the idea of supplying considerable quantities of American airplanes to China was unrealistic. Clearly, these early talks did not bode well for the formation of a Special Air Unit.

WHY WOULD ROOSEVELT WANT CHINA TO BOMB JAPAN?

By the fall of 1940, America and Japan were already at war—albeit, a war of economy. Japan was an emerging power in the Orient and had designs on colonies of the French, the British, and the Dutch. Japan was fast becoming one of the most developed nations in Southeast Asia; by 1936, nearly half of all United States exports to Asia were received by Japan. Japan was dependent on raw materials and petroleum from the United States in order to feed its growing economy. However, when Japan invaded China in 1937, it became clear that this powerful country's ambitions would eventually place it in direct conflict with the United States.

Although Japan began its conquest by invading Manchuria in 1931, it soon turned its attention southward. In the summer of 1937, Japan attacked southeastern China, including the port city of Shanghai and the exotic and sophisticated capital, Nanking. A Japanese aerial attack on the gunboat USS *Panay* almost plunged Japan into war with the United States. The *Panay* was involved in evacuating Americans from Nanking as the Japanese army approached. Despite the fact that an American flag was prominently displayed, she was attacked and sunk on Sunday, December 12, 1937. Three Americans were killed while forty-three sailors and five civilians were wounded. On Christmas Eve, Japan made a formal apology but maintained the attack was unintentional. A U.S. Navy court of inquiry determined several American flags were clearly visible during the attack. Four days before the Japanese apology reached Washington, Japan admitted Japanese Army planes had strafed the survivors after Japanese Navy planes had bombed and sunk the vessel. On April 22, 1938, Japan paid indemnity of $2,214,007.36 to the United States. American Ambassador to Japan Joseph Grew feared war would break out and was surprised to see that so many Japanese appeared to be extremely remorseful; there were "two Japans," one sincere and apologetic, and the other focused on conquest. Interestingly, individual Japanese made donations to America as an expression of remorse, but Secretary Hull maintained that none of the families of those killed or wounded would receive the contributions. It is perhaps remarkable that the *Panay* incident did not plunge Japan and America into war four years before Pearl Harbor.

The sinking of the *Panay* also had a connection to Chennault, since he had provided a collection of Japanese equipment salvaged from wrecked planes to an American intelligence officer attached to the U.S. Embassy. Marines dutifully crated the equipment and carried it to what was believed to be the safest place to store it, the *Panay*. Chennault's efforts to alert American authorities to Japanese aeronautical advances were frustrated with the sinking of the American ship.

For decades prior to the outbreak of what Japan called "the China Incident," America had enjoyed good relations with China, and Americans were horrified by the newsreels that depicted the indiscriminate bombing of Chinese villages and execution of Chinese civilians at the hands of the Japanese military. These atrocities received worldwide attention in 1937 with the "Rape of Nanking," where several hundred thousand helpless Chinese were raped, murdered, bayoneted, and shot, only to be dumped in mass graves.[74]

The Western press reported on the carnage, and Americans sat horrified in theaters, watching the destruction of Chinese cities and the death and annihilation of innocent Chinese civilians—soon deemed acts of genocide. By January of 1938, newsreel accounts of the Japanese bombing of the *Panay* had reached U.S. theaters, causing quite an up-roar before Japan apologized and made restitution for the deaths and the damage. Americans were receptive to the pleas for help that came from Madame Chiang Kai-shek, popularly hailed as "China's Joan of Arc" in newsreel coverage.

The conduct of the Japanese army in Nanking demonstrated that Japan was a menace to peace in the Orient—a rogue nation engaged in the wholesale bombing and barbarous slaughter of helpless Chinese civilians.[75] Japanese troops entertained themselves by raping Chinese women, dousing people with gasoline and lighting a match, forcing sons to rape their mothers, and cutting off the heads of the Chinese, which became a sick form of competitive sport.[76] If the Japanese troops ran short of food, they improvised by eating the remains of dead Chinese. It has been estimated that as many as thirty million Chinese died during the Japanese occupation of China.[77] The late Iris Chang in *The Rape of Nanking* and James Bradley in *Flyboys* wrote extensively about the brutal occupation of China by the Japanese military.

By March of 1940, Japan had set up a puppet government in Nanking. On July 16, 1940, Japan pressured the French, who controlled Indochina, to close the Yunnan railway, which had been used to transport food and war supplies to the Chinese army. Immediately after the railway was closed, America reacted by imposing an embargo on the sale of aviation fuel to Japan. No doubt, America could have reacted with more onerous sanctions, but President Roosevelt clearly appreciated the mood of isolationism prevalent in America and was wary of anything that might provoke armed conflict between the two powers.

On August 2, 1940, Japan demanded transit rights for its troops and the use of airfields in French Indochina. On August 18, 1940, the British closed the Burma Road—China's last remaining lifeline to the outside world—for a short time. They made this decision out of concern for possible Japanese initiatives if they failed to do so. On August 30, 1940, Japan recognized French sovereignty over Indochina in return for economic and military concessions.

On September 27, 1940, Japan took another important step when it joined the Axis powers of Germany and Italy by signing the Tripartite Pact. The United States responded by imposing an embargo on scrap-iron sales to Japan. In October of 1940, Japan coerced the Dutch government into requiring that between 75 and 100 percent of the exports leaving the Dutch East Indies be sold to Japan. Of particular interest to the Japanese was oil extracted from the Dutch East Indies. In November of 1940, America imposed an embargo on the sale of tin and steel to Japan. While the initiatives of the Japanese government appeared increasingly hostile to Western interests, President Roosevelt obviously felt constrained by the weight of public opinion to limit America's retaliatory initiatives to those of an economic as opposed to a military nature.

Japanese ambitions were nothing new. The world had watched as Japanese military initiatives had escalated over the past decade, reaching the boiling point in 1940. Japan had left the League of Nations in 1931, claiming its only desire was to maintain peace in the Far East. However, Japan had been using military force to develop its "Greater Southeast Asia Co-Prosperity Sphere" in which the only people prospering were Japanese. Furthermore, as Great Britain was fighting for its survival with Nazi Germany, and Holland had been invaded by the German Wehrmacht, the abilities of both countries to protect their colonies in Southeast Asia were substantially diminished. There was a military and political vacuum in Southeast Asia ready for Japan to exploit. Japan made its intentions clear when it signed the Tripartite Pact with Germany and Italy on September 27, 1940. With the Japanese execution of the Tripartite Pact, any hopes the Western powers had that Japan might turn away from her ambitions of conquest faded. The battle lines for the next great world conflict were being drawn.

It is little wonder that President Roosevelt and members of his cabinet were giving serious consideration to the idea of assisting the Chinese government by providing American-built aircraft, pilots to fly them, and technicians to maintain and service them.

SOONG'S RESPONSE TO MORGENTHAU'S QUESTION

In his diaries, Morgenthau relates a conversation he had with Dr. Soong following his lunch with President Roosevelt on that December day in 1940. Interestingly, this conversation took place in the presence of Mrs. Morgenthau and Mrs. Soong:

I then said that we might get him planes by 1942, but what did he think of the idea of some long-range bombers with the understanding that they were to be used to bomb Tokyo and other Japanese cities? Well, to say he was enthusiastic is putting it mildly. He [Soong] said, "This would give us a chance to hit back." I asked, "Would you be afraid of their bombing you?" and he said, "They are doing it anyway." I told him that I had not discussed this with the President, but intimated it was the President's idea, which it is in part, because he has mentioned to me that it would be a nice thing if the Chinese would bomb Japan. I told him that if we let American planes be flown to Canada, I did not see why these bombers could not be flown to China via Hawaii and the Philippines.

I told Soong that I noticed in Chiang Kai-shek's memo that they have airfields within 650 miles of Tokyo and that he also offered to furnish me with this information.

I said that I thought this could be done by January, and it would be possible to arrange to hire pilots who are experienced in flying this kind of bomber.

Soong is to let me know just as soon as he hears from Chiang Kai-shek.

If the Chinese would do this, I am convinced that overnight it would change the whole picture in the Far East. Soong is convinced that it would have a very decided effect on the Japanese population, because he said that they are at present in a very critical political state at home . . ."[78]

THE SECRET MEMO FROM CHIANG KAI-SHEK

Chiang Kai-shek's memorandum—the subject of discussions between Soong and Morgenthau (and almost certainly, President Roosevelt) following Sunday's lunch on December 8, 1940—consisted of four typewritten pages.[79] The memo is, of course, marked SECRET and bears a handwritten notation on the top of the document: "T. V. Soong sent this over after his meeting with the Secretary—12 noon—11/30/40." Since the notation declares that there was a meeting between Morgenthau and Soong on November 30, 1940, we know the first meeting between

Morgenthau and Soong was prior to Sunday dinner at the White House on December 8, 1940. While not conclusive evidence, these facts suggest, circumstantially, that the secret memorandum from Chiang Kai-shek (or possibly written by Soong, in Washington, at the generalissimo's direction) was composed sometime during November of 1940.

The generalissimo's secret memo reported that Japan had lost 1.1 million soldiers in combat due to death or invalidation (i.e., were no longer physically fit to serve in the military), and that Japan was required to keep 1.25 million soldiers in China as an occupational force exclusive of the forces in Manchuria. Chiang Kai-shek's strategy of yielding ground (and the lives of Chinese) and engaging in guerrilla warfare is confirmed in this memorandum. Furthermore, the generalissimo indicated that Japan desired to withdraw its troops from China for *southward expansion* and conquests in Indochina, the Dutch East Indies, and Malaya. Chiang Kai-shek hypothesized that the Japanese government desired to negotiate an "easy" peace with China so that if and when the Japanese government prevailed over the British Empire in Southeast Asia, Japan could renounce the peace with China.

The memo also revealed that Germany was trying to mediate the conflict between Japan and China. In this regard, it is important to note that while the Tripartite Pact was in effect between Germany, Japan, and Italy, Germany still had ties with the Chinese government. For example, German officers had trained and organized the Chinese army. Chiang Kai-shek's son had served in the German Wehrmacht for training purposes. Chinese troops wore helmets that looked exactly like German helmets. Chiang Kai-shek had an inner circle of soldiers protecting him, very much like Hitler's vaunted SS troops. Chinese ace pilots had received flight training in Germany.

We know from Chiang Kai-shek's secret memo that the drain on China's resources was substantial, with an army of 2.5 million men in the field and 2 million more guerrilla fighters. He further related that the Chinese people had suffered inflation of seven- or eightfold. Despite these economic sacrifices, their resistance to Japan's invasion had been maintained in the belief that the democratic countries would eventually prevail in their combat with the Axis powers. However, with the success of the German army in France and throughout Western Europe, the faith of the Chinese people was being shaken. As a result, the generalissimo had turned his attention to the need for a Chinese air force, and went on to state:

Russia has stopped sending planes, and since September [sic] this year, Japanese planes are much superior in quality, as well as in absolute numbers, so that today no existing Chinese planes could take the air [sic]. The effect of constant bombing on the Chinese troops, and especially on the civilians in the principal cities, without the possibility of any defense, is telling on the general morale.[80]

As aviation historian Richard Dunn has noted in his monograph, *The Vultee P-66 in Chinese Service*, ". . . in November, 1940, it was not literally true that the Russians had stopped supplying aircraft to China."[81] However, the *last* shipment was *en route* and the Russian supply of airplanes was drying up.[82]

In the fifth paragraph of Chiang Kai-shek's secret memo, he suggested the formation of a Special Air Unit composed of two hundred bombers and three hundred fighter planes that would be operated by pilots and mechanics "from the British and American training centers."[83] Noting there could be complications in having British and American pilots flying combat planes in China, the generalissimo observed, "Special consideration must be given to the status of this force, according to the political development of the situation in the Far East."[84] He then went on to say, "This air force should be created at once, so as to be assembled in China and ready to operate before the start of the Japanese spring offensive on Singapore."[85]

Approximately one year later, following the attack on Pearl Harbor, President Roosevelt's address to Congress stated that the Japanese had embarked upon a "*surprise* [emphasis added] offensive extending throughout the Pacific area." However, we learn from Chiang's memo that the U.S. government had known about Japanese designs on Singapore and territories in the Far East at least one year earlier.

In paragraph six of his memo, we see Chiang Kai-shek attempting to entice the American government into providing long-range bombers for operation in China:

There are 136 airfields available in China, more than half of which are in excellent condition, and all serviceable for both bombers and pursuits. Several of these airfields are within 650 miles from Japan; and they are so located that they are not easily vulnerable to army attacks. Japanese garrisons are nowhere in proximity and land attacks would require, in most cases, the concentration of several divisions over extremely difficult terrain without communications, thus leaving adequate time for defense or for transfer of menaced airbases.

This Special Air Unit could operate in conjunction with the Chinese army which, so supported, could effectively take offensive actions against Canton, to relieve Hong Kong; against Hankow, to clear the Yangtze Valley; or again the Unit could *operate independently in attacking Japan proper* [emphasis added], Formosa and Hainan.

According to the political strategic necessities of the war in Asia and Europe, it will be possible to take [sic] a decision as to the advisability of carrying the air war into Japan proper. One should not be dogmatic as to the reaction bombing will have on [the] Japanese psychology, but every day evidences accumulate of growing internal dissensions in Japan, and the severe strain and privations the Japanese people are put to by the prospect of a war without end, when at the beginning of their Chinese adventure they were told that hostilities would only last a few months.[86]

The generalissimo added a footnote to his secret memorandum, saying that a confidential map could be provided to the American government showing the location of the air bases in China from which bombing raids might be mounted on Japan. Finally, Chiang Kai-shek again requested that the Special Air Unit be organized within the next two weeks in order to start operations in the spring of 1941.

SOONG'S LETTER TO MORGENTHAU, DECEMBER 9, 1940

Further evidence of the substance of discussions at the White House luncheon of December 8, 1940, is found in Dr. Soong's handwritten letter to Morgenthau, dated the day after the luncheon.[87] Soong wrote: "In connection with General Chiang Kai-shek's secret memorandum to the president concerning China's air needs, I take the pleasure of enclosing a map of China, showing the location of the airfields now in the possession of our Air Force, which, I hope will prove of interest."[88]

Soong further related in a postscript: "This map is of course very secret, and is for your personal information."[89] Included with the Soong letter in the Morgenthau diary is a two-page map of China (identified as Exhibits 7 and 8 in Appendix 1), consisting of rectangles that identify the location of airfields in China. A number of these airfields were located in eastern China so as to minimize the flight time for bombers attacking Japan.

Chiang Kai-shek, in an attempt to forestall the collapse of China to Japan, had seized upon a bold plan to mount bombing raids on Japan from China. If desperate times call for desperate measures, one can certainly appreciate why he would take such extraordinary action as to send his American military advisor Chennault to Washington in hopes of forming an American guerrilla air corps whose function would be to curtail and hopefully preempt further Japanese aggression in Southeast Asia.

Chapter Five

TEACH THE JAPANESE
A LESSON

"Find a way to have them drop some bombs on Tokyo."

—Secretary of State Cordell Hull, December 10, 1940

By December of 1940, officials at the highest levels of America's government were giving serious consideration to China's request for a Special Air Unit. Secretary of the Treasury Henry Morgenthau called on Secretary of State Cordell Hull at 8:40 A.M. on Tuesday, December 10, 1940.[90] That morning the following conversation took place (as recorded by Morgenthau):

Hull: What we have to do, Henry, is to get five hundred American planes to start from the Aleutian Islands and fly over Japan just once. That will teach them a lesson. If we could only find some way to have *them* drop some bombs on Tokyo.
Morgenthau: Well, who do you mean?
Hull: The Chinese.
Morgenthau: Well, Cordell, you leave me speechless. I didn't know you felt this way. Sunday I suggested to T. V. Soong in the greatest of confidence and secrecy that he wire Chiang Kai-shek that we could make available to him a limited number of long-distance bombers provided that they were used to bomb Tokyo.

Hull: Fine. That proviso doesn't have to be part of the contract, does it?

Morgenthau: Of course not.

Hull: How would you get them over there?

Morgenthau: We are letting them fly planes from San Diego to Halifax. Couldn't we let them fly the planes to Hawaii and the Philippines and then to their destination in China?

Hull: Absolutely. I will be for that. They have airfields in China within six hundred miles of Tokyo. But couldn't we fly them to the Philippines ourselves in order to make a demonstration to Tokyo, and then let the Chinese take title for them in the Philippines?

Morgenthau: It might be worked out, but I think it is more difficult.[91]

Implicit in the Morgenthau/Hull discussion was the idea of providing bombing aircraft to China, with the understanding they would be employed to bomb Tokyo. However, they did not want any *evidence* of this understanding.

Following Morgenthau's chat with Hull, he noted that he had told Hull he would need Hull's help in persuading (Secretary of War) Stimson to release more planes. Hull had responded by saying he had already asked Stimson for a meeting with the Defense Commission, ". . . so that he could tell them that unless they really got the U.S. industry producing that it would be too late by the spring to keep Hitler from winning."[92] Morgenthau went on to say:

> He [Hull] has been talking to the head of the American Manufacturers' Association. He is just a bundle of fervor and vitality on this thing . . . What has come over Hull I don't know, but his whole talk is that unless we get this country really producing that we can't help England.
>
> I am going to see a lot more of Hull because we evidently are thinking absolutely along the same lines as to what are the necessary steps to take to get this country ready to defend itself.[93]

It is understandable that Secretary of State Hull would seize upon the idea of having Tokyo bombed as a means of curtailing Japanese designs in the Pacific and Southeast Asia. American theories on airpower at the time were shaped by General Billy Mitchell and the Italian war theorist, General Giulio Douhet, who maintained that strategic bombers were the

weapon of choice to destroy the will and productive capacity of a belligerent nation. In fact, upon America's entry into World War I, the Congress
passed an enormous aviation appropriations bill, believing that large ar-
madas of American warplanes would bring a prompt end to the conflict
with Germany and its allies.[94]

However, in 1940, America grossly underestimated the Japanese in
terms of their technology and their will to fight. In addition, the Air
Corps leadership seems to have ignored the ability of fighter planes to intercept and destroy bombers.

THE COMPETITION BETWEEN CHINA AND BRITAIN FOR AMERICAN BOMBERS

While the thought of hitting Japan was tantalizing, there were tremendous obstacles to be overcome if the plan was to succeed. Providing long-
range bombers to China presented America with significant problems.
U.S. aircraft production capacity was not unlimited, and the needs of
Great Britain had to be considered. Six days before the White House
luncheon involving President Roosevelt, Morgenthau, and Dr. Soong,
Morgenthau and British ambassador Philip Kerr, 11th Marquess of
Lothian, had discussed the option of supplying China with "three- or
four-engine bombers . . . with the understanding that these bombers
[were] to be used to bomb Tokio [sic] and other big cities."[95]

Ambassador Lothian was a very distinguished British politician and
diplomat. He was appointed private secretary by British prime minister
David Lloyd George in 1916 and was active in the Paris Peace Conference at the conclusion of the First World War. In response to Morgenthau's suggestion, Ambassador Lothian was "very enthusiastic, and said it
might change everything."[96] Lothian agreed to discuss the matter with
Dr. Soong, but he failed to do so.[97] After discussing it with his people, the
British officials ". . . felt it was *impracticable* [emphasis added] and that the
Chinese wouldn't want it, because it would mean the Japanese would only
retaliate harder than ever."[98]

The British reaction to Morgenthau's suggestion—that America employ China as a surrogate to bomb Japan—must be put into proper context. England was fighting for her own survival. The Luftwaffe had
commenced bombing operations against England on August 13, 1940
(also known as "Eagle Day").[99] German submarines roamed the Atlantic

in "wolf packs," slaughtering merchant ships bringing food and war materiel to England. While England required 43 million tons of goods per year in imports, only 36 million were getting through.[100] Britain needed American long-range bombers to patrol the Atlantic and combat the German submarine menace. Clearly, Britain had her own needs to consider, even at China's expense. Hull, Stimson, and Morgenthau recognized that given the limitations of America's war production efforts, providing long-range bombers to China would work against Britain and her prospects for survival.

THE ISOLATIONIST VERSUS INTERVENTIONIST DEBATE BETWEEN LINDBERGH AND ROOSEVELT IN 1939–40

To fully appreciate the political dilemma presented by China's request for combat aircraft, and American airmen to fly them, we must look to the year 1939.

On April 20 of that year, President Roosevelt met with Charles Lindbergh, the heroic airman who had made the first solo flight from New York to Paris in 1927.[101] Lindbergh's remarkable achievement had catapulted him onto the world stage. He was an authority on aviation matters, had pioneered air routes for Pan American Airways, and engaged in international and exploratory flights accompanied by his wife, Anne. In addition to his aviation achievements, Lindbergh was involved in the development of technology that was the precursor to the artificial heart.

Unhappily, Lindbergh paid a high price for his fame when his son was kidnapped and murdered. The murder trial that followed and the subsequent media attention prompted Lindbergh to move his family to Europe for a period of self-imposed exile. While living in England, Lindbergh met with Major Truman Smith, military attaché to the American embassy in Berlin. On behalf of the German government, Major Smith invited Lindbergh to inspect and fly the latest aircraft in the inventory of the Luftwaffe.[102] After this experience, Lindbergh was uniquely qualified to provide information to the United States on the military threat Adolf Hitler presented to the world.

When General Hap Arnold, who commanded the Army Air Corps, learned that Lindbergh was coming back to live in America in April of

1939, he radioed Lindbergh's ship. Arnold asked that Lindbergh contact him as soon as possible following his arrival in the U.S.[103] The day after he returned, Lindbergh drove to West Point for a meeting with Arnold, who acknowledged that Lindbergh's reports had provided "the most accurate picture of the Luftwaffe, its equipment, leaders, apparent plans, training methods, and present defects."[104] General Arnold requested that Lindbergh return to active duty as a colonel in the United States Army Air Corps to "make a study of an attempt to increase efficiency of American [aeronautical] research organizations."[105]

Before Lindbergh met Roosevelt, he met Secretary of War Harry Hines Woodring to discuss his general thoughts on military aviation in Europe and America. Afterwards, Lindbergh met with President Roosevelt. Although we do not know everything that was said that day, we do know that following the meeting, Lindbergh wrote of Roosevelt: "I liked him and feel that I could get along with him well. Acquaintanceship would be very pleasant and interesting."[106] Following the meeting with the president, Lindbergh was besieged with a flock of press photographers on the White House steps. When Roosevelt was interviewed by the press following the meeting with Lindbergh, the president stated that Lindbergh's information corroborated facts already known to the American government.[107]

Lindbergh was given a Curtiss P-36A fighter based at Bolling Field in Washington, D.C. After flying the plane for a few hours to become comfortable with his new charge, Lindbergh embarked on a three-week inspection tour with twenty-three stops. During the summer of 1939, Lindbergh visited laboratories, airfields, factories, and educational facilities from coast to coast. One of Lindbergh's stops was in Roswell, New Mexico, where he renewed contact with his old friend, Dr. Robert Goddard, America's pioneer in rocket development. When Lindbergh explained how guarded the Germans were in discussions of rocket technology, they concluded the Germans must have great plans for its development. Meanwhile, Goddard was forced to resort to his own devices and grants from benefactors in his rocket development work. In addition to his aerial odyssey, Lindbergh headed a NACA committee charged with coordinating two dozen organizations engaged in aeronautical research, and he sat on an Air Corps board that was revising proposed specifications for military aircraft that would be produced within the next five years. Lindbergh accepted only two weeks' pay for his months of work on behalf of the Air Corps.[108]

However, Lindbergh's pursuits in the summer of 1939 were not *solely* aeronautical. He also renewed his acquaintance with William R. Castle, a conservative associated with the Republican National Committee who had served as ambassador to Japan and undersecretary of state.[109] Castle introduced Lindbergh to Fulton Lewis Jr., a conservative news commentator. Lindbergh's belief that America ought to avoid war should it develop in Europe was reinforced by these men of like minds. The opportunity to express these beliefs came after September 1, 1939, when Germany invaded Poland.

Wasting no time, Lindbergh addressed the nation on September 15, in remarks entitled, "An Appeal for Isolation."[110] Lindbergh proclaimed: "We must either keep out of European wars entirely, or stay in European affairs permanently."[111] However, Lindbergh's thinking evidenced a racial component when he said, "This is not a question of banding together to defend the White race against foreign invasion."[112] While Lindbergh was a gifted aeronautical pioneer who made remarkable advances in aviation and science, his views on race and culture would not be generally accepted today.

Prior to this first radio address, Lindbergh had met with General Arnold, saying he would return to inactive status in view of his decision to take an active role in politics. Truman Smith, now a colonel in G-2 (Military Intelligence) had also met with Lindbergh on September 15, 1939, before the first radio address. Smith related that the Roosevelt administration had concerns about the Lone Eagle's taking to the national airwaves in an address expressing a conviction that America should remain detached from the war in Europe. In fact, the administration was so concerned it was prepared to appoint Lindbergh to a cabinet position of secretary of state for air if Lindbergh would *not* voice his political opinions. Laughing, Smith conceded the administration was worried. However, Lindbergh's response to the administration's offer was a foregone conclusion. Smith knew Lindbergh to be a man of conviction and principle. There is no indication Lindbergh ever seriously entertained the offer.

Following Lindbergh's first radio address, he received hundreds of telegrams and letters, the majority of which were favorable. However, at least one news commentator who had previously written that Lindbergh had spoken "bravely" before the Berlin Aero Club[113] now portrayed him as a "pro-Nazi recipient of a German medal."[114] However, General Arnold wrote that Secretary Woodring thought Lindbergh's speech "was very well worded and very well delivered."[115]

On October 13, 1939, Lindbergh gave his second national radio address, entitled "Neutrality and War."[116] He maintained that America should refuse "credit to belligerent nations or their agents."[117] Lindbergh's second address came at a time when President Roosevelt was advocating legislation that would relax the American Neutrality Law and allow the sale of war materiel to combatants on a "cash and carry basis." On September 21, 1939, Roosevelt had reassembled the Congress during an extraordinary session, seeking a repeal of the embargo provisions of the Neutrality Law, which advocated that America "require all purchases to be made in cash, and all cargoes to be carried in the purchaser's own ships, at the purchaser's own risk."[118] Lindbergh's words conflicted with those of President Roosevelt. However, Lindbergh did not relent in his opposition to American involvement abroad, even if it was only selling materials to belligerent nations.

Lindbergh met with a half-dozen Democratic senators who sought to place language in the legislation then under consideration that would minimize the chances of the United States becoming embroiled in foreign wars.[119] He also met with Republican leaders, including former president Herbert Hoover, William Castle, and Carl Ackerman, the dean of the Columbia University School of Journalism. Senator William E. Borah suggested Lindbergh would make a good candidate for president. Lindbergh's efforts notwithstanding, the Neutrality Law was relaxed by legislation enacted on November 4, 1939, allowing the sale of materiels to belligerents provided they paid in cash, and provided American vessels were not employed in the transportation of the goods.

Continuing his clash with the Roosevelt administration, Lindbergh's isolationist essay, "Aviation, Geography, and Race" appeared in the November 1939 issue of *Reader's Digest*.[120] Although Roosevelt had won the first round in the debate with Charles Lindbergh, as we shall see later, the debate between the president and the Lone Eagle over the topic of U.S. foreign policy was far from over.

With the relaxation of the Neutrality Law, England spent vast sums of money in America buying planes, guns, ammunition, and food to sustain itself during its "darkest hour." China had been allowed to "borrow" money from America to finance her war with Japan. It is submitted that Britain spent substantially more money on weapons purchased from America than China did.[121] Eventually, America would provide food and war materials to its allies in World War II, employing a concept of "lend-lease," this being the subject of further debates between Roosevelt and Lindbergh. However, in the fall of 1940, foreign combatants were to *pay* for the materials required to wage war.

This explains why Morgenthau oversaw a "loan" of $100 million to China. After all, America was ostensibly neutral in the Sino-Japanese War. If America admitted that it was subsidizing China's war effort, the American government would be in violation of the Neutrality Law. More important, America—a nation allegedly at peace with Japan—would have to admit to the world that she was a non-belligerent ally of China. Only by employing a loan to China could America *legally* provide that country with the weapons needed to fight Japan.

Providing American airmen to man and fly the aircraft was an entirely different matter. America would need a plausible cover story for an efficient guerrilla air corps, or, as Chiang Kai-shek called it, a Special Air Unit operating in China. What about Pawley, Leighton, and their business concerns, CAMCO and Intercontinent? Would the American government take them up on their offer to fund a guerrilla air corps as a commercial venture, thereby paying lip service to the American Neutrality Law?

While the Roosevelt administration was pondering a bombing initiative directed at Japan, Chennault decided to try, once again, to return to service in the Air Corps. He met with Elwood R. (Pete) Quesada, who would eventually attain the rank of Lieutenant General and command the Ninth Air Force in Europe. Chennault, then making $15,000 a year, was offered a non-flying job making $4,300 a year at the same coast-artillery post position he had declined nearly a year earlier. In his biography, Chennault wrote about the experience: "Pete was slightly piqued at my ingratitude. I never did convince the Air Corps that I was not just looking for a regular pay check but really wanted to do a specific job that I knew was being badly neglected." As war with the Axis Powers loomed on the horizon, the Air Corps *still* lacked the vision to avail itself of Chennault's experience in China and his theories on air interception and fighter tactics.

CHIANG KAI-SHEK'S TELEGRAM TO ROOSEVELT, DECEMBER 12, 1940

On Thursday, December 12, 1940, the generalissimo telegraphed the president to thank him for his "generous and timely announcement of a substantial loan to China," which "has infinitely increased China's powers of resistance, strengthened its social and economic structure, and enhanced the confidence of the army and the people in its final victory over the aggressor."[122] Turning to the proposal for an air force for China, Chiang Kaishek requested that the president convey his views "on these grave matters" to Dr. Soong, "as soon as possible."[123] The generalissimo explained that his purpose in seeking a powerful air arm in China was "to prevent the spreading of the war to Southern Asia, and to accelerate its termination."[124]

Then, on December 16, 1940, the generalissimo dispatched a telegram to Morgenthau[125] in which he was quite explicit about China's objectives in securing a substantial air force:

> . . . I am most anxious to acquire as many of your latest Flying Fortresses as you could spare, which from our air bases could effectively bomb all the vital centers of Japan, and harass their fleet and transports. The effect of this upon the Japanese people who are already much divided and dispirited will certainly be far-reaching.
>
> The Flying Fortresses should be complemented by a proportionate number of pursuits and medium bombers, so that the air force thus constituted could also support the counteroffensive which I am preparing with a view of taking Canton and Hankow, and of forcing the Japanese to recall their troops, transports, and airplanes from the contemplated attack on Singapore, the safety of which is vital to us as to the British.[126]

Chiang Kai-shek's request for Flying Fortresses was audacious. The Boeing B-17 Flying Fortress was a marvel of American technology. Boeing had designed the four-engine bomber based on its experience with the Boeing Model 247 commercial airliner. Powered by four Pratt & Whitney R-1690-E Hornet radial engines, the prototype was designated the Boeing Model 299 and first flew on July 28, 1935. The bomber had four blisters for machine guns, a dorsal position on the fuselage above the wing, a ventral position on the fuselage behind the trailing edge of the wing, and waist blisters on either side of the fuselage. Legend has it that a reporter, upon seeing the 48,000-pound behemoth, remarked: "Wow, it's a flying fortress!" Another explanation given for the B-17's name was the fact that its original mission was to attack enemy warships off the coast of the United States, thereby becoming, in effect, a "flying fortress." Regardless of which story is correct, the name stuck.

The prototype could carry 4,800 pounds of bombs, and on its maiden flight in 1935, it flew 2,100 miles at a cruising speed of 232 miles per hour and an average altitude of 12,000 feet. It could fly higher, faster, and with greater range and heavier bomb loads than any large bomber in service at that time, with any other air force in the world. Its only rival in 1940 was the relatively new Consolidated B-24 Liberator. The Liberator prototype had first flown on December 29, 1939, and had not been in service as long as the B-17. While the Liberator did not have the same level of operational experience as the B-17, Liberators would be supplied to the Royal Air Force when President Roosevelt's request for Lend-Lease authority was authorized by Congress in March of 1941.

Not only was the B-17 the weapon of choice for all of the reasons mentioned above, but it also featured that triumph of American technology, the Norden bombsight, which was essentially an analog computer comprised of motors, gyroscopes, mirrors, levers, and gears, along with a small telescope. The Army Air Corps would brag that the bombsight could put a bomb in a pickle barrel from 30,000 feet. The capabilities of the Norden bombsight were a carefully guarded military secret, to such an extent that the following Bombardier's Oath was administered to any airman who had knowledge of its workings:

> Mindful of the secret trust about to be placed in me by my Commander-in-Chief, the President of the United States, by whose direction I have been chosen for bombardier training . . . and mindful of the fact that I am to become guardian of one of my country's most priceless military assets, the American bombsight . . . I do here, in the presence of Almighty God, swear by the Bombardier's Code of Honor to keep inviolate the secrecy of any and all confidential information revealed to me, and further to uphold the honor and integrity of the Army Air Forces, if need be, with my life itself.

On December 19, Morgenthau gave the first of the generalissimo's two telegrams, dated December 12, 1940, to President Roosevelt, and the second, dated December 16, 1940, to Hull.[127] In the interim, however, Morgenthau had been busy working on the Special Air Unit for China.

On the previous day, he had a phone conversation with the president asking for a meeting the following day.[128] When the president inquired as to the purpose of the meeting, Morgenthau replied, "It has something to do with a very secret message from Chiang Kai-shek."[129] The president then asked: "Is he still willing to fight?"[130] Morgenthau replied: "That's what the message is about."[131] Morgenthau then reports on the president's reply: "Wonderful. That's what I have been talking about for four years."[132] In a single-spaced, typed note dated December 18, 1940, Morgenthau placed the president's remarks in context, noting: "When he said that that is what he had been talking about for four years, I had just made the remark that Chiang Kai-shek's message was that he wanted to attack Japan."[133]

Morgenthau concluded his summary of his conversation with the president, commenting: "Undoubtedly, the President was in grand humor. He said, 'There's one other thing I want to talk to you about and I'll tell you about it in the morning.'"[134]

Not only had Morgenthau spoken with the president about the Special Air Unit on December 18, but he had also had two phone conversations with Dr. Soong on the same day about this very urgent topic.[135] Morgenthau summarized the substance of the first conversation in his notes:

T. V. Soong called and said that General Chiang Kai-Shek [sic] feels that the only way to stop the Japanese from going down and attacking Singapore in April is for the Chinese to attack Japan and Chiang Kai-Shek [sic] is ready to do so provided that we can furnish him with Boeing bombers and the escort planes necessary to accomplish it. He said it is important that they be given the materiel to build up a ground organization. He left with me a map, which he says is very secret, which shows the various airfields in China. There is a big field located at *Chekiang* which he says is only *500 miles from Japan* [emphasis added].

He is leaving at my house tonight a more detailed memorandum on just what General Chiang Kai-Shek [sic] said. I promised him I would lay the whole thing before the President sometime tomorrow. He also asked if I could deliver to the President a personal message from General Chiang Kai-Shek [sic] rather than go through the State Department and I said I could.[136]

Why was Soong requesting that Morgenthau deliver a note from Chiang Kai-shek to President Roosevelt? There appears to be several possible answers to this question.

First, Soong knew how to use his influence. While he was a close friend of Morgenthau's, he may not have enjoyed such a close friendship with Cordell Hull. Second, Morgenthau appears to have been closer to Roosevelt than Hull. Third, Morgenthau acted outside his portfolio, becoming involved in foreign policy matters, especially when it came to China. Finally, it has been suggested that Roosevelt did not think Hull was sufficiently firm with the Japanese. In any case, so far as Soong was concerned, Morgenthau was the means by which he could gain access to Roosevelt, not Hull.

In their second conversation of December 18,[137] Morgenthau recounts their discussion in a single-page, typewritten note:

> I told T. V. Soong that Cordell Hull has brought up the question himself of the advisability and feasibility of bombing Japan from China. When Hull did this, I told him of my conversation with Soong. I also told Soong that not only did Hull approve the plan of their having these bombers with which to bomb Japan, but he also approved the idea of having them fly from the West Coast via Hawaii, Wake Island, and the Philippines directly to China. I told him that Hull was the only person who knew of this besides myself, but I would be in touch with the President tomorrow.
>
> He told me that he had information that the Germans and Italians expect to go right ahead with their campaign, irrespective of temporary reverses that they are having in Greece and Africa.[138]

While Dr. Soong was lobbying with Morgenthau for bombers to be flown to China, Chennault was visiting Air Corps staff officers at the Munitions Building in Washington. When General Arnold asked Chennault to give a lecture on the Sino-Japanese War, Chennault had to sketch in the locations on a poorly detailed map. While Washington war planners were focused on the situation in Europe, little thought and few resources were being devoted to the war in China.

The Air Corps staff officers' indifference to affairs in China was illustrated by the fact that a dossier Chennault had provided on the Nakajima

Army Type 97 fighter was missing. Chennault discussed the matter with Haywood "Possum" Hansell, who, before Billy McDonald, had flown with Chennault in the Flying Trapeze act. According to Air Corps records, no one had ever seen the dossier. Air Corps technical manuals in use at the time devoted a blank page to the Japanese Zero.

How were personnel in the American State Department feeling about the Chinese government's efforts to obtain a Special Air Unit? The answer is found in a letter from the Division of Far Eastern Affairs to Secretary Hull, dated December 3, 1940. In that letter, State Department personnel requested that Secretary Hull deliver an oral statement to Dr. Soong with the following six components.

The first component stated: "This government has recently taken steps toward making available to China within the comparatively near future fifty modern military aircraft and is giving its best thought and attention to the problem of making a substantial additional number of airplanes available as soon as practicable."[139] The oral statement also indicated that on November 30, 1940, President Roosevelt had "announced that this Government contemplated a credit to the Chinese government of $100,000,000."[140] Soong was to be told that supplying these airplanes was "not easy to arrange." Also, it was to be impressed upon Soong that "they [the airplanes] constitute solid and very substantial assistance to China. Their importance will be recognized by all."

The second component in the oral statement directed that Dr. Soong be told it was the "traditional policy of the United States to avoid entering into alliances or entangling commitments."[141] This element seems curious. How could America provide China with a credit of $100 million and fifty modern military aircraft, but somehow *not* have an "alliance" with China? It would appear that along with the provision of such extensive resources to the Chinese, there was a de facto—if not a formal—alliance.

The third item to be conveyed to Dr. Soong is particularly interesting. This point indicated that there were criminal penalties for foreign nationals who entered the United States to recruit personnel for service in foreign armed forces. In fact, Sections 21 and 22 of Title 18 of the United States Code were referenced in the oral statement. However, it was declared: "But there is no penalty in the general laws of the United States where citizens of the United States go abroad *and while abroad enter the armed forces of a foreign state* [emphasis added]."

Because of revisions made to criminal provisions of the United States Code, this would mean that if American aviators and technical personnel were to be recruited for service in China, the recruiters must be American, not Chinese. The oral statement also referred to considerations under the Selective Service Law, and went on to relate: "The Department of State would probably issue passports to American citizens who desire to proceed to China for the purpose of serving as aviation instructors."

The fourth element to be communicated to Dr. Soong was that the announcement date of November 30, 1940, was no accident, since that was the same day the Japanese signed a treaty with the Nanking regime. Even though the Japanese had established a puppet regime in Nanking, America still recognized the Nationalist government of China as located in Chungking.

The fifth item to be shared with Dr. Soong was that the "number of airplanes is receiving our best attention. This will not be an easy matter to arrange." The sixth and final item to be conveyed was the American government's desire that this information be delivered to the Chinese government by Dr. Soong and the Chinese ambassador.

It is interesting to note that at this time, Department of State personnel were already reflecting on the legal impediments involved in providing American airplanes and pilots to fly them. By elevating form over substance, it was suggested that American citizens could avoid any violations of the United States Criminal Code by allowing them to first go abroad, and *then* to enter the employ of a foreign state.

Chapter Six

"THIS COLONEL CHENNAULT, WHERE IS HE?"

Hundreds of Americans were slipping across the Canadian border to join the R.C.A.F. and fight in Europe, but the idea of American volunteers in China seemed fantastic. Virtually everybody to whom I broached the subject told me, with varying degrees of courtesy, that I was insane.

—General Claire Lee Chennault[142]

THE PRESIDENT WAS DELIGHTED

The China Bomber File created by Morgenthau contains his notes, memoranda, and records of conversations, both in person and via telephone. This file is found in the archives of the Roosevelt Presidential Library in Hyde Park, New York. As reflected in a memorandum in the China Bomber File, Morgenthau met with Soong in the presence of Morgenthau's assistant, Philip Young, and Morgenthau's secretary, Mrs. Klotz, at 4:00 P.M. on December 20, 1940, wherein Morgenthau related that he had delivered both of Soong's memoranda to the president on December 19.[143] Morgenthau and Soong then had the following exchange:

Morgenthau: He [the President] was simply delighted, *particularly with the one about the bombers* [emphasis added]. Yesterday, after Cabinet,

I asked for a chance, and the President had Hull, Stimson, and Knox stay, and we all had your map out, and the President gave it his approval. I said, "Should we work it out and come back?" and he said that it was not necessary. He said, "The four of you work out a program." Just how we're going to do it, I do not know, but I wanted you to know that the President was delighted. I am meeting again with these gentlemen on Monday. I wanted you to get word to Chiang Kai-shek that he has the approval of the President, and the President said he had been dreaming about this for years . . . I understand that the Japanese Navy has a new kind of fighting ship which takes off from an aircraft carrier, which is so much better than anything you have.

Soong: I understand that they do not take off from the decks of ships but from the water.

Morgenthau: This Colonel Chennault, where is he?

Soong: He is here now in Washington.

[At this point in the conversation, Morgenthau put a call in to Frank Knox, Secretary of the Navy who was in a meeting. Then he continued his discussion with Dr. Soong.]

Morgenthau: I have not told anybody about this outside of Mr. Young and Mrs. Klotz. I have told them because I need their assistance. I said, and I hope you will back me up, that if they could get a man who knew how to fly these four-engine bombers, that China would be glad to pay up to $1,000 a month in United States dollars. Was that too high?

Soong: No. Not at all.

Morgenthau: What are your plans for the next two days? Something might break over the weekend.

Soong: I will be available at any time.

Morgenthau: Find out whether a four-engine flying boat will be any use to you.[144]

Soong: It is the best news I have had since I came here.

Morgenthau: I am going to put all of my energy behind this because it has to be done at once.[145]

As a point of interest, while Chennault had retired from the Air Corps in 1937 with the rank of captain, he was referred to as "Colonel Chennault" in 1940. While it has been reported that Chennault became "a colonel, and foremost ace in the Chinese Air Force,"[146] it appears Madame Chiang Kai-shek felt he required a more prestigious honorary title so he could "deal as an equal with the generals."[147] Chennault had his good friend, Governor Jimmie Noe of Louisiana, bestow upon him the honorary title of colonel.[148]

MORGENTHAU PHONES KNOX AFTER THE MEETING WITH SOONG

Shortly after the meeting with Dr. Soong concluded, Morgenthau reached Navy Secretary Knox at 5:13 P.M. on a beautiful Friday evening in Washington. Washington had been enjoying an Indian summer, and Frank Knox was in an upbeat mood as he received the call from Morgenthau. They discussed a meeting of the "Plus Four" that was scheduled to be held in Hull's office at 9:30 on Monday morning, December 23. From the transcript of their telephone conversation, it is clear that Morgenthau was still moving full speed ahead with the program of arming China with long-range American bombers—what Morgenthau and Knox refer to as the "hush-hush thing" in the following transcript of their telephone conversation:

Morgenthau: I see. Well, I am delighted. Now, Frank whenever you're ready on that hush-hush thing which we've been talking about . . .

Knox: Yeah. I'm worried about that. I wanted to talk to you about that today but the President kept me pretty busy on this other thing.

Morgenthau: Well, when are you going to be ready?

Knox: I'll be ready any time. We must do it quickly if we're going to do it at all.

Morgenthau: Well, shall we do it Monday morning in Hull's office?

Knox: Yeah.

Morgenthau: Whoever's there we can "shush" them all out after we get through dividing up these three hundred Curtiss P-40s.

Knox: Where—what office, Henry?

Morgenthau: I sent you a list—I don't know whether you've got it. There are 300 Curtiss P-40s which can be ordered . . .

Knox: Three hundred Curtiss P-40s.

Morgenthau: Yeah.

Knox: For the British?

Morgenthau: Well, for anybody. They've got the engines.

Knox: Well, by God, we ought to grab some of those for the Chinese.

Morgenthau: Well, that's the point, and I sent you a list of all the requests from all the countries for the various things.

Knox: When did you send it to me?

Morgenthau: Oh, two days ago.

Knox: Well, then I've got it here. There's a lot of stuff here I haven't had a chance to . . .

Morgenthau: Two days ago—at the point—I mean, I'm sick and tired of all this hemming and hawing, you see, and I thought I'd lay the whole thing and decide what you're going to do with this new order. See?

Knox: Yeah.

Morgenthau: And I'll keep pushing for these foreign orders and playing nurse to them until the President tells me not to.

Knox: Uh-huh.

Morgenthau: I suppose, as far as I know, he wants me to continue doing this as I have.

Knox: Why sure. I don't know why not. There's nothing in this new set-up [sic] that interrupts that. You're, as I've always recognized your efforts, to help the British get what they want.

Morgenthau: Or any other foreign country where it doesn't interfere with our own progress.

Knox: That's right.

Morgenthau: Well, there are three hundred Curtiss P-40s that this fellow can still make. The English have got the engines 'cause they've cancelled the Lockheeds, you see.[149] Now, we've got the Greeks and Chinese and South Americans—I sent the whole list over and I thought the four of us would get together with Hull at 9:30. Did you get the note?

Knox: I got that note. Hull called me up about it. That's the one—9:30 A.M. at Hull's office. Okay. I've got that.

Morgenthau: Now, what we'll do is this, when we get through with that, I'll ask Hull to ask the other people to step out and we'll talk about the hush-hush mission.

Knox: All right. That's fine.

Morgenthau: How's that?

Knox: That's okay.

Morgenthau: Thank you.

Knox: All right, Henry.

Morgenthau: Good-bye.[150]

Morgenthau's reference to the Lockheeds was a reference to the Lockheed P-38 Lightnings which the British had ordered. This magnificent airplane suffered degraded performance after removing the turbosuper-chargers that gave it superior high altitude capability. Rather than having counter-rotating propellers as featured on American aircraft, the British Lockheed Lightnings had propellers which turned in the same direction. Equipped with the turbosuperchargers, the Lockheed P-38 Lightnings (which had originally been called "Atlantas") were a match for Axis fighters at high altitude. However, the aircraft was experiencing developmental problems, such as compressibility (inability to control the aircraft when approaching the speed of sound) during diving maneuvers. It is truly unfortunate the British were not allowed to properly equip these aircraft with the turbosuperchargers that gave them such outstanding performance at high altitude. With the outbreak of World War II, P-38 fighters shot down more Japanese planes than any other U.S. fighter.

CHENNAULT PRESENTS HIS PLAN TO MORGENTHAU TO BOMB JAPAN

As was the case with so many of the activities related to this Special Air Unit for China, the meeting about this "hush-hush" subject took place not in a government office building, but at Secretary Morgenthau's home at 5:00 P.M. on the evening of Saturday, December 21, 1940. Morgenthau, Dr. Soong, and now, General Mow—who had originally recruited Chennault to serve in China—assembled around the table in Morgenthau's dining room. Also in attendance were Claire Chennault and Morgenthau's aide, Mr. Philip Young. Chennault was a chain smoker, so it's easy to picture him puffing away on a Camel cigarette in what was very likely a smoke-filled room.

As the discussions began, Morgenthau explained to his confederates that President Roosevelt "was seriously considering trying to make some four-engine bombers available to the Chinese in order that they might bomb Japan."[151] Morgenthau then reported that the discussions had focused on the B-17 Flying Fortress, and he needed more information to find out just exactly what China had needed before going further.

When Dr. Soong requested that General Mow respond to Morgenthau's questions about China's needs, General Mow referred the question to Chennault. According to Morgenthau's "Notes on Conference at Home of Secretary," included in the China Bomber File: "Chennault . . . got out some maps of China and gave a brief discourse on the location of the Chinese airfields and the parts of China occupied by the Japanese."[152] Morgenthau then asked Chennault about "the type of equipment needed in order to reach Japan."[153] Chennault responded "that long-range bombers would be required and that it would be necessary to have pursuit ships to accompany them."[154] Dr. Soong interrupted, voicing his opinion that "the bombers were more important than the pursuit ships, but both General Mow and Colonel Chennault disagreed."[155]

Pressing the issue, Morgenthau asked these members of the Chinese lobby exactly what kind of bombers they needed. Chennault indicated that either the Lockheed Hudson (a bomber derivative of the Lockheed Model 14 Super Electra civilian airliner, equipped with an internal bomb bay and a machine-gun turret positioned on top of the aft fuselage) or the Boeing B-17 Flying Fortress would be acceptable. Chennault said that: "the Lockheed Hudson had a radius [of action] of 1,000 miles with a good load but that it was 1,200 miles to Tokyo, so that the Lockheed [Hudson] would not be able to reach that city. However, Nagasaki, Kobe, and Osaka were within range of the Hudson bomber."[156] When Morgenthau asked Chennault if the bombing could be conducted at night, Chennault said that would have to be the case, because the "pursuit ships did not have sufficient range to defend the bombers in daytime on such a long tour."[157]

According to his notes, Morgenthau then suggested spreading the large bombers around at different air bases, remarking that they could be moved from base to base so the Japanese would not know where they were.

"Chennault said that could be done, as there were two fields near the border of occupied China which were good enough for the Flying Fortresses and four fields good enough for the Lockheed Hudsons. One of the big fields had a[n] 1,800-yard runway which was plenty for the Flying Fortresses."[158] Chennault pointed out that "China should have about 130 pursuit ships in order to defend the bomber bases."[159] Then, General Mow said China needed "another 100 pursuit ships to keep the supply line open along the Burma Road and hold back Japanese operating from Indo-China."[160]

Chennault asked Morgenthau whether it would be possible to fly the planes into China from the Philippines. Morgenthau answered that it would not be a problem. Chennault noted that each American bomber should have an American pilot, an American bombardier, and about five mechanics. Morgenthau replied that the matter had been discussed, and that "the Army would release enough men from active duty at $1,000 per month to help the Chinese with the ships."[161] Soong and Mow both agreed that "$1,000 per month was all right [sic] to pay."[162]

General Mow pressed the issue of China's needs for pursuit planes. Morgenthau responded by saying that he believed China would require "at least a hundred, as ten or twenty would not do any good."[163] Morgenthau then asked General Mow what could be done about the bombs. Chennault replied that China had lots of bombs that could be adjusted to fit the Flying Fortresses.

When Morgenthau asked if it was a pipe dream to spread these bombers around in various fields and hide them from the Japanese, Chennault responded that it was not sound tactically, but he felt it could be done, and that "a terrific amount of damage could be accomplished before the Japanese found them."[164] Soong volunteered that "it was the only practical thing to do."[165]

The discussion then turned to the kinds of bombs to be employed on these bombing raids on Japan. Morgenthau recommended dropping incendiary bombs, since the Japanese cities were made up of just wood and paper. Chennault agreed that a lot of damage could be done, and even if the Chinese lost some bombers, the losses would be well justified.

Morgenthau's comments about employing incendiary bombs were understandable. Report Number 161-40 from the American Naval Attaché in Tokyo, dated September 30, 1940, noted:

> Fire-fighting facilities are woefully inadequate. Hoses are old, worn, and leaky. Water mains are shut off at night. Little pressure is available. Fire hydrants are few and far between. Sluggish canals and drainage pools are used for suction of hand-pumped and hand-carried fire apparatus. . . .
>
> Nine-tenths of Japanese houses are roofed with tiles. Ninety-nine out of a hundred are constructed of flimsy wooden materials which catch fire with alarming rapidity. Incendiary bombs sowed widely over an area of Japanese cities would result in the destruction of the major portions of these cities. . . .
>
> Bomb shelters are few in number and totally inadequate to accommodate even a minute percentage of the population.
>
> Transportation facilities are already overcrowded, and the evacuation of civilian population would be attended by

tremendous difficulties. Since every home in Japan is already crowded, few accommodations for refugees are available.

A complete list of important bombing objectives, including aircraft factories, steel and gas works, main transportation systems, and government buildings will be prepared and forwarded.

The discussion of whether to employ incendiary bombs on Japan suggests Morgenthau had more than a casual understanding of Japan's vulnerability to such weapons. Indicating the level of thought Morgenthau had given to this issue, he then asked about weather-reporting capabilities in China. Both General Mow and Dr. Soong said the Chinese were getting adequate weather reports.

Chennault commented to Morgenthau that incendiary bombs were lighter than conventional bombs. If they were used, the aircraft could carry more fuel, thereby increasing their range. As Morgenthau and members of the Chinese lobby continued their discussions that evening, it was felt "that nothing would do the Chinese much good except the big bombers if they were going to go after Japan."[166]

It is clear from this meeting with Chennault, Soong, and Mow that Morgenthau intended to move forward with plans for the Special Air Unit. According to legend, at some point while members of Roosevelt's cabinet were discussing the Chennault/Chinese initiative for provision of a Special Air Unit to China, Chennault sent a copy of A. E. Housman's poem, "Epitaph on an Army of Mercenaries" to President Roosevelt.

MARSHALL BLUNTS AMBITIONS OF THE CHINA LOBBY TO ACQUIRE FLYING FORTRESSES

At 5:00 P.M. the next day, Morgenthau, Stimson, and Knox met with General Marshall at Stimson's home.[167] Morgenthau proposed the idea of providing Flying Fortresses to China. General Marshall then revealed that he had had two meetings with Dr. Soong, Chennault, and General Mow. Morgenthau, in a memorandum to the China Bomber File, summarized the remarks of General Marshall:

General Marshall questioned the advisability of simply letting them [the Chinese] have the bombers. He also questions the advisability of taking these bombers away from the English at this time. During the long, dark nights in England, these bombers would be most useful. He is going to work on a plan for China. He thinks the English might give up some of their pursuit ships rather than these bombers.[168]

Daniel Ford tells the story in his book, *Flying Tigers—Claire Chennault and the American Volunteer Group*:

Stimson also had second thoughts. The bombing scheme was "half-baked," the Army Secretary decided, so he asked Marshall, Knox, and Morgenthau to his home that Sunday—a beautiful afternoon, virtually a second Indian summer—"to get some mature brains into it." The brains were Marshall's, and the Treasury secretary immediately capitulated to the general's cool logic. By Monday morning, only fighter planes were still on the table.[169]

Morgenthau returned home at 6:30 that evening and found Sir Frederick Phillips from the British Air Mission waiting for him. Sir Frederick related that Britain was "ready to put down $14,000,000 for 300 Hawke [sic] 81—As known as the Curtiss P-40s."[170] Sir Frederick and Morgenthau discussed just how perilously close Britain was to bankruptcy. Sir Frederick said that Britain was down to about $400,000,000 in gold and was spending $50,000,000 a week. Sir Frederick told Morgenthau, "[I]f something doesn't come forth from America soon in the way of assistance, they will have to do something else."[171]

Sir Frederick, noting that there was $360 million in Canadian gold in Canada, indicated it was the intention of his government to take all the money even though it might mean trouble with the Canadian government.

On Sunday, December 22, Philip Young, Morgenthau's devoted aide, prepared a three-page memorandum summarizing the aircraft available to equip the Special Air Unit for China, including their performance figures, bomb loads, operational altitudes, number and nature of machine guns, and their production schedules as allocated for the Royal Air Force and the Army Air Corps.[172] The only heavy bombers discussed in the Young memorandum are the Boeing B-17 Flying Fortress and the Consolidated B-24 Liberator (including the export versions sold to the Royal

Air Force, known as the LB-30). Mr. Young did not put any information in his memorandum about the Lockheed Hudson.

Phillip Young had attended the meeting with Morgenthau, Soong, Chennault, and Mow on the previous evening, and it is clear from his memo that he believed the B-17 and B-24 were the ideal aircraft for China. He felt they had adequate range to be employed on bombing missions to Tokyo. The Young memo also provided Morgenthau with information on pursuit planes that would be needed to protect the bomber bases and keep the vital supply line—the Burma Road—open. The only two pursuit planes mentioned were the Curtiss P-40 Tomahawk and the Republic P-43 Lancer.

Whether it was a pipe dream or a stroke of tactical brilliance, Chennault's plan to firebomb Japan had been shot down by General Marshall—at least for the moment.

JAPANESE ANXIETY OVER THE POTENTIAL FOR AMERICAN BOMBING RAIDS

While the Chinese-American bombing initiative appeared to have suffered a setback in late December of 1940, Report Number 18-41 from the American naval attaché in Tokyo, dated February 5, 1941, strongly suggests that the Japanese government, military, and civilian population were experiencing anxiety about the potential of an American bombing initiative. According to the report, the Japanese cabinet met on January 10, 1941, to discuss "the imminent danger of air raids, and the total lack of a proper air defense . . ." According to the report, the Japanese authorities had investigated the ability of Japanese cities to withstand aerial bombardment. The cover page of the report contains provocative language: "The authorities, from the prime minister down to the common people, are scared to death of air raids and know Japan is totally unprepared with AA defenses." The Japanese war minister, General Hideki Tojo, commented at the cabinet meeting: "We must take urgent measures to defend our air against enemy planes." The war minister further declared: "No matter how superior the defending air force is, the possibility cannot be forestalled that enemy aircraft will invade after dodging the air cordon. Although our air defense facilities have made rapid developments in connection with the China Emergency, we must be prepared for the danger of incessant air raids in time of emergency."

An investigation by the Japanese Home Office concluded:

> The majority of Japanese houses are made of wood and paper
> . . . If a 5 kilo bomb is dropped, it is absolutely impossible to
> extinguish the fire unless five or more people begin pouring
> on water constantly within the first five minutes. If the fire is
> not got under control within the minute, then it will spread to
> the entire structure within the next five minutes, a fact which
> is proved beyond doubt by recent tests. In large cities in Japan,
> there is practically no space between the houses, with the re-
> sult that a blaze will quickly spread from house to house and
> eventually will cause a huge conflagration.

The naval attaché report concluded with this telling language:

> Despite the grandiose plans of Japanese authorities for air de-
> fense, their inflammable cities, poor fire-fighting equipment,
> and lack of both money and materials to alter the case will
> continue to be the gravest dangers to Japanese life and secu-
> rity. Deep within their hearts the people believe it impossible
> for "enemy" aircraft to reach the Japanese islands proper,
> propaganda and ever-victorious "Wild Eagles" of the armed
> services having reaped excellent and significant fruit.

Without a doubt, the *possibility* of aerial bombardment of the Japanese
home islands was a source of great concern to Japan, at least as early as
January of 1941.

LINDBERGH AND ROOSEVELT DEBATE
THE LEND-LEASE POLICY OF 1941

While Chennault, Morgenthau, Hull, and Soong were planning air raids
on Japan, the Roosevelt administration struggled to find a way to openly
subsidize the wars of foreign belligerents. The battle between Roosevelt
and Lindbergh for public opinion did not end with relaxation of the Neutrality Law in 1939. Lindbergh became the champion of the Committee
to Defend America First ("America First"). The chairman of America

First was General Robert E. Wood, who was also chairman of Sears, Roe-buck and Company. No fewer than seven United States senators sought Lindbergh's support for their anti-interventionist views. Among the supporters of the America First movement was a law student named Gerald R. Ford, who would later become President of the United States.

The America First movement included Republicans, Democrats, and independents, national leaders connected with the Roosevelt administration, a daughter of former president Theodore Roosevelt, and even Captain Edward ("Eddie") Vernon Rickenbacker, the highest-scoring American fighter pilot of World War I, then president of Eastern Airlines.

With the advent of the America First movement, Lindbergh enjoyed the support of scholars, university presidents, and other men and women who influenced public opinion. A radio address by Lindbergh generated more mail than any other person in America at the time. While Lindbergh could speak with authority on the strength of the Luftwaffe, he had incorrectly declared at Yale University in October of 1940, "no nation in Asia has developed their aviation sufficiently to be a serious menace to the United States at this time . . ."[173] He also raised three rhetorical questions: "Do we intend to attempt an invasion of the continent of Europe? Do we intend to fight a war in the Orient? Do we intend to try both at the same time?"[174]

With America in economic despair, Roosevelt must have understood why many people would be attracted to the America First movement and its message of isolationism. A poll taken in the summer of 1940 indicated that Americans believed Germany would defeat Britain and Russia and dominate Europe. How could America, ranked *fourteenth* in global military power in 1940, expect to defeat Japan?

While the Roosevelt administration was fulfilling Chiang Kai-shek's request for a Special Air Unit, President Roosevelt, in a State of the Union address on January 6, 1941, asked Congress to pass legislation that would empower the president to transfer war materials to nations deemed vital to United States interests. This was viewed as giving the president the power to wage war without a declaration of war by Congress. Lindbergh, surrounded by motion-picture cameras, testified before the House Committee on Foreign Affairs on January 23, 1941, maintaining that Roosevelt's proposed Lend-Lease policy would weaken the American military when the Air Corps was already in "deplorable condition."[175]

Lindbergh's testimony failed to prevent passage of Roosevelt's Lend-Lease policy, which became law in March of 1941. Its enactment signaled the transfer of supervision of aid to China from Morgenthau's Treasury Department to the White House. Roosevelt could now dispense with the fiction of a "loan" to China and allow his aides to execute this American foreign-policy initiative. During an interview in April, when asked why Lindbergh had not been asked to rejoin the Air Corps, the president declared he viewed Lindbergh as an "appeaser." This prompted Lindbergh to resign his Air Corps commission.[176] Lindbergh paid a high price for exercising his First Amendment right to freedom of speech, noting: "Here I am stumping the country with pacifists and considering resigning as a colonel in the Army Air Corps when there is no philosophy I disagree with more than that of the pacifist, and nothing I would rather be doing than flying in the Air Corps."[177]

In the midst of personal disappointment, Lindbergh spoke to a rally of fifteen thousand in St. Louis on May 3, and on May 23, 1941, he made a speech at Madison Square Garden. There were twenty-five thousand people inside, with an equal number standing outside. Among those standing outside the Garden were followers of the pro-Fascist American Destiny Party. Lindbergh arrived for the America First rally accompanied by a police escort. As Lindbergh and other speakers appeared on the stage, a gathering of photographers rushed toward him. The scene was one of hysteria as people shouted "Lindy!" and "Our next President!"[178] With Lindbergh's introduction, there was thunderous applause. He proclaimed: "With adequate leadership we can be the strongest and most influential nation in the world."[179] In a remark that could only be considered threatening to the Roosevelt administration, he told the audience to "demand an accounting from a government that has led us into war while it promised peace."[180]

With Lend-Lease policies under way, the president had prevailed over the isolationists. No longer would the administration be required to provide weapons to friendly nations under the pretext of a "loan." Yet, Roosevelt's administration remained under the watchful eyes of Charles Lindbergh and the America First movement. Plans for aid to China and the concept of a preemptive air strike on Japan would have to be kept top secret.

As the members of the Roosevelt cabinet pondered the international situation of countries friendly to America, the very existence of the British and Chinese governments was in question in 1941. German U-boats were devastatingly successful in sinking merchant ships carrying food, clothing, and war supplies to England, which was desperately struggling for its survival. The Japanese occupied the ports and much of eastern China, as well as French Indochina. There was grave doubt about the future of these nations. How much more could they endure?

America was still feeling the effects of the Great Depression and was far from the superpower we know today. While Germany and Japan had swollen the ranks of their armed forces to accompany plans for or actual initiatives of conquest and domination, America's focus on her domestic troubles had led to budget cuts for armed forces that labored under the most austere conditions. The war in Europe, more so than the Sino-Japanese War, had awakened the United States from her isolationist slumber as factories turning out war machinery were expanding not only to meet the demands of the American military but also the needs of the U.S.'s de facto allies, Britain, Russia, and China. In contrast to the compromises America would be forced to make as she undertook to more fully arm herself while also seeking to satisfy needs abroad, Japan, ruled by Emperor Hirohito, who had ironically pronounced his reign *Showa* or "enlightened peace," was singularly focused on military expansion regardless of the domestic hardships imposed on her people.

Chapter Seven

THE GENESIS OF THE JAPANESE PLAN FOR A PREEMPTIVE STRIKE

We need not repeat that at present oil is the weak point of our Empire's national strength and fighting power . . . As time passes, our capacity to carry the war will decline and our Empire will become powerless militarily.

—Transcript of Japanese Imperial Conference,
September 6, 1941[181]

While American war planners in Washington had entertained—but for now, tabled—Chennault's plan for bombing raids on Japan by American planes and pilots, Japanese war planners were not so tentative. Her military leaders drew upon Japan's historical memory of defeating adversaries with economic and military resources greater than hers. Japanese military leaders were well acquainted with the execution of preemptive strikes. In her war with China (1894–95) and her war with Russia (1904–05), she had attacked *without* a formal declaration of war.

By launching preemptive strikes, Japan had used her navy to quickly gain command of the seas. By securing for herself an advantageous position, she forced both China and Russia to accept the futility of fighting a war they were incapable of carrying to the Japanese home islands. Both adversaries acquiesced in compromising peace agreements.

The reward for Japan in the First Sino-Japanese War was to wrest control of Korea from China. Prior to the Japanese initiative, Korea had been a tributary state of China. In the Treaty of Shimonoseki (April 17, 1895), China abandoned its claims to Korea, as well as ceding Taiwan and Lüshunkou (Port Arthur) to Japan.

Almost immediately, Russia, the German Empire, and the French Third Republic applied pressure on Japan to give up Port Arthur. Both Russia and Japan were trying to take over Korea. Japan sent an ultimatum on February 6, 1904, and attacked the Russian fleet at Port Arthur two days later. President Theodore Roosevelt mediated the Treaty of Portsmouth, a settlement signed at Portsmouth Naval Shipyard in Kittery, Maine. Russia surrendered her twenty-five-year lease to the naval base at Port Arthur, as well as the peninsula around it. Russia also agreed to evacuate Manchuria and recognize Korea as a Japanese sphere of influence.

In light of Japan's previous successes over China and Russia, one can understand why some Japanese leaders would have imagined that a preemptive strike on the American Pacific Fleet—followed by successful invasions of the Philippines, Malaya, the Dutch East Indies, Wake Island, Burma, Singapore, and other territories in Southeast Asia and the Pacific—would force America to resolve a war with Japan by a negotiated peace. While today, the idea of Japan taking on an industrial giant like America may sound fantastic, the reader must appreciate the military balance of power in 1941. America had only three advanced aircraft carriers in the Pacific; Japan had eight. While Japan lacked the industrial and manufacturing capacity of America, if war erupted in the Pacific, Japan would clearly have the initial military advantage.

THE GREAT PACIFIC WAR, A NOVEL

In 1925, Hector C. Bywater, a Far-East correspondent for the *London Daily Telegraph*, published a novel entitled *The Great Pacific War*. Bywater's novel hypothesized simultaneous attacks on Pearl Harbor, Guam, and the Philippines. This literary work became interesting reading for cadets at Eta Jima, the Japanese Naval War College. In fact, in 1936, Eta Jima published *The Study of Strategy and Tactics in Operations against the United States*. That study advised intrepid Japanese cadets: "In case the enemy's main fleet is birthed [sic] at Pearl Harbor, the idea should be to open hostilities by surprise attacks from the air."

Leading naval theorists in Japan had been inculcated in this strategy, essentially derived from a novel. Among them was Admiral Isoroku Yamamoto, who would assume command of the Japanese Combined Fleet on August 30, 1939. In addition to Bywater's novel, Yamamoto's thinking was influenced by the events of November 11, 1940, when twenty-one Swordfish biplanes launched from the British carrier *Illustrious* crippled seven Italian vessels, including three battleships at the heavily protected naval base in Taranto, Italy.[182] Only two British planes were lost in the raid of this shallow-water port. However, the balance of power in the Mediterranean shifted to the Royal Navy for six months.

Japan dispatched Commander Minoru Genda, an assistant naval attaché, who flew in from Berlin to inspect Taranto.[183] He concluded that the British had succeeded in realizing a tactical victory with their surprise attack, and had proven that properly configured torpedoes could operate successfully in shallow waters. Impressed by this information, Yamamoto dispatched a letter to Japanese navy minister, Admiral Koshiro Oikawa, arguing that a surprise attack on American military installations in Hawaii should be part of any Japanese military attack to the south. In fact, in December of 1940, at approximately the same time the Roosevelt administration was entertaining Chiang Kai-shek's request for preemptive bombing raids on Japan, Yamamoto had related to Rear Admiral Shigeru Fukudome: "I want to have [Rear Admiral] Onishi study a Pearl Harbor attack plan as a tentative step. After studying the result of his report, the problem may be included in the fleet training program, and I want to keep it a secret until that time."[184]

Like America, Japan had talented pilots and military strategists. Among them was Genda. Besides investigating how the British had ambushed the Italian fleet anchored in Taranto Harbor, Genda had served in the oldest Japanese fighter squadron and had gained a reputation as a superior fighter pilot. His group was called "Genda's Circus," and he soon rose to prominence in the Japanese navy. In early February of 1941, Genda was summoned by Rear Admiral Onishi to fleet headquarters, where Genda read the following letter from Admiral Yamamoto:

> In the event of outbreak of war with the United States, there would be little prospect of our operations succeeding unless, at the very outset, we can deal a crushing blow to the main force of the American Fleet in Hawaiian waters by using the

full strength of the 1st and 2nd Air Squadrons against it, and thus to preclude the possibility of the American Fleet advancing to take the offensive in the Western Pacific for some time.

And it is my hope that I may be given command of this air attack force, so that I may carry out the operation myself. Please make a study of the operation.[185]

Rear Admiral Onishi asked Genda: "Please make this study in utmost secrecy, with special attention to the feasibility of the operation, method of execution, and the forces to be used."[186] Amazingly, in the midst of the secret work of the Japanese navy, American ambassador Joseph C. Grew had heard a rumor from the head of the Peruvian legation, minister Ricardo Rivera-Schreiber, "that the Japanese military forces planned in the event of trouble with the United States, to attempt a surprise attack on Pearl Harbor using all of their military facilities." Grew dispatched a message to the American State Department which consulted with ONI, the Office of Naval Intelligence for the Far Eastern Section headed by Lieutenant Commander Arthur McCollum. McCollum, who was the author of an eight point action memorandum dated October 7, 1940, arguing for, among other things, the provision of aid to Chiang Kai-shek, had a message dispatched to Admiral Kimmel. In a strange point of irony, the message from ONI reached Kimmel on February 1, 1941, the day of his change of command ceremonies aboard his flagship the U.S.S. *Pennsylvania*. While ONI disclosed the rumor of a possible attack on Pearl Harbor heard by Grew in Tokyo, Kimmel was further instructed: "The Office of Naval Intelligence places no credence in these rumors." As Kimmel pondered this message from ONI on February 1, across the International Date Line in Japan, it was February 2, where Japanese Navy planners were pondering the very attack ONI told Kimmel he should disregard as an unfounded rumor."[187]

Only days before Genda was requested to develop a feasibility study concerning an attack on Pearl Harbor, Navy Secretary Knox sent a memorandum to Secretary of War Stimson (with a copy going to Admiral Kimmel, Chief of the Pacific Fleet) [CINPAC] in Hawaii, relating:

If war eventuates with Japan, it is believed easily possible that hostilities would be initiated by a surprise attack upon the

Fleet or the Naval Base at Pearl Harbor. In my opinion, the inherent possibilities of a major disaster to the fleet of this naval base warrant taking every step, as rapidly as can be done, that will increase the joint readiness of the Army and Navy to withstand a raid . . . [A]n air bombing attack . . . and air torpedo attack . . . might be initiated without warning prior to a declaration of war.[188]

Perhaps a week or ten days later, Commander Genda paid another visit to Rear Admiral Onishi at the Kanoya Naval Air Base.[189] In answer to the question put to him by Rear Admiral Onishi, Genda, as related in Goldstein and Dillon's *The Pearl Harbor Papers*, gave his answer in six parts:

1) This attack must be a perfect surprise attack. And the result of this attack must be such that the main force of the American Fleet will not be able to advance to the Western Pacific for a period of at least six months.

2) The main target of the attack must be against the American aircraft carriers and land-based planes.

3) We must use the entire carrier strength that we have.

4) In order to continue the attack by carrier-based planes, we must have sufficient means of supplying the carriers.

5) An attack by torpedoes will be the best, but when it is not possible due to antisubmarine or anti-torpedo obstructions in the deeper waters and near harbors, we must use dive-bombers for the attack. In that case, we must change the type of planes on the carriers. Whether the torpedo attacks be in shallow or deep waters, plans for such attacks must be made.

6) This attack will be difficult but not impossible. The success of this attack lies in the success of the initial attack; therefore, the planning of the attack must be done in strict secrecy.[190]

As Genda and Onishi discussed Genda's proposal, Genda insisted that Japan needed to mount a landing operation on Hawaii and deprive America of her largest and most advanced base. Onishi demurred: "With our present strength, we are not able to take the offensive in both the eastern and southern areas. First, we must destroy the larger part of the American fleet."[191] Genda was directed to continue his planning for an attack on the American carrier force, and Commander Akira Sasaki, a staff officer to the Japanese Combined Fleet, was developing similar plans with a focus on the American battleships.[192]

BASES FOR AMERICAN BOMBERS IN CHINA

While the U.S. Department of State postured that there was no "alliance" between America and China, a "strictly confidential" dispatch of February 8, 1941, from the American naval attaché for air, Major James M. McHugh, USMC, confirmed: "THEY BUILDING [sic] ONE NEW AIRFIELD NEAR CHENGTU COSTING THIRTY MILLION AND ENLARGING MANY OTHERS."[193] McHugh also confirmed China was receiving three hundred planes from Russia, half of which were twin-engine bombers "with a range of seven hours."[194]

In fact, there were five airfields in the vicinity of Chengtu. Taipingssu was home to a Chinese bomber group. Shuangliu was home to two pursuit groups. Fenghuangshan was a commercial field. Wenkiang was another bomber base. Finally, Hsinching is described in a report by Major F. J. McQuillen, USMC, assistant naval attaché for air, circa June 1941, as follows: "2000 x 2200 meters, has newly-constructed surfaced runway 150 x 1800 meters. This field has been constructed since December, 1940, and is intended to serve as a base for the heaviest bombardment planes that the Chinese can obtain."[195]

Chuchow (also known as Zhuzhou) was a forward air base in southeastern China only seven hundred miles from the nearest targets on Kyushu, and approximately eight hundred miles from the Yawata Steel Works.[196] Tokyo was only 1,300 miles away. A Flying Fortress with a full bomb load could reach naval targets at Nagasaki and Sasebo, and with a lighter bomb load and a heavier fuel load, Tokyo was within range. Kweilin (also known as Guilin) was an intermediate base well-positioned for attacks on French

Indochina, Canton, and Hainan Island. Interestingly, Kweilin was surrounded by rock spires that "furnish[ed] caves in which almost any
amount of supplies can be stored, machine shops can be protected from
bombing, and practically the whole installation of the field rendered immune from enemy raiders."[197] Historian Daniel Ford has described the intermediate and forward bomber bases as follows: "Guilin had a mile-long
runway surfaced with crushed rock, and revetments large enough to hide
a B-17 Flying Fortress. (For which purpose, indeed, Guilin and Zhuzhou
had been built in the fall of 1940) . . . The operations center and radio station were built into sugarloaves, impervious to bombing . . ."[198]

McHugh's dispatch confirmed that the Chinese were concerned about
the shortage of gasoline.[199] Finally, he wrote: "MAO [sic] WILL COMMAND
THE AIR FORCE AFTER IMPENDING SHAKEUP."[200]

A JAPANESE SPY IN HAWAII

In March of 1941, Lieutenant Takeo Yoshikawa (alias "Tadashi Morimura") sailed for Honolulu. His purpose was to spy on American military
facilities[201] as he was driven about the island by a chauffeur attached to the
Japanese consul. He spied on American army and navy bases, and developed an appreciation for the low level of activity at the bases on week-
ends.[202] He persuaded employees of Japanese descent who were working
on the bases to provide him with information on activities at the facilities. Members of the Japanese consulate gave radio reports to Tokyo concerning the location of American ships.[203] In this way the Japanese came
to know the movements of the American Pacific Fleet and the location of
each battleship.

While Yoshikawa was spying on American military facilities in Hawaii,
reports in the Japanese press of March 12, 1941, contemplated the possibility of air raids on Japan and war with the United States. In relation to
a perceived threat of American bombing raids, Japanese naval aviators
suggested the bombing of United States bases at Midway Island, Wake
Island, and Cavite in the Philippines. Also, Admiral Sankichi Takahashi
addressed the Shumeikai, a private cultural society, declaring: "Japan's
Navy . . . is fully prepared for any eventuality. Our Navy is convinced it
cannot be defeated by a navy of any other nation."

JAPANESE PLANS FOR SINGAPORE

Colonel Masanobu Tsuji—a reputed tactical genius in the Japanese army who would survive the war and go into hiding for fear of being tried as a war criminal—surveyed the Malay Peninsula in anticipation of the Japanese southern expedition. His protégé, Shigeharu Asaeda, who had been recruited by the colonel because of his reckless fighting ability, was put in charge of the surveillance of Thailand. At this time, it was realized that while Singapore (Britain's fortress of the Pacific) had substantial fortifications facing seaward, it was virtually defenseless if approached from the rear.

In April 1941, Japanese navigators studied the courses set by ships that had been traveling the Pacific for the past ten years. The study indicated that between November and December, there were virtually no ships traveling north of 40 degrees latitude. It appeared that more southward courses were taken to avoid the rough seas.

AMERICA BEGINS STUDYING BOMBING OBJECTIVES IN JAPAN

While Japanese war planners were hard at work in the spring of 1941, their American counterparts were studying their war options with Japan. For example, the Steering Committee of the Export Control Commodity Division of the U.S. Department of Commerce had been engaged in studies on how to interfere with "1) What Japan needs; 2) How Japan can pay for what she needs; and 3) How Japan can transport what she needs."[204] Now it turned its attention to "studying bombing objectives and providing this data to the Army and Navy." Those Americans, including Charles Lindbergh, who subscribed to an isolationist worldview would likely have been shocked by the extent to which bureaucrats had embarked on initiatives that extended beyond economic policy and included a plan to bomb Japan. America's economic and military initiatives were complementary and were on the minds of American war planners, as evidenced by the discussion in the next chapter.[205]

Chapter Eight

"AN ECONOMIC BLOCKADE OF JAPAN"

The United States announced an embargo on iron and steel scrap exports except to nations of the Western Hemisphere and Britain. Japan, the largest importer of American steel, would get no more.

—Edwin P. Hoyt, *Japan's War: The Great Pacific War* [206]

On May 13, 1941, Captain W. R. Purnell wrote a secret memorandum to President Roosevelt that accurately described Japan's ambitions for Southeast Asia and the Pacific.[207] When the memorandum was written, Captain Purnell served under Admiral Thomas Hart, the commander of the U.S. Navy Asiatic Fleet in the Philippines. In the memorandum, Captain Purnell noted: "The concept of a war with Japan is believed to be sound."[208] While American strategy against Japan would be premised upon an "economic blockade of Japan,"[209] Purnell also pointed out that there were "several psychological and tactical factors which it is desired to submit for consideration."[210] Japan's most critical need in relation to strategic war materials was oil.[211]

Ironically, thanks to the benevolence of the United States, Japan enjoyed an eighteen-month oil reserve "including lubricants, including those for aircraft use."[212] The captain, writing from his station on the USS *Houston*, went on to point out that "The United States has been shipping large quantities of petroleum products to Thailand, including an abnormal quantity of 85–86.9 octane gasoline, and there can be little doubt that it is for Japanese use."[213] While Japan enjoyed a substantial reserve of oil, it had only a one-month supply of rubber, excluding its war reserve.[214] Without vast supplies of rubber, production for the Japanese war machine would grind to a halt.

At the time Captain Purnell prepared his secret memorandum, no doubt with the advice and encouragement of Admiral Hart, there had been economic conferences between Japan, French Indochina, Thailand, and the Dutch East Indies, in which Japan had made substantial demands for materials vital to its economy.[215] If Japan were going to wage war, she could not "hope to sustain a protracted campaign without recourse to supplies in Southeast Asia and outlying islands."[216] Accordingly, Japan would (as indeed, she did) secure resources of supplies and destroy Dutch and British military bases from which resistance or counterattacks could be mounted. After conquering areas rich in the resources Japan required for her economy, as in the Dutch East Indies and British-controlled Malaya and Burma, "Her primary effort in that geographical locality becomes protective," Purnell surmised.[217]

Looking upon a secret memorandum six decades old, and living in a country possessing sufficient nuclear devices (both airborne and on submarines) with the power to destroy civilization many times over, it is hard to imagine that America was so poorly equipped to respond to the threats of the Japanese menace. Taking into consideration the "limited forces available," Captain Purnell did point out to the president "certain offensive operations that [could] be conducted."[218]

First, American and Dutch submarines could engage in offensive operations in the area of Luzon (the Philippines) and in the South China Sea. Second, high-level bombing, scouting, and reconnaissance operations offered some promise. Third, fighter aircraft operations offered the prospect of inflicting damage on Japanese interests in a more restricted sphere than bomber operations. Fourth, army and guerrilla operations along the Malayan and Burma frontiers and in China offered promise. Fifth, American naval forces, although (comparatively) weak, could engage in opportune raids on Japanese sea communications.

However, there were substantial impediments to American military operations in Southeast Asia and the Western Pacific. The Vichy French government in Indochina, following a proclamation of June 23, 1941, that Indochina was a Franco-Japanese protectorate, allowed Japanese troops to occupy their country on June 26, 1941. This included naval installations at Camranh Bay from which Japanese assaults on the Philippines could be easily mounted. On July 28, 1941, the United States government imposed an embargo on all oil sales to Japan, froze Japanese assets, and closed American ports to Japanese vessels. This course of action was entirely in keeping with the American strategy outlined in Captain Purnell's secret memorandum. The objective of America's economic blockade was to reduce Japan's supply of strategic materials and force her to consume her reserves.[219] The sooner Japan's reserves were consumed, "the earlier a critical situation is forced on an enemy."[220] An economic embargo by the United States would force Japan to maintain her supply lines from China and French Indochina, and, in the case of oil, from Borneo and Sumatra.[221]

In coordination with an economic blockade, submarine attacks on Japanese interests would be conducted on all communications from Borneo southward. Attacks by American submarines on Japanese merchant vessels and supply ships would be relatively simple after they sailed into the open sea.[222] However, in relation to shipments to French Indochina, the Japanese vessels needed to be forced away from the coast and beyond the range of Japanese aircraft that could interdict American submarines.

While American airpower held promise, Captain Purnell cautioned the president that "too much weight is given this arm in present done with a wish born of expediency."[223] However, the captain did admit that air weapons should be developed in that theater to their maximum value, with bombers operating from land bases—provided there was sufficient fighter protection. Conceding the importance of aircraft operations, Captain Purnell related the following in the same memorandum to President Roosevelt:

> Under present conditions and allocation [sic] of military forces, the air weapon is the only one about which our prospective allies have offensive determination and it should be supported to the *utmost* [emphasis added]. If opinions and reports can be credited, and advance precautionary measures taken as a criterion, one of Japan's *greatest fears* rests upon the *bombing of the homeland* [emphasis added].[224]

Fighter and pursuit squadrons offered promise for offensive and defensive operations in northern Malaya and Burma due to the distances from enemy activities. For example, at the time Captain Purnell wrote his memo, the Japanese had occupied eastern and southeastern China as well as French Indochina. Japanese air strength was therefore not physically close to the Allied air operations that could be staged from Malaya or Burma. Fighter and pursuit squadrons from America, Britain, China, and the Dutch—the "ABCD Powers," or "Associated Powers"—would force "the enemy to come to them."[225]

THE POTENTIAL OF FORWARD AIR BASES IN CHINA

Army and guerrilla operations along the Malayan and Burma frontiers were being organized by the British, and these were to include operations in China.[226] At or during the time Purnell authored his memorandum, there was an understanding between the Associated Powers that they would fight together in the event of war with Japan. The alliance of the Associated Powers came to be memorialized in the British Memorandum dated September 19, 1941, entitled: "The Problem of Defeating Japan— Review of the Situation," discussed in Chapter 14 of this text.

During meetings between Roosevelt and Churchill—as well as senior American and British military officers aboard the British battleship, the *Prince of Wales*, beginning August 9, 1941—Churchill would call for the following ultimatum to be delivered to the Japanese: If Japan advanced south into the Malay Peninsula or the Dutch East Indies, all means necessary would be employed to force Japan's withdrawal by Britain, America, and the Soviet Union.[227]

Operations in China of the guerrilla armies would relate to the acquisition and maintenance of forward air bases—disbursed airfields in southeastern China and Burma—"where bomber squadrons may stop overnight for refueling and rearming during a series of raids from a main base."[228] The maintenance of these forward air bases by guerrilla army forces and their use as staging bases for offensive operations by bombers was believed to offer "the greatest feasible method of waging offensive warfare against Japan available to the Associated Powers *particularly during the early stages of the war* [emphasis added]."[229]

Regarding these forward air bases, the captain went on to report:

> The hinterland of Southeastern China, except in the vicinity of Canton, has not been penetrated to any great depth by the Japanese. It is believed many sites are available and suitable, and

that the Chungking Government would be more than willing to furnish assistance in turning them into airfields. This procedure would offer a progressive advancement of airfields past Formosa towards Japan as more planes become available.[230]

The provision and maintenance of forward air bases in southeastern China would not take place without difficulty, since accommodations would have to be improvised, and initially supply drops would have to be made by air.[231] However, bombers of the Associated Powers operating in southeastern China would be able to drive Japanese convoys offshore, making them "more vulnerable to submarine attack."[232] Because Japan was making every effort to "close out the China affair," the captain believed that "[e]very possible aid should be extended to the Chungking Government to keep its army in the field."[233] Japan was hoping for a successful conclusion to the Sino-Japanese War and was directing its attention toward the oil- and mineral-rich lands to the south, such as the Dutch East Indies, Malaya, and Burma. With the Chinese government being supported by military aid from America, Captain Purnell "earnestly believed that the rejuvenated Chinese would keep more Japanese troops planted on Chinese soil than had been there heretofore, and would keep in continuance a threat from the southwest."[234]

If the efforts of the Associated Powers in developing forward air bases in southeastern China were fruitful, this would have the salutatory effect of forcing the Japanese to focus their air and surface forces on meeting this threat in China, thereby diminishing their ability to interdict American naval forces attacking Japanese convoys on the high seas.[235]

Captain Purnell's secret memorandum to President Roosevelt outlining his and Hart's conception of Japan's intentions was substantially consistent with the war plans being developed by the Japanese. For example, Captain Purnell speculated that should the United States' Pacific Fleet move westward, the goals of the Japanese would be to cripple the American fleet in a war of attrition by submarine and air attacks, "until superiority [was] established for the Japanese main fleet."[236] However, Purnell may not have read Bywater's *The Great Pacific War*. Whatever the case, the U.S. Navy had, on several occasions, executed mock air raids on Pearl Harbor. The vulnerability of the American Pacific Fleet based in Hawaii at the time the Purnell memorandum was written was not considered an issue of concern for President Roosevelt.

The imminent Japanese attack on Pearl Harbor was a situation in which life would imitate art.

JAPANESE AMBITIONS TO THE SOUTH

While Captain Purnell was not cautioning President Roosevelt in May of 1941 about a possible surprise attack by the Japanese on Pearl Harbor, he did accurately foretell Japanese designs on the Philippines. He foresaw the Japanese reducing American forces by naval and air attacks and expeditionary landing forces, to be accompanied by land- and carrier-based bombers and carrier-based fighters.[237] He also accurately foretold events that would unfold in Malaya and the Dutch East Indies, since these countries would also be invaded by Japanese troops accompanied by surface and air attacks. He even anticipated that the operations would take place on the Kra Isthmus in Malaya, a land mass south of Thailand and Burma where Malaya extended southward to Singapore.

It was Captain Purnell's impression that "southward expansion has been the hobby of Japanese planners for years."[238] However, it was the captain's assessment that Japanese war planners had failed to consider the defensive measures that would be required if they were to be successful in consolidating their conquests in Southeast Asia and the Western Pacific.

JAPANESE AIRCRAFT PRODUCTION

Captain Purnell was aware of the Japanese ability to manufacture aircraft. Assuming the eleven Japanese aircraft factories listed in his secret memorandum were working twenty-four hours a day, it was Captain Purnell's assessment that the Japanese could manufacture 3,000 aircraft per year. At the time of Purnell's memorandum to the president, Japan had approximately 3,000 combat aircraft in commission, equally divided between the Japanese army and the Japanese navy.[239] However, knowledge of Japanese aviation production was somewhat limited, since there were no details available on the allocation of aircraft production of Japanese fighter planes versus Japanese bomber planes (the latter being more time-consuming and more expensive to construct).

The president was advised that America should make every preparation to ensure the destruction of Japanese aircraft carriers, submarines, and bombers.[240] Purnell further admonished: "The primary need in this theater to support offensive operations is fighting in pursuit planes. Their number is woefully inadequate to fulfill the missions of protection to our bombers, attacking enemy bombers, and meeting the enemy fighter attacks. It is urgently recommended that they be supplied to our prospective Allied Forces at the earliest possible time."[241]

AMERICA'S IGNORANCE OF THE CAPABILITIES OF JAPANESE FIGHTER PLANES

Captain Purnell revealed his ignorance of the capabilities of the Japanese aviation industry—as well as the flying qualities and performance capabilities of the Japanese Zero (Mitsubishi's Japanese Navy Type 0 series) and Oscar (Nakajima's Japanese Army Model Type 1)—when he optimistically made the following statement in the same secret memorandum to President Roosevelt:

> Her [Japan's] air force has never encountered serious opposition in the air. It is of paramount importance that the fighting planes supplied should excel the latest Japanese planes in performance. When that *fact* is implanted in the Japanese pilot's mind, then it is *confidently* [emphasis added] believed the morale of their air force will rapidly deteriorate.[242]

Captain Purnell's statements demonstrate the arrogance and contempt with which the American military viewed the Japanese military. The Japanese were thought to be ignorant and unsophisticated people, incapable of manufacturing fighter planes with performance that would equal or surpass American-made fighter planes. This turned out to be a grave mistake.

The ignorance of American military planners about the performance of Japanese fighters is truly unfortunate, especially considering the fact that Chennault had test-flown a captured Nakajima Army Type 97 in 1939.[243] Chennault "noted all its specifications, took numerous photographs, and compiled a thick dossier on its construction and performance."[244] It is reported Chennault remarked it climbed like a rocket and turned like a squirrel. After turning over his data to the War Department, Chennault later received a letter explaining that "aeronautical experts" concluded "that it was impossible to build an aircraft of the performance [Chennault] cited with the specifications submitted."[245] Even more disturbing is the fact that Chennault "brought back the data on the first Model Zero in the fall of 1940."[246] With a top speed of 322 miles per hour and the ability to climb to 16,000 feet in six minutes, the Zero would prove to be a formidable opponent for Allied aircraft.[247] Perhaps if the Air Corps had paid more attention to Chennault's recommendations for a fast-climbing interceptor, America would have had fighters capable of dogfighting with the Zero. "Air Corps technical manuals on Japanese aircraft in use at the time of Pearl Harbor devoted a blank page to the Zero."[248]

The summary of strategic considerations for President Roosevelt was first to maintain the threat of the United States fleet in the Pacific for as long as possible, and then to increase the threat from China by every and all possible means. It would be necessary to supply the latest-type fighters to the Associated Powers' air forces in order to sufficiently protect Wake Island, and to maintain as America's primary objectives against Japan, the destruction of its aircraft carriers, submarines, and bombers.

The extent to which America would make its latest fighter planes available to China will be apparent in the next chapter. The Hawk 75 fighter Chennault had flown in China had been refined by Curtiss-Wright into the Hawk 81 series. The blunt radial engine had been removed and replaced with a more streamlined and compact Allison V-1710, inline engine. The Air Corps designated it the P-40 Tomahawk. Vast supplies of Tomahawks were being provided to Great Britain. While no match for the Zero in a turning dogfight at lower airspeeds, it would be more than a match for the Japanese fighters if properly flown.

Chapter Nine

"YOU NEED A HUNDRED OF THESE"

The initial step in resolving priority conflicts was the agreement of the British purchasing mission to let the Chinese have 100 P-40Bs allocated for Britain . . .

—Charles F. Romanus and Riley Sunderland,
*China-Burma-India Theater: Stillwell's Mission to China
(United States Army in World War II)*[249]

THE P-40 DEMONSTRATION FLIGHT

It was April of 1941 when members of the China lobby traveled to Bolling Field in Washington, D.C., to observe a demonstration flight of the P-40B Tomahawk. Dr. Soong, General Mow, and Claire Chennault were warmly greeted by Lieutenant John Alison, who had agreed to give a demonstration of the aircraft.

The Tomahawk was an imposing machine with its long, sharklike nose, which housed the 12-cylinder Allison V-1710-33 engine. Lieutenant Alison acquainted the visitors with the features of the aircraft. The engine developed in excess of 1,090 horsepower. The aircraft had a maximum airspeed of 352 mph and a cruising speed of 273 mph. The initial rate of climb would be in excess of 2,860 feet per minute. It featured six machine guns, two 50-caliber machine guns in the cowling, and four 30-caliber machine guns in the wings. A rubber membrane surrounded each fuel tank in the event a bullet should pierce any one of them. This membrane would seal a leaking tank and increase the prospects of the aircraft's survival in combat. The aircraft had an empty weight of 5,590 pounds and a maximum weight of 7,645 pounds. It carried 160 gallons of fuel internally.[250]

Having flown the P-36 (export model Hawk 75) in China, Chennault was not unfamiliar with the aircraft being demonstrated. However, he had not flown this new streamlined aircraft with the bullet-pointed spinner and the chin-mounted radiator, which gave the machine's nose its sharklike profile.

With members of the China lobby standing on either wing beside the cockpit, Alison explained the cockpit layout to them, including the landing-gear lever, the flap lever, and the trigger on the stick which activated the hydraulic system that pumped the gear and flaps up and down. Alison then requested that his guests deplane the aircraft so that he could start the engine. Moving quickly through his preflight checklist, Alison verified that:

- the landing-gear selector and flap selector were in the neutral position;
- the throttle was advanced one inch;
- the mixture was at the idle-cutoff position;
- the fuselage tank was selected on the fuel selector;
- the magneto switches were off;
- the prop control was full forward;
- the three right-hand circuit breakers were on;
- the gun switches were off;
- the battery and generator switches were turned on; and
- the fuel boost pump was turned on and indicated more than fifteen pounds.

He then gave the engine three shots of primer, turned off the boost pump, positioned the magneto switch to turn both magnetos on, and engaged the starter.[251] With a great roar, the Allison engine came to life with a cloud of blue-gray smoke pouring from the exhaust stacks. The roar from the engine was deafening. Dr. Soong held his hands over his ears, and General Mow smiled gleefully and clapped his hands to signal approval. As usual, Chennault said virtually nothing. However, there was a twinkle in his eye as he glanced at Mow and Dr. Soong.

Alison advanced the throttle in the aircraft and taxied to the active runway. Dr. Soong and Chennault discussed how soon the one hundred P-40s earmarked for China could be made available. As members of the China lobby stared intently at the lone P-40 sitting at the end of the runway, they heard the throttle advance, and the aircraft accelerated, announcing its intention to fly with a thundering roar that could be heard by the audience a quarter of a mile away. As the P-40 became airborne, Alison held the aircraft about fifteen feet above the runway and retracted the landing gear. The aircraft quickly accelerated to nearly 250 miles per hour indicated airspeed. Just beyond the end of the runway, Alison pulled back on the stick and the aircraft climbed skyward, performing one-half of a loop, rolling out on top in an Immelman turn. The roar of the P-40 could be heard as the aircraft accelerated 3,000 feet above the runway. Then, banking to his left and diving sharply, Alison brought the P-40 down the runway at over 350 miles per hour, flashing over the heads of his guests and blasting them with his propeller wash. Again, climbing skyward, Alison performed loops, rolls, and Cuban Eight maneuvers to demonstrate the agility of the P-40.

His demonstration flight complete, Alison taxied in on the tarmac and cut the engine. Climbing from the cockpit and meeting his guests, Alison saw Dr. Soong and General Mow pointing toward the P-40, both of them exclaiming, "We need a hundred of these."[252] Chennault then turned to Alison, putting his right index finger on Alison's chest, saying: "No, you need a hundred of *these*."[253] Chennault recognized a great pilot when he saw one. Alison could wring every ounce of performance out of the P-40 and display the fighter's strengths, which included a terrific diving speed.

GOVERNMENT-FURNISHED EQUIPMENT

While the China lobby had succeeded in obtaining a commitment from Curtiss-Wright to provide one hundred P-40s, the airplanes would come without government-furnished equipment (GFE), including engines, guns, and radios. The absence of GFE presented additional obstacles to be overcome by members of the China lobby if China was to survive in her defense against Japanese aggression.

China Defense Supplies, Inc. had been established to finance the Special Air Unit. This company presented one more corporate layer in the machinations developed to obscure the source of financing for the Special

Air Unit. The corporation was established by President Roosevelt's former speechwriter and confidant, Tommy Corcoran. President Roosevelt's uncle, Frederic Delano, was enlisted to serve as "honorary counselor." Corcoran's brother, David, became the company's president. While having all the appearances of a private business venture, money to finance the project actually came from the United States government, and its "corporate" office was located in the Chinese Embassy. Make no mistake—with the president's elderly uncle, Corcoran, and Corcoran's brother involved, China Defense Supplies had President Roosevelt's fingerprints all over it. One is left to wonder what the public reaction would have been in the spring of 1941 if the American people had realized Roosevelt's confederates were involved in a scheme to set up a guerrilla air force in China. However, Universal Trading Corporation would represent China Defense Supplies in its negotiations to acquire aircraft engines.

Allison engines were in short supply, but a number of "off-dimension parts" that met neither British nor U.S. Army Air Corps specifications were employed, using fitting, machining, and repairing techniques to build engines from these parts that would power the P-40s. In the parlance of high-performance engine builders, these hand-assembled engines were essentially "blueprinted," resulting in engines that had more power than standard engines, more exacting tolerances, and ultimately, lasted longer in the field.[254] Ironically, the salvaged engines outperformed standard Air Corps engines; in fact, when the engine controls were altered in an unauthorized manner, the Allison engines that were originally designed to generate 1,050 horsepower were actually producing 1,500 horsepower at altitude.[255] While altering the throttle linkages and engine settings was contrary to pertinent technical manuals, a fighter pilot in combat is more concerned with having enough power to outrun his adversary if he's being chased. The niceties covered in safety and technical manuals are of no significance if the pilot is killed because his engine does not afford him the necessary power to escape.

PAWLEY THREATENS CHENNAULT WITH AN INJUNCTION

In February of 1941, William Pawley learned that China Defense Supplies, through its agent, Universal Trading Corporation, had arranged to purchase one hundred P-40 Tomahawks for a purchase price of $4.5 million.

In a confrontation with Chennault, Pawley insisted on his 10 percent commission as the Curtiss-Wright sales agent to China, threatening Chennault with an injunction unless he was paid. Two months were lost in negotiations and bickering as Pawley insisted upon his payment. Finally, on April 1, 1941, Secretary Morgenthau convened a conference in which Dr. Soong offered to pay Pawley his 10 percent commission out of Chinese funds. Morgenthau would hear nothing of it. Morgenthau threatened Pawley, telling him the American government would confiscate the fighter planes as war materials. If Pawley was going to interfere with the fighters' shipment to China, it would be a simple matter for the American government to impound them and transfer them either to the Air Corps or to the British, the original purchaser of the planes. After arguing throughout the afternoon, Pawley finally relented and agreed to accept payment of $250,000, with the proviso that CAMCO would assemble, service, and test-fly the P-40s in China and Burma. In late April of 1941, the planes were shipped aboard a Norwegian freighter bound for Rangoon. However, when a cargo sling broke, one P-40 fuselage was dumped into the New York harbor, leaving the Special Air Unit with ninety-nine Tomahawks.

RECRUITING PILOTS AND TECHNICIANS

While Chennault and the China lobby were busying themselves with acquiring airplanes for the Special Air Unit, Commander Harry Claiborne, Commander Rutledge Irvine, and Captain Richard Aldworth scouted military installations across the United States for pilots and technicians who would fly and operate the fighter planes of the American Volunteer Group.

In March 1941, pilots Tex Hill and Ed Rector were coming off the flight line at Norfolk Naval Air Station when they were approached by a CAMCO recruiter, who gave them a pitch about flying fighters to protect the Burma Road.[256] Hill remarked that they didn't even know where Burma was.[257] The discussions took place in the operations office at the airfield.[258] After being sold on the spirit and adventure of flying in defense of China, Hill and Rector, along with Bert Christman, a newspaper illustrator who had joined the navy, signed documents resigning their commissions in the navy to go to work for CAMCO.[259] None of them actually believed they would ever be released to fly and fight for China.[260]

A month later, however, they were once again approached by the CAMCO representative and were told their paperwork had come through.[261] When the base commander flew to Washington to protest the robbing of experienced navy aviators from one of its squadrons, he was rebuffed by Admiral Towers, who said the entire operation was "presidentially approved."[262]

Charlie Bond, an Air Corps pilot, joined the AVG because he had been trained to fly fighters and felt he was wasting his talents ferrying bombers to Canada.[263] Also, the money was very enticing. Gregory Boyington, a Marine Corps lieutenant in financial trouble, was the only regular officer to join the AVG. Boyington was recruited by Richard Aldworth. As Boyington tells the story, the discussions were as follows:

> He said we'd be flying against people who wore thick lenses and were not mechanical, like we boys were . . . He said we'd be getting five hundred bucks besides a good salary—twice what we were getting in the service—for knocking down Japanese planes . . . These would be unarmed transports, nine out of ten of them. Well, I wasn't above picking up money like that to pay off bills.[264]

Alluding to the glamour, allure, and adventure of fighting for the besieged Chinese, and summoning up parallels to America's foreign legion of World War I (the Lafayette Escadrille), Chennault's confederates succeeded in recruiting pilots, mechanics, and technical personnel to man the Special Air Unit. Besides the romantic appeal, recruiters used racial prejudice and pejorative characterizations of the Japanese to help persuade men to join the unit. Chennault's volunteers would not be ordinary men. Adventurers, romantics, mercenaries, and idealists, these men would require a stern taskmaster if they were to survive the harsh combat conditions of China.

Chapter Ten

"KEEPING THE THING QUIET"

This major development in the tactics of clandestine intervention was inaugurated in the decisive months preceding Pearl Harbor and should not be rationalized or dismissed as merely another development of the Cold War. The long-term implications of Chennault's AVG were of course imagined only dimly . . . in December of 1941.

—Michael Schaller, *The U.S. Crusade in China, 1938–1945* [265]

THE SECRET FORMATION OF THE AMERICAN VOLUNTEER GROUP

While Soong, Chennault, and Mow had secured one hundred P-40 fighter planes, there was still the matter of recruiting American pilots to fly them and technicians to service them. Since recruiting by Chinese officials would be a criminal act contrary to sections 21 and 22 of the United States Criminal Code (Title 18 of the United States Code), China would have to employ American recruiters to enlist American personnel. Further, if any of the American volunteers were going to sign agreements to serve the Chinese Nationalist government, they would have to be signed *after* they left the United States.

A collection of materials at the National Museum of Naval Aviation (called "the Pensacola Papers")[266] provide a paper trail that outlines the recruitment efforts in terms of U.S. Navy personnel as well as the policies adopted by the navy for the "volunteers."

Among these materials are secret or confidential letters, memoranda, and handwritten notes between such notable figures as President Roosevelt, Secretary Knox, Admiral Chester Nimitz, and Dr. Currie. At the time the Pensacola Papers were formulated, Admiral Nimitz served as the commander of the Navy's Bureau of Navigation, which, in reality was the navy's personnel office. Of German descent and with extensive experience in naval operations dating back to the First World War, Nimitz was an officer focused on efficiency and practicality. After the Japanese surprise attack, it was Nimitz who would take command of U.S. naval forces in the Pacific. The Pensacola Papers also include secret correspondence between United States navy officers and representatives of CAMCO, Pawley and Leighton's concern in China that was assembling and servicing American aircraft, as well as a report from CAMCO to personnel in the Navy Department.

The Pensacola Papers tell a tale of political intrigue in which officers and members of the U.S. government went about the business of organizing a Special Air Unit for China while keeping the entire affair a secret from the American people.

In Commander Bruce Leighton's statement, circa 1941, it is apparent that the Chinese government sent a special mission to Washington in 1941 to arrange loans and other assistance to develop a Chinese air force.[267] Commander Leighton related that a loan of $100 million was arranged from the United States to China, and that the United States would release one hundred P-40 pursuit planes from aircraft then allocated to Britain.[268] Because the P-40 aircraft were of a complex nature with very high performance capabilities, it was decided that these aircraft had to be flown by former U.S. military pilots, to ensure they were effectively operated in combat and not consumed in training accidents. Further, Commander Leighton related: ". . . for obvious reasons individuals engaged in operations of the nature contemplated in China must have no connection with the U.S. Government Services . . ."[269] Apparently, Intercontinent Corporation was an American (District of Columbia) corporation, while it appears that CAMCO was a Chinese firm, and included as stockholders H. H. Kung, the generalissimo's brother, and William Pawley. Obviously, the generalissimo's brother had an interest in CAMCO, which assembled and serviced aircraft employed by the Chinese Air Force. Madame Chiang also had a vested interest for several reasons: she served as spokesperson to the world on the suffering of China; she was the nominal head of the Chinese Aeronautical Commission; her brother, Dr. Soong, was acting as China's special envoy; and of course, as the wife of president Chiang Kai-shek, she had substantial power and influence behind the scenes. Clearly, the operation of the Chinese government and its military appears to have been a family affair.

In his statement, Leighton declared that the Intercontinent Corporation was a concern with long experience in China of manufacturing and servicing aircraft. Intercontinent functioned in China through its subsidiary, CAMCO,[270] which had trained Chinese mechanics and established repair and maintenance facilities in China since the Sino-Japanese War had begun in Shanghai in 1937.[271] CAMCO maintained offices in New York, Chungking, Rangoon, and Hong Kong, in addition to operating a factory and repair facility near the Burma Road.[272] Commander Leighton explained that he was a retired naval officer with twelve years of active duty, and the vice president of CAMCO, and William D. Pawley was CAMCO's president.[273]

Leighton's statement was filled with references to Intercontinent and CAMCO, suggesting that only by making CAMCO the employer of the volunteers would the program work effectively. For example, he noted: "Successful results have been obtained only where the personnel are employed and paid by some responsible American concern having long experience in China." He also noted: "The Intercontinent Corporation is such a concern." Was this a suggestion that graft and corruption in the Nationalist Government would prevent all of the funds from being allocated to their intended purpose? To ensure the guerrilla air corps functioned effectively, CAMCO was to be used as a "blind" by the United States government to conceal their activities in providing China with an air force. As Leighton explained it, CAMCO would offer its services as a vehicle to employ the pilots and ground personnel who would operate "ostensibly as civilian employees . . ."[274] Commander Leighton also noted that CAMCO had an agreement with the Chinese government to be reimbursed for its expenses.[275]

Leighton reported that the formulation of the project with the American government was "handled orally" with no file record of any kind. The reason for this course of action is obvious: if there were no papers, there would be no paper trail. Leighton's desire to accomplish his objective without such evidence is the same reason personnel in the State Department had briefed Dr. Soong orally in keeping with the letter to Secretary Hull from the Division of Far Eastern Affairs of December 3, 1940. America was ostensibly neutral in the Sino-Japanese War. A paper trail would have been an embarrassment for President Roosevelt, both with the American people and also with the Japanese.

On April 14, 1941, the aide to Navy Secretary Frank Knox, Captain Frank E. Beatty, issued a memorandum of introduction to the commanding officers of five naval air stations, declaring: "1) This letter introduces Mr. C. L. Chennault, who has permission of the Navy Department to visit your station. 2) He will explain the purpose of his visit."[276]

On the same day, Captain Beatty composed a memorandum of introduction addressed to the commanders of five naval air stations and one Marine Corps air station with the same language on behalf of CAMCO recruiter, Rutledge Irvine.[277] Similar memoranda or letters of introduction allowed CAMCO recruiters to visit Air Corps bases.[278] CAMCO employees were allowed to make contact with individual reserve officers and enlisted men soliciting their applications for employment as ostensible employees of CAMCO in the service of China.[279] Further, Commander Leighton related that the American military had agreed to these resignations and discharges to allow the military personnel to accept employment with CAMCO.[280] While the American military personnel would officially sever their connections with their particular branch of the military, upon completion of their tour of duty with CAMCO, they would be accepted for recommission or reenlistment in the active reserve in such rank or grade and with *the same seniority* and other benefits (including disability) they would have enjoyed *had they remained on active duty* in the Army or Navy Reserve.[281]

While Leighton envisioned (and the recruiters no doubt promised) time in China would serve toward seniority with the branch of the service from which the volunteers had resigned, the United States breached its agreement. When Admiral Nimitz took over the China Project from Captain Beatty, Nimitz decreed that former naval personnel would *not* accrue retirement benefits or seniority during the time they served the Chinese Nationalist government.

Leighton spelled out three steps that were necessary in order for an American "volunteer" to participate in the service of China: First, the individual would resign his commission or enlistment in the armed forces. Second, he would complete a passport application. Third, the American State Department would obtain the required visas from the British and Chinese embassies.[282] Visas from the British would be required because the American volunteers would pass through Singapore and Rangoon, both British colonies. CAMCO arranged for the transportation of the volunteers to China, telling them when and where to report. CAMCO agreed to provide weekly summaries on this special project to the Secretary of the Navy and to the special Chinese Affairs Desk in the State Department. Further, interested persons in Washington (Dr. Lauchlin Currie) would be kept constantly informed on the progress of this project.

Although General Marshall had blunted Chennault's plans for bombers, Leighton's statement clearly indicates otherwise. It appears the option to supply China with bombers was kept open, since Commander Leighton reported:

> The original program called for the shipment to China of 100 Curtiss P-40s. Subsequently, arrangements have been made under Lend-Lease Act [sic] for the supply to China of substantial additional numbers of aircraft and extension of the original project, and further plans are at present under consideration for the supply of bomber type planes, as soon as personnel and facilities are available to handle [sic].[283]

According to a confidential memorandum from one W. L. Keys for Secretary Knox, dated February 3, 1941,[284] William Pawley and Claire Chennault called Keys on that day telling him that an agreement had been reached between Curtiss-Wright Corporation, Intercontinent, and the Chinese, for the servicing of one hundred P-40s for China. It was further related by Keys that the requirements of this Special Air Unit would consist of 100 pilots and 150 enlisted ground crew. Then, Keys included this ominous language: "They realize the necessity for *keeping the thing quiet* [emphasis added] and will take due precautions."[285]

Keys further conveyed that personnel resigning from the navy would do so without detriment to their future status in the service. Interestingly, this memorandum suggests that the initiative in securing personnel for the AVG came from the navy, since the author relates:

> Note: BuNav [Bureau of Navigation] is ready to do this, but it will have to be taken up with the Army, and I understand that General Arnold has not yet been informed by Secretary Stimson. I suggest that you personally take this up with Secretary Stimson and also with Admiral Towers, who is not very enthusiastic about this idea, I believe.[286]

The memorandum goes on to explain that members of the AVG would be deferred from the draft, would receive their passports from the State Department as employees of "Central Aircraft Corporation" [sic], and that they would be *bona fide* employees of "Central Aircraft" [sic].[287] Further, Keys related that Pawley, Leighton, and Chennault would require letters of passage from the War and Navy Departments, "authorizing them to visit the various Air Stations."[288]

Further evidence that the one hundred P-40 aircraft and their personnel were only the first wave of this Special Air Unit is found in the last paragraph of the memorandum of February 3, 1941: "It was pointed out to me that this considerable organization would hardly be worth sending out and establishing unless there were excellent prospects for further release of planes to carry on the work. They will have to start more or less from scratch in Burma and work their way in against probable opposition."[289]

The Pensacola Papers reveal that Captain Beatty was organizing the Special Air Unit for China from the office of Navy Secretary Knox, as the captain wrote memoranda of introduction for Claire Chennault[290] and Rutledge Irvine[291] on April 14, 1941, allowing them to visit naval air and/or marine stations around the country.

A number of authorities on the formation of the American Volunteer Group have related that President Roosevelt signed a secret executive order on April 15, 1941, authorizing the group's formation. Among these authorities is General Claire Chennault, who, in his autobiography, related: "On April 15, 1941, an unpublicized executive order went out under his signature, authorizing reserve officers and enlisted men to resign from the Army Air Corps, Naval, and Marine Air Services for the purpose of joining the American Volunteer Group in China."[292] Also, Professor Duane Schultz, who wrote *The Maverick War: Chennault and the Flying Tigers*, has maintained that President Roosevelt "*signed* [emphasis added] a secret executive order that permitted men on active duty with the army and navy to sign contracts with CAMCO for one year of service in China, after which they could rejoin the military with no loss in rank."[293] However, there is no evidence President Roosevelt issued a *written* executive order authorizing the formation of the AVG.[294]

The letter of introduction by Captain Beatty, aide to Secretary Frank Knox, of August 4, 1941, to Captain James Shoemaker, the commanding officer of the United States Naval Air Station at Pearl Harbor, introduced

Lieutenant C. B. Adair.[295] Captain Beatty's letter made a representation that was simply incorrect:

> It has been the policy of our government *for some time* [emphasis added] to facilitate the hiring by the Chinese Government of pilots and mechanics from our services. The above-mentioned officer is a representative of the Intercontinent Company, of which company is doing the hiring for the Chinese Government. The cooperation of the Commanding Officer is requested in permitting this representative to interview pilots on your Station to see if they are interested in being hired by the Intercontinent Company for service in China.[296]

Hiring American pilots to fly for China had *not* been an American policy "for some time." In fact, Chennault and other mercenaries had been advised to leave China by the American consul in August of 1937 after the outbreak of the undeclared Sino-Japanese War. This prompted Chennault to write a letter published in the *Montgomery Advisor* in Alabama, in which he related: "The majority of the American pilots and other employees of C.N.A.C. quit the job, on advice of American consuls . . ."[297] At best, the suggestion that America had been providing China with pilots could only have been directed at the American mission headed by Colonel Jack Jouett in 1932. However, that was to *train* Chinese pilots, not to fly in combat against Japan.

Next, Commander J. B. Lynch wrote a secret memorandum to Admiral Nimitz on August 7, 1941, concerning "Releases of naval personnel to accept employment in China with the Central Aircraft Manufacturing Company."[298] Commander Lynch reported to Admiral Nimitz that about two months earlier, he had been called into a meeting with a number of naval officers as well as Bruce Leighton and a Captain Aldworth, retired from the Army Air Corps. Commander Lynch then reported: "It was indicated that the plan to release personnel for the purpose indicated had been approved by the Secretary of the Navy. My distinct impression was that the Secretary in turn had received his instructions *from the President* [emphasis added]."[299]

Even though there is no written executive order, there can be little doubt that President Roosevelt *orally* ordered the formation of a Special Air Unit for China. Commander Lynch also reported: "It was determined that all Naval personnel, regular and Naval Reserve, who were accepted for such employment must first be discharged from the Navy or Naval Reserve so that they would have *no connection whatever* with the Armed Forces of the United States [emphasis added]."[300]

To compound the confusion about the futures of these "volunteers," Commander Lynch stated:

> It was agreed that Reserve Officers who resigned might later apply for re-appointment in the same rank as at the time of separation. At the direction of the Department, they might even be re-appointed to a *higher rank* [emphasis added], or be required to serve *less time* [emphasis added] than the normal period and grade for promotion to the next higher rank.[301]

If volunteers were injured in service with the AVG, there were no provisions for supporting them or their families while they recovered. It was further determined that personnel physically disabled during their China service could still legally reenlist,[302] and the request of naval personnel to resign to join the AVG would be delivered by CAMCO representatives, or naval officers would "act as courier messengers."[303] The intention was for two-thirds of the volunteers to come from the army and one-third from the navy.[304] The AVG would initially consist of approximately three hundred members—one hundred pilots and two hundred technicians and support personnel. As of the date of Commander Lynch's secret memorandum to Admiral Nimitz, twenty-three naval officers and three marine aviators had resigned for service in China.[305]

Commander Lynch noted that the number of pilots or enlisted men released for this program might increase three-, or even fourfold.[306] The reason for this statement is because the first one hundred pilots were destined to fly the one hundred P-40 fighters. As China received bombers and more fighter planes, more pilots would be required. Finally, he concluded with this telling remark: "I have at *no time* seen anything *in writing* [emphasis added] regarding this program."[307]

On August 7, 1941, Aubrey W. Fitch, the commander of Carrier Division I, the USS *Saratoga*, reported to the chief of the Bureau of Aeronautics, giving the names of the pilots under his command who were resigning from the navy to serve with CAMCO in China.[308] The pilots identified in the Fitch letter were among the thirty-eight "required to complete the original program of 100 pilots."[309] Fitch went on to relate: "It is also understood that a program of 266 additional Navy and Air Corps pilots will be initiated in the near future."[310]

In a secret memorandum to Admiral Chester Nimitz, chief of the Navy Bureau of Navigation, dated August 8, 1941, Captain H. N. Briggs reported on enlisted personnel who had been discharged for service in China.[311] Captain Briggs stated that he had been called into a conference with Captains John F. Shafroth and Good, and Commander Lynch, along with Leighton and two other civilians (ex-army pilots).[312] During the meeting that took place in May of 1941, Captain Briggs related: "We were told that the Secretary of the Navy had directed that a certain number of reserve officers and an undetermined number of enlisted men who desired it should be separated from the service for employment in China to help the Chinese Government with their aircraft."[313] It was agreed that "civilians would be given necessary authority to interview officers and enlisted men in various aeronautical units of the Navy."[314] Captain Briggs further confirmed it was his "understanding . . . that the Chief of Bureau would be asked to recommend to the Secretary of the Navy that men, who returned (from China) and desired it, would be permitted to re-enlist regardless of their physical condition. They would then be allowed to serve until they had sufficient time in service to retire."[315] The request for discharge would state that the men desired "to take employment with Central Aircraft Manufacturing Co., which would signify that they were going to China."[316] Noting that forty-five men had been discharged under that program to date, Captain Briggs said simply, "The matter was secret."[317]

In a handwritten memorandum to Admiral Dunfield of August 14, 1941, we learn that fifty-six pilots and forty-five enlisted personnel had been released from the navy for service in China.[318]

Apparently, Captain Frank E. Beatty, Navy Secretary Knox's aide, had been quietly organizing this guerrilla air force from his office in Washington. In his confidential memorandum to Dr. Currie of August 15, 1941, Beatty related that Dr. Currie was "the representative of the President with regard to the China Project, and has been in direct contact with the Aide to the Secretary of the Navy regarding it."[319] However, the administrative burden was becoming more than Captain Beatty could handle with the resources available in his office. Captain Beatty reported to Secretary Knox in the confidential memorandum:

> With the approval of the Secretary of the Navy, the Naval Aide
> to the Secretary has assisted the representatives of Central Air-
> craft Manufacturing Company to obtain the acceptance of res-
> ignations of certain volunteering Naval personnel, for the
> purpose of accepting employment with CAMCO, the idea
> being to permit this [sic] personnel to ultimately accept em-
> ployment under the Chinese Government for the purpose of
> operating a number of P-40 planes to operate against the
> Japanese over China . . . this has been carried on in a secret
> manner.[320]

While the China Project, as originally contemplated, had envisioned
that two-thirds of the volunteers would come from the army and one-
third from the navy, Captain Beatty confirmed that "this ratio is not
being maintained, particularly as regards to pilots."[321] The ratio had become skewed because relatively high numbers of naval aviators had volunteered in comparison to volunteers from the Army Air Corps. This
suggests that there was a greater emphasis on supporting the China Project among naval officers as opposed to those in the Army Air Corps.

The personnel who were busy recruiting volunteers included retired
Air Corps captain Aldworth, retired navy commander Rutledge Irvine,
and retired navy lieutenant Harry G. Claiborne.[322] The recruiters for the
enterprise were dealing directly with Lauchlin Currie, Captain Beatty,
and Army Air Corps major Goodrich.[323]

As Beatty's report continues, we see that one hundred pilots and
fighter planes would not satisfy the expectations of Lauchlin Currie. In
fact, Captain Beatty told Secretary Knox:

> Although it is felt that the present set-up will suffice to accom-
> plish the recruiting of the first 100 pilots mentioned above, Mr.
> Currie [sic] is setting up a *far more extensive program* projected
> into the future, which envisions sending a *far larger number of
> pilots* [emphasis added] to China, as well as the training of Chi-
> nese pilots in this country. Brigadier General Louis B. Her-
> shey, Deputy Director, Selective Service System, has been
> advised of the names of all men accepting employment with
> CAMCO.[324]

On August 15, 1941, in requesting that he be relieved of the administrative burden of forming this guerrilla air force, in secret, from his office in Washington, Captain Beatty wrote: "Due to the *expansion of the project* [emphasis added], as well as the change of status of its formerly secret classification, it is recommended that the entire project be transferred to the Office of the Chief of Naval Operations."[325]

On August 18, 1941, there was a meeting in the office of Navy Secretary Knox,[326] attended by Admirals Nimitz, Stark, and Ramsey; Captain Beatty; Commander Lynch; and Dr. Lauchlin Currie.[327] The subject of the meeting was CAMCO recruiters and what the recruiters could tell volunteers about the navy's position on their status.[328] Admiral Nimitz further confirms that the secretary of the navy had "directed that all officers—Navy & Marine Corps who had applied for resignation—should be let go for Camco [sic]."[329] Evidence that Dr. Currie was spearheading the China Project for President Roosevelt is found in the note of Admiral Nimitz, who said Mr. Currie would be satisfied with the release of sixty-three navy and marine officers "for the present."[330]

While the Nimitz note relates that the meeting with Dr. Currie, Admiral Stark, and others took place on August 18, 1941, a memorandum from Commander J. B. Lynch to Admiral Nimitz states that meeting actually took place one day later.[331] The Lynch memo confirms that the meeting between Admiral Nimitz and Lauchlin Currie took place, along with the fact that there would be "a total of sixty-three aviators as a quota for subject employment."[332]

NIMITZ TAKES COMMAND OF "THE CHINA PROJECT" FOR THE NAVY

When Captain Beatty relinquished control of the China Project, Admiral Nimitz took over the command of this secret venture. Admiral Nimitz confirmed this in a secret memorandum written to Secretary Frank Knox on August 15, 1941[333]: "Because of the nature of the project, all matters had been considered as *secret* and any promises made to those whose release from service were effected have been or will be made *orally* [emphasis added]."[334]

One problem with oral commitments is that the persons striking the bargain may each recall their agreement differently. This was the case in the formation of the AVG. While Commander Bruce Leighton had declared that persons volunteering for the Chinese venture would be allowed to return with "the same seniority and other benefits, including disability benefits as they would have enjoyed *had they remained on active duty* [emphasis added] in the Army or the Navy Reserve,"[335] Admiral Nimitz phrased the commitment differently. He said that when volunteers for the China venture returned to the military, they would do so "with the identical seniority in the grade held *at the time of separation* [emphasis added]."[336]

The tour with the AVG was to be a one-year commitment. Contemporaries of the volunteers could be promoted to higher grades while the volunteers were serving in China. Bruce Leighton believed that the volunteers would have the same seniority as their contemporaries. In fact, Commander Lynch had written on August 7, 1941, that the volunteers "might even be reappointed in a *higher rank* [emphasis added], or be required to serve less than the normal period in grade for promotion to the next higher rank."[337] The absence of a clear policy with respect to the seniority of these pilots at the conclusion of their one-year tour of duty would lead to dissent and disagreements when the Army Air Corps attempted to induct members of the AVG following the outbreak of World War II.

In writing to Secretary Knox, Admiral Nimitz confirmed that the volunteers would not be entitled to bonuses that would accrue to them for continuous service while they were serving in China.[338] Volunteers would be authorized to reenlist in the navy regardless of their physical condition after serving their one-year tour of duty.[339] The navy would be authorized to deny reinstatement to personnel "known to be guilty to a charge involving moral turpitude" (during their China service).[340] Death of a volunteer in China would not entitle him to any benefits from the United States Government.[341] While it appears to have been harsh not to provide survivors of Americans killed in combat with any benefits, the "fiction" that the guerrilla air corps was a commercial venture without any direct ties to the American government had to be maintained. The payment of government benefits would have undercut President Roosevelt's cover story. Entries would be made in the personnel records of the volunteers to reflect their separation from service.[342] In the bottom left-hand corner of the Nimitz memorandum, we see the handwritten notation *OK—Knox*, indicating that Secretary Knox had agreed with the terms outlined in the memo.[343]

THE PRESIDENT'S SECRET MEMORANDUM TO FRANK KNOX AND HENRY STIMSON, SEPTEMBER 30, 1941

President Roosevelt dispatched a secret memorandum to Navy Secretary Knox and Secretary of War Stimson on September 30, 1941.[344] This memorandum is one of the few documents we find that confirms the president's participation in the China Project. Also, it is instructive, since it signaled the resurrection, after a lapse of about ten months, of the plan for a preemptive strike against Japan. Because of its significance, the full text of President Roosevelt's secret memorandum to Knox and Stimson is set forth below:

> I have been informed that the Chinese Government has hired 100 pilots and 181 ground personnel to man and service 100 P-40s. In the next few months we are delivering to China *269 pursuit planes* and *66 bombers* [emphasis added]. The Chinese pilot training program here will not begin to turn out well-trained pilots until next summer. In the interim, therefore, I think we should facilitate the hiring by the Chinese Government of further volunteer pilots here. I suggest, therefore, that beginning in January, you should accept the resignations of additional pilots and ground personnel as care to accept employment in China, up to a limit of 100 pilots and a proportional number of ground personnel. I am directing Mr. [*sic*] Lauchlin Currie to see that representatives of China carry out the hiring program with the minimum of inconvenience to the Navy and also to see that no more are hired than are necessary.[345]

The president's memorandum is a clear indication that the plan for preemptive bombing raids against Japanese interests had been resurrected.

NEGOTIATIONS BETWEEN DR. CURRIE AND THE NAVY DEPARTMENT CONCERNING THE CHINA PROJECT

After Admiral Nimitz took charge of the China Project, he received a letter from Harry Claiborne of CAMCO, who related that Captain Beatty had declared Admiral Nimitz was taking over "the foreign project."[346] Mr.

Claiborne further stated: "We have been sending out a confidential 'Weekly Progress Letter' to those closely associated with the project, of which this is the current issue."[347]

To say that volunteering to serve China was a challenge would be an extreme understatement. While the military can use concepts of duty and honor to motivate servicemen in a positive fashion, and concepts of guilt and shame to preclude their disobeying orders, when you have a civilian operation of volunteers serving a foreign warlord, conventional military discipline techniques are not necessarily effective.

Not all of the volunteers possessed the requisite character traits to sustain them in combat operations in China and Burma. The "Weekly Progress Letter" referenced by Harry Claiborne discussed six pilots and three enlisted men who had elected not to fulfill their AVG commitments after resigning from the military.[348] With regard to the men who had abandoned the AVG project, Claiborne made the following suggestions to Dr. Currie and Admiral Nimitz:

> It is most strongly recommended that punitive action be taken against all these officers and men. This is mandatory if the Project is to expand or even if we are to be charged with the obtaining of replacements. If pilots and others can come and go at pleasure either through a real or fancied grievance, or run out on their obligations through fear or discomfort or a belated realization that this is a serious matter and not a picnic staged for their enjoyment and enrichment, it will be impossible for us to do our job. I looked for at least ten percent desertions and malingerers. The ratio up to now is far below that, but to my mind, positive action is indicated.
>
> I recommend that these officers and men be drafted immediately on their return to the United States, that they be sent in enlisted status to some station such as Iceland or Newfoundland, and that this action be taken before they can poison the minds of such personnel as may be interested in our program.[349]

In a confidential memorandum written to Admiral Nimitz, Captain V. D. Chapline discussed the navy's need of pilots.[350] While the navy as a whole would need 7,500 pilots as of January 1942, it would, in fact, only have 6,800 pilots. Of those pilots, only 3,194 would be experienced—

meaning, pilots with a year or more in service in operating squadrons. Because of this, a notation was made by someone in the bottom left-hand corner of the letter, indicating that resignations should be limited to those pilots who had graduated from training centers before they began their pre-fleet training.[351]

Because the navy needed its most experienced pilots, Secretary Knox wrote Lauchlin Currie, declaring: ". . . I feel eligibility for release should be confined to recent graduates of the Naval Flight Training Centers in the first three months immediately after completion of training and designation as Naval Aviator."[352] This letter bore the initials "CWN," for Chester W. Nimitz.[353]

Currie wrote Knox on November 8, 1941, saying, ". . . the arrangement you suggest, namely, that eligibility for release should be confined to recent graduates of the Naval Flight Training Centers in the first three months immediately after completion of training and designation as Naval Aviator, is perfectly satisfactory."[354] The letter from Dr. Currie has a notation that it was first to be given to Secretary Knox and then to Admiral Nimitz.[355] Dr. Currie's letter of November 8, 1941, was, in turn, circulated for approval by Admiral Nimitz and Admiral Towers.[356]

Three days before the attack on Pearl Harbor, Dr. Lauchlin Currie dispatched a letter to Admiral Nimitz that said: "I have been advised by Mr. [sic] T. V. Soong, Chairman of China Defense Supplies, that Richard Aldworth, H. C. Claiborne, and F. L. Brown are persons who are authorized to contact pilots and enlisted men in our Services for purposes of acquainting them with the possibilities of securing employment with the American Volunteer Group in China."[357]

How were Chennault and the CAMCO representatives faring in securing the services of pilots? How was the China lobby faring in its need to acquire fighter planes? These questions are answered in the next chapter.

Chapter Eleven

JOINT BOARD 355

These Flying Tigers were hotheads, soldiers of fortune, adventurers, and, like Chennault himself, highly individualistic. Behind them and supporting them, however, was something that was anything but individualistic: a massive, organized, systematic effort on the part of the U.S. Government to prepare for the bombing of Japan.

—Robert Smith Thompson, historian, *A Time for War: Franklin D. Roosevelt and the Path to Pearl Harbor* [358]

ROOSEVELT EQUIVOCATES ON BOMBERS FOR CHINA

In the spring of 1941, the champion for the Special Air Unit was Lauchlin Currie, PhD. A Canadian by birth, Dr. Currie had been educated at the London School of Economics and had received his doctorate from Harvard. He eventually became an American citizen and served as an aide to President Roosevelt. This fascinating personality, who would wield such influence and power in shaping the destiny of America and China under the auspices of the president, would someday leave America in political disgrace and move to Latin America.[359]

While there is evidence Currie provided confidential information to Russia, his conduct as a representative of the American State Department in China suggests he was loyal to American and Chinese interests. Although trained as an economist, Currie became one of Roosevelt's experts on China. After Chennault pitched the bombing initiative, Currie visited China in February and March of 1941. He appeared to enjoy a good working relationship with the Generalissimo and Madame Chiang. While the Japanese invasion of China had forced a temporary armistice in the fighting between the Chinese Communist Party and Chiang Kai-shek's Nationalist Government dominated by the Kuomintang Party, Currie was concerned that renewed internal conflict would weaken China and benefit Japan. For this reason, Currie recommended that Chiang emulate Roosevelt by promoting liberal economic reforms, thereby undercutting criticism from the left and the right. However, Chiang was not interested in following Currie's advice. The fact that Currie worked to strengthen Chiang's regime demonstrates that if, in fact, Currie was a Communist sympathizer, he was not a doctrinaire Communist.

Following his return from China, Dr. Currie wrote a memorandum to President Roosevelt on May 9, 1941, about providing aircraft, including bombers, to China. On May 15, 1941, Roosevelt wrote Currie a letter telling him to proceed with the program involving aircraft for China; this letter was later published in the Pearl Harbor Hearings.[360]

In the meantime, on May 12, 1941, Currie dispatched a letter to General George C. Marshall (at whose insistence Chennault's bombing plan had been deferred the previous December[361]). Currie's letter included a strategic estimate advocating bombing Japanese industrial areas in the Kobe, Kyoto, and Osaka triangle, as well as Yokohama and Tokyo. The letter included a proposal to supply China with 350 fighters and 150 bombers by October 1, 1941. Also included with the proposal was the argument that when a railway along the Burma Road was completed, it would be possible to supply and maintain one thousand combat planes in China. Currie explained to Marshall that the Joint Aircraft Procurement Committee had referred "the Chinese aircraft program" to the Joint Army/Navy Board.

On the same day that Currie wrote to Marshall, Lieutenant Colonel E. E. MacMorland of the Office of the War Department had dispatched a letter to Colonel Orlando Ward, secretary to the General Staff. According to the MacMorland memorandum, the matter of providing fighters and bombers to China was being placed before the Joint Board because it was "believe[d] [to be] a strategic question involving diversions from British and United States plane deliveries which should be settled by the Joint Board."[362]

In connection with a meeting of the Joint Board scheduled in mid-May 1941, Lieutenant Colonel MacMorland of the Ordinance Department, Defense Aid Division, related:

For the information of General Marshall, I am attaching a strategic estimate which I obtained from Mr. Currie, indicating the interest which the British should have in a strong Chinese air force on the flank of any attack on Singapore. I make this remark because I have heard that the *British will be invited to attend the Joint Board Meeting* [emphasis added], and if diversions are seriously discussed, it would be very desirable to emphasize the importance of a Chinese air force to them.[363]

Dr. Currie's strategic estimate, provided for consideration by General Marshall as the chairman of the Joint Chiefs of Staff, contained the following *tactical objectives*:

1) Defense of all establishments in Yunnan Province.

2) Attack Japanese air bases in Indo-China and on Hainan Island.

3) Attack Japanese supply dumps in Indo-China and attack Hainan Island.

4) Attack Japanese supply vessels, transports, tankers, and small naval vessels in harbors of Indo-China and Hainan Island and at sea between those places.

5) Occasional raids on Japanese industrial establishments in Japan.

6) Attack Japanese supply vessels on Yangtze River.

7) Support of offensive operations of Chinese armies.

The strategic estimate also contained the following *strategic objectives*:

1) Force diversion of considerable portion of available Japanese air force to defense of Japanese establishments on South China coast and in Japan and to counteroffensive operations in interior of China.

2) Enable Chinese armies to assume offensive operations which will make them necessary [sic] heavy reinforcement of Japanese troops in China.

3) Destruction of Japanese supplies and supply ships in order to handicap operations of an expeditionary force to the south of Indo-China.

4) *Destruction of Japanese factories in order to cripple production of munitions and essential articles for maintenance of economic structure in Japan* [emphasis added].[364]

In addition, the strategic estimate contained the following time schedule: "The increase of the air force from 300 to 500 airplanes (350 pursuit and 150 bombardment) *should be completed by October 31, 1941* [emphasis added]."[365]

Having the Special Air Unit operational by October 31, 1941, made tactical sense, since this would be the end of the monsoon season and would provide suitable weather for airborne operations.

Dr. Currie's strategic estimate was complete with tables showing the distances in statute miles between Chinese cities or provinces possessing airfields in relation to potential targets of opportunity such as Nagasaki, Kobe, Osaka, or Tokyo. Also, since the Japanese occupied Hainan, Formosa, Hanoi, and Saigon, distances to those targets of opportunity were also listed.

For example, from Chuchow to Nagasaki was 730 miles, or about 3.5 hours for a B-17 or Lockheed Hudson cruising at 200 miles per hour, which was easily within their performance capabilities. From Chuchow to Tokyo was 1,355 miles, or about 6 hours. From Chuchow to Kobe was 1,060 miles, or about 5 hours. From Chuchow to Osaka was 1,085 miles, or about 5 hours.[366] From Kunming to Hanoi (the capital of French Indochina) was only 335 miles, or roughly 1 hour for a B-17 or Hudson. Hainan was within easy striking distance of air bases in Kweilin, since the distance was only 380 statute miles.

Three days after the provision of substantial numbers of bombers and fighters was referred to the Joint Board, President Roosevelt wrote a short letter to Currie:

It is quite all right to go ahead and negotiate regarding the air program or any other thing that the Chinese request, but I don't want to imply that I am at this time in favor of any of the proposals. Obviously that can only be finally worked out in relationship to our whole military problem and the needs of ourselves and the British. This should be taken up with General Burns and General Arnold.[367]

While Currie was moving forward with efforts to supply China with large numbers of warplanes, including bombers, Roosevelt was still not fully committed to the provision of bombers as part of the China Project.

Roosevelt's equivocation on providing bombers for China must be put in context. Everyone was crying out for bombers in 1941. General F. L. Martin and Admiral P. N. L. Bellinger, air commanders in Hawaii, wrote a report on March 31, 1941, calling for 180 B-17 Flying Fortresses for air patrols to protect Hawaii from a surprise air attack. Secretary Stimson had become enamored with heavy bombers like the B-17 and B-24 Liberator as the means of launching air strikes against the Japanese home islands from bases in the Philippines, and also as weapons to attack Japanese ships approaching the Philippines as part of an invasion force.

In the competition between Hawaii and the Philippines for heavy bombers, General Douglas MacArthur in the Philippines had prevailed on the theory that the Philippines could successfully be defended with an umbrella of airpower. Britain, too, required heavy bombers to attack Germany and patrol the North Atlantic, scouting for U-boats. However, bombers that were less expensive and potent than American four-engine bombers (like the B-17 and B-24) were viewed as being capable of inflicting damage on Japan from airfields in eastern China.

With regard to whether or not the Japanese home islands could be successfully attacked by Lockheed Hudson bombers, General Hap Arnold made the following report in a memorandum of June 11, 1941:

> The Chinese believe that bombers are very essential if the Japanese transport lines are to be attacked effectively. They call attention to the congested life lines, usually rivers, used by the Japanese for transporting their supplies deep into isolated sections of China. In one case, about 1,400 boats a month went up one river just for supply purposes. The A-20s or DB-7s can be used for this purpose; that is, destroying boats and trains on lines of communications. The Lockheed Hudsons have ample

range to perform missions against targets in Japan. It is their desire to use incendiary bombs on the Lockheed Hudsons. Advance bases are available in Eastern China. It is 1,300 miles from these advance bases to industrial Japan.[368]

Dr. Currie's strategic estimate indicated that 500 aircraft should be provided to China in three stages. The *first stage* consisted of one hundred P-40s that were already *en route* to China at the time of his request.[369] He reported that pilots and ground crews were volunteering for service in China.[370] Dr. Currie believed that the initial batch of one hundred P-40s could begin providing the air cover that would protect the Burma Highway as early as July 1941.

The *second stage* suggested that by September 1941, there would be two hundred pursuit aircraft and one hundred bombers that "could be constituted if immediate decision were taken and intense preparations were made to supply an additional 100 pursuits and 100 bombers to be shipped during the month of May."[371]

The *third stage* was to be completed by the first of November 1941, and would include the shipment in June and July of an additional 150 pursuits and fifty bombers for a full force of five hundred aircraft, taking into account replacements at a loss rate of 15 percent.[372]

Dr. Currie indicated in his strategic estimate that pilots and crews for the P-40s already on their way to China had been secured, and "[I]f permission is given to recruit an additional 150 pilots and 300 technical men for ground crews, the personnel of the force could be in the field by the end of July."[373]

Another page of Dr. Currie's strategic estimate speaks in terms of phases rather than stages of deployment. The *first phase* would consist of one hundred Lockheed Hudson bombers, one hundred Curtiss P-40 fighters, and one hundred Republic P-43 Lancer fighters. The personnel accompanying the first phase would include one hundred pilots and 160 technical and clerical personnel. The Curtiss P-40s would be operational by July 1941, and the Republic P-43 fighters and *the Lockheed Hudson bombers would be operational by early September 1941.*[374] Again, under this alternate plan of phases, the *second phase* would consist of one hundred additional Republic P-43 or P-47 aircraft, fifty additional Bell P-39 pursuit aircraft, and fifty additional bombardment aircraft consisting of

Lockheed Hudsons, the Martin B-26 Marauder, or the Douglas B-23 Dragon.[375] The second phase would also require an additional 150 pilots and 250 technical and clerical personnel.[376]

Dr. Currie recognized that Singapore was the key to the Western Pacific, and that the Japanese had made clear their intentions to move against that British colony.[377] At the time Dr. Currie was submitting his strategic estimate, Japan and Russia had recently finalized a Neutrality Pact that would eliminate the need for Japan to station ten divisions of Japanese soldiers and five hundred Japanese airplanes in Manchuria.[378] An efficient air force in China would serve to threaten Japanese expansion to the south. Japanese forces could be bombed and strafed by fighter and bomber aircraft throughout occupied China and French Indochina. The Strategic Estimate found in Joint Board 355 declared: "With the initial strength of the new air force, the Chinese troops could launch counterattacks, the main purpose of which would be not only to hold existing Japanese forces in China, but to compel the continuous dispatch of strong reinforcements."[379] An efficient air unit operating in China would provide assistance to Singapore and the Dutch East Indies by occupying the Japanese troops and aerial forces with combat operations over China and Southeast Asia.[380]

CURRIE'S ARGUMENTS FOR DIVERSION OF AIRCRAFT FROM THE BRITISH

Dr. Currie wrote Navy Secretary Knox on May 28, 1941, enclosing a document entitled "A Short-Term Aircraft Program for China."[381] In the attachment to the Currie letter, Dr. Currie argued for the provision of thirty-three Lockheed Hudsons and thirty-three Douglas DB-7 (or A-20) aircraft to China, with twelve Hudsons and twelve Douglas DB-7 aircraft shipped immediately, and the balance of twenty-one to be shipped during the remainder of the year.[382]

As relates to President Roosevelt's secret memorandum to Knox of September 30, 1941—indicating that sixty-six bombers were being sent to China, along with 269 additional fighter planes[383]—Dr. Currie's short-term aircraft program for China explains the figures contained in the president's memorandum. With the exception of the one hundred P-40s already in China,[384] the president's statement was more of a wish than a reality. The 269 fighter planes (over and above the one hundred P-40s) were to consist of 144 Vultee P-48s and 125 Republic P-43s. However, the Vultee fighters' deliveries would not be completed until December 1941 or January 1942. The Republic P-43 fighters would not be delivered until November 1941 through March 1942.[385]

The situation with the bombers was similar. Dr. Currie anticipated shipping twelve Lockheed Hudsons and twelve Douglas DB-7s (or A-20s) immediately, with twenty-one additional aircraft of each type over the balance of the next year. In point of fact, the Lockheed Hudson bombers were sitting on the tarmac in Burbank, California, when the Japanese attacked Pearl Harbor. Ironically, crewmen who were to service the Lockheed Hudsons left San Francisco en route to Southeast Asia on November 21, 1941, four days before the Japanese task force set sail for Pearl Harbor.

The Vultee P-48C and D model was an attractive low-wing monoplane with a radial engine. Nicknamed the "Vanguard," this aircraft was built of components that bore a strong resemblance to other Vultee products, such as the Vultee BT-13 basic trainer aircraft. According to pilots who flew her, the Vanguard had delightful flying qualities, was quite nimble, and had a respectable top speed substantially in excess of 300 mph true airspeed. However, Dr. Currie indicated, "The British have signified their willingness to release these ships."[386]

Apparently, the British did not think the Vanguard was suitable for combat over European theaters, and they were probably right, as it did not perform well at high altitudes in comparison to German fighters. With the exception of the Lockheed P-38 Lightning, most American fighter aircraft produced during this period (like the Curtiss-Wright P-40 and the Bell Aircraft P-39) lacked two-stage superchargers (or turbo-superchargers) that would enable them to operate with full engine power at high altitudes. Aircraft powered by engines without turbo-superchargers or superchargers (there is a difference) will have a lower "critical altitude" than aircraft equipped with one of the devices. While a turbo-supercharger is driven by a turbine connected to engine exhaust, a supercharger is driven by gears that obtain their power from the engine's crankshaft. Both the British and Germans had fighters capable of operating effectively at altitudes higher than 20,000 feet. In time, America would also produce a number of fighters that possessed very good high altitude performance. One of these, the North American P-51 Mustang, would be powered by a Merlin engine designed by the British and built under license in America by Packard Motors. With the outbreak of World War II, the Vultee pursuit aircraft were pressed into service with the Army Air Forces and given the Army designation of P-66. They flew in defense of the West Coast of the United States.

With regard to the DB-7 (the export version of the Douglas A-20 attack aircraft), Dr. Currie said: "These ships have a low rating on the British priority list and it is proposed to cancel a substantial part of the British order. The ships are, however, ideal for China."[387]

Dr. Currie's assessment was correct. With the fall of France, 130 DB-7s ordered by the *Armée de l'Air* were supplied to Britain and referred to as the "Boston" when used as a bomber, and as the "Havoc" when used as a night intruder. Boston I aircraft equipped with single-stage superchargers and restricted to operations below 12,000 feet had been a disappointment to the British. However, by early 1941, Boston II aircraft equipped with Pratt & Whitney R-1830 Twin Wasp engines and two-stage superchargers, five machine guns, and carrying 2,400 pounds of bombs—along with night fighter versions with eight machine guns— were roaming over the continent of Europe, inflicting considerable damage with few losses. DB-7s were fast and very maneuverable, and would have served China well in the role of a light bomber and a ground-attack aircraft. They did, however, lack the range of the Lockheed Hudson.

What about the coveted Lockheed Hudson bombers? Dr. Currie had an answer for that as well. He declared there were one hundred Lockheed Hudson bombers awaiting delivery and ". . . Britain has neither enough pilots to ferry the ships immediately nor to man them upon arrival."[388] So the British did not care for the Vultees, placed a low priority rating on the Douglas DB-7s, and were not taking timely delivery of the Lockheed Hudson bombers. Dr. Currie could justify diversion of these aircraft from the British to the Chinese. The mission of this fleet of bombers and fighters would be to "a) protect strategic points, b) permit local army offensive actions, c) permit the bombing of Japanese air bases and supply dumps in China and Indo-China, and the bombing of coastal and river transport, [sic] and d) *permit occasional incendiary bombing of Japan* [emphasis added]."[389]

Ever the astute politician, Dr. Currie sought to assuage British concerns before they were raised. To the extent airplanes otherwise destined for Britain were diverted to China, Dr. Currie declared: "The Chinese have expressed their willingness to make any planes diverted from the British available for the defense of Singapore, if it is attacked. Air and supply bases in Indo-China can easily be bombed from airdromes in Yunnan Province."[390]

When war did break out in Southeast Asia, the Chinese did send (on a rotational basis) each of the three squadrons of the American Volunteer Group to defend the skies over Rangoon, Burma (a British colony). However, in the face of the "Japanese juggernaut," there was little hope that China, or any other nation, would be able to come to the aid of Singapore, which, in reality, quickly fell to Japan. History would prove Currie's representations to American strategists to be little more than wishful thinking.

Because of the unorthodox nature of the Special Air Unit that was to operate in China, Dr. Currie's short-term aircraft program makes the following comments about personnel:

> Ships comprised in the above program would all be flown by American reserve officers and maintained by American technicians and mechanics. They would be under the command of an American reserve officer, Captain Chennault, directly under Chiang Kai-shek. To improve discipline and efficiency, four or five staff officers from the Army Air Corps are urgently desired. The opportunity for our men to acquire actual combat experience appears to be a factor that should be given some weight.[391]

Although Dr. Currie speculated that four or five staff officers would be given to Chennault to improve discipline and efficiency, this never happened. In fact, Chennault noted in his memoirs that his request to General Hap Arnold for staff officers was denied.[392] General Arnold is somewhat obscure on this subject. In his report of June 11, 1941, he said: "*Observers* to be sent over would *really* serve on Colonel Chennault's staff as staff officers and supervise operations of American aviators. If this is approved, they would have to be selected with *extreme care* [emphasis added]."[393]

Why did General Arnold never give Claire Chennault any staff officers? Was he concerned about the political repercussions? Was he unable to find anyone who met his expectations in terms of their ability to function in such a politically complicated environment? There are several explanations that may account for this lack of support. First, with war clouds on the horizon, the Air Corps was engaged in a massive buildup and training program. Arnold probably felt he could not afford to provide Chennault the requested assistance. Second, Chennault had not endeared himself to Arnold or any of the other bomber advocates. Chennault's criticism of Air Corps tactics and policy may be another reason Arnold refused to assist with the provision of staff officers. However, as was the case with the Condor Legion, the group of "volunteers" from Germany who fought in Spain in support of a fascist government, Arnold should have appreciated the substantial value in having pilots acquire actual combat experience, during a time when the United States was not at war. Providing staff officers for Chennault's expedition would have benefited American interests.

DR. CURRIE'S CONTINUED QUEST MEETS WITH APPROVAL OF BOMBERS FOR CHINA

A meeting chaired by Dr. Currie was held in the State Department on May 28, 1941. Among those in attendance were Admiral Towers, General Leonard Gerow (a graduate of Virginia Military Institute and a veteran of World War I), and Colonel Clayton Bissell, a former instructor with Chennault at the Air Corps Tactical School at Maxwell Field.[394] A memorandum confirming the meeting relates that while one hundred P-40s had been shipped, Dr. Currie was seeking aid for China that would eventually increase to 1,300 aircraft.[395] "The American main-spring appears to be Major Chennault [sic], a former Air Corps officer. Chennault is competent, but lacks personnel of staff qualifications to coordinate the effort he is organizing and supervising."[396] The conclusion drawn from the meeting was that Dr. Currie would prepare a revised project with hope that it would be approved by General Marshall and Admiral Stark.

Dr. Currie was urgently seeking to have Chinese pilots trained in the Philippines. However, a report from the commanding general in the Philippines stated that there were no facilities available for such activities.[397]

Currie's quest for transport planes resulted in a suggestion by Pan American Airways that ten DC-3 aircraft be taken into inventory by the army and navy and loaned to the Chinese National Airways Company for operation in China.[398] Dr. Currie, in turn, forwarded the letter from Pan

American to Secretary of War Stimson on June 7, 1941, for a recommendation from the Joint Board.[399]

An element of Dr. Currie's short-term aircraft program involved the provision to China of 125 Republic P-43 aircraft. These were powered by the Pratt & Whitney R-1830 Twin Wasp engine. This engine powered a number of navy and army aircraft. After discussion by the Joint Aircraft Committee (Subcommittee of the Allocation of Deliveries) on June 3, 1941, the special subcommittee recommended approval of the production of the additional 125 Republic P-43 aircraft despite the demands it would make on the Pratt & Whitney R-1830 inventory.[400]

Dr. Currie's original short-term aircraft program for China was submitted on May 12, 1941. He then revised it on May 28, 1941, deleting requests for P-47 Thunderbolts, P-39 Bell Air Cobras, and restricting his recommendations (in addition to the one hundred P-40s already en route) to 144 Vultee P-48s, 125 Republic P-43s, 36 Lockheed Hudsons, 36 DB-7s (or A-20s), 70 primary trainers, and 35 DC-3s. He also wanted three to four hundred Chinese pilots processed through advanced training centers in America.[401] Dr. Currie's revised request indicated that the British had released the Vultee P-48 fighters, and that Republic Aircraft Corporation had said that production of the additional P-43 Lancers would permit an expansion and greater production of the P-47 Thunderbolt, then in development.[402] He again maintained that Lockheed had declared the British were not picking up their Hudsons as they were being produced,[403] and he sought approval of his revised short-term aircraft program for China.

Dr. Currie and Chennault met with General Hap Arnold on June 11, 1941, to discuss Dr. Currie's revised plan.[404] General Arnold's memorandum about the meeting confirms Chennault's request for four or five staff officers. In terms of the Lockheed Hudson bombers, Arnold's notes declared, "They understand that 12 of these might be delivered at once were pressure applied, and three could be delivered each month thereafter."[405] Republic's filling the order for 125 P-43 fighters would serve its interest to keep their employees active and the factory running until production of a P-47 aircraft could begin. There were also discussions about the government-furnished equipment (radios, machine guns, and engines) required for the Vultee P-48s and Republic P-43s.

Nearly one month later, on July 9, 1941, the Joint Planning Committee of the Joint Board recommended approval of Lauchlin Currie's revised aircraft program for China,[406] and on July 12, 1941, they *finally* approved it.[407] While Currie had traveled to China, visited with Chiang Kai-shek, returned to America, and formulated an ambitious program that would allow America to provide China with a guerrilla air corps, Chennault spent the first six months of 1941 working in the Chinese Embassy on the myriad of details and problems presented by establishing an air force in China. As Chennault recalled in his autobiography: "Most of my time in Washington was spent flying a desk in the brick building on V Street that was the headquarters of China Defense Supplies Incorporated. There I sat during the winter in civilian clothes, as an employee of the Chinese government, planning the basic strategy that I was destined to use during the next three years as a general in the Army of the United States."

The initial batch of one hundred P-40 fighter planes was provided without engines, machine guns, or spare parts. All of the supplies that would be needed to support an American expeditionary force in China would have to be secured if Chennault's efforts were to be successful. As he noted in his autobiography: "There was no precedent for this kind of an air force. Every policy and detail had to be thoroughly examined in advance."

PRESIDENT ROOSEVELT APPROVES THE JOINT BOARD PLAN

On July 18, 1941, Acting Secretary of War Robert P. Patterson and Navy Secretary Knox dispatched a secret letter to President Roosevelt indicating the Joint Board had approved the Joint Planning Committee Report of July 9, 1941, in reference to J.B. 355 (serial 691) *placing the matter before the president* for his consideration.[408] President Roosevelt dealt with the letter with a simple handwritten note, which read: *July 23, 1941. OK—but restudy military mission versus the attaché method. FDR*.[409] If America could have provided military airplanes to China employing an *attaché method*, an American military presence in China would, arguably, have been more obscure and thus, less obvious to the Japanese than a military mission. A military attaché is merely associated with a diplomatic embassy. A military mission suggests more officers and more extensive advice being given to the country being visited.

On the same day President Roosevelt authorized the implementation of Joint Board 355, secret memoranda were dispatched to Admiral Stark as the chief of naval operations and General Marshall, chief of staff, alerting them to President Roosevelt's approval of the plan to supply China with additional American warplanes and American pilots, including bombers that would bomb Japan.[410]

In contrast to the efficiency with which the Japanese had prepared for their attack on Pearl Harbor, here we perceive what appears to be a failure of the Navy Department to appreciate President Roosevelt's authorization of J.B. 355 on July 23, 1941. This lack of coordination is clearly suggested in a letter from Lieutenant Colonel Scobey, secretary for the Joint Board, to Admiral Turner dated August 28, 1941 (more than one month after President Roosevelt had given his approval).[411] In his memo to Admiral Turner, Scobey outlines the procedural history and actions taken in relation to J.B. 355, the president's approval of July 23, 1941, and his activities in communicating this information to both the Navy and War Departments.[412]

Scobey wrote his letter to Admiral Turner following a telephone conversation held on the same day—the clear import of which is that Turner had complained about a lack of information provided to the Navy Department. It is clear that Lieutenant Colonel Scobey refused to take responsibility for any failure by the Navy Department to implement or act upon the president's authorization of J.B. 355. Scobey's letter concludes: "May I say in this connection that my records of this case indicate that my action as Secretary in connection with this paper was complete. I feel that a failure on the part of either the War or Navy Department to implement approved recommendations is no fault of mine."[413]

THE FIRST AMERICAN AIR MISSION TO CHINA AND THE INSPECTION OF SPECIAL BOMBER BASES

While Currie was doing battle with the army and navy to divert American warplanes to China, the first American air mission to China took place in June 1941. Headed by Brigadier General H. B. Claggett, the group made a survey of Chinese airfields, aircraft, and airmen. General Claggett was the commander of U.S. Army Air Forces aircraft in the Philippines, but would, in time, be replaced by General Lewis Brereton. Claggett was accompanied on his mission by Colonel H. H. George and Lieutenant Colonel D. D. Barrett, who were both Army Air Force officers, as well as the assistant naval attaché for air, Major F. J. McQuillen. They also spent time with and acquired information from the American naval attaché in Chungking, Major James McHugh, who had previously dispatched information to the U.S. State Department on February 8, 1941, about China's progress in building airfields.

On June 5, 1941, at 5:00 P.M., there was a conference between General Claggett and members of his staff, as well as Major McHugh. Generalissimo Chiang Kai-shek, Madame Chiang, General Chou Chih-jou, and Colonel C. H. Wang also joined the group. The discussions at this meeting were summarized in a memorandum by McHugh of June 9, 1941.[414] While Claggett had told the generalissimo the best airfield he had seen was in Chuchow in southern Chekiang province, the generalissimo said he hoped Claggett would state that the best airfield was in Chengtu, "since it was built especially to receive American Flying Fortresses."[415] This was clearly a reference to Hsinching Airfield in the vicinity of Chengtu.

The plan of action for the infusion of American aircraft into China was to start with the organization of pursuit groups for the defense of bases in Yunnan (southwest China and the Burma Road), then, to increase air operations northward to cover Szechuan, and finally, to locate aircraft in southeastern China to attack Formosa, Canton, Hainan Island, and ultimately, the Japanese home islands.[416] Colonel George expressed the opinion that the Chinese Air Force was capable of supporting and operating a force of five hundred planes, but the principal problem would be supplying pilots who would be lost due to attrition when operations commenced. Madame Chiang inquired of Colonel George as to whether he thought Chinese pilots "were capable of flying the modern American equipment."[417] George said that he thought the Chinese pilots could fly the American airplanes, since "they would find the new P-40 easier to fly than the present Russian equipment they were flying."[418]

The generalissimo asked George to comment on the shortcomings of the Chinese air force, but ever the diplomat, George declared the Chinese pilots "to be fully as capable as the majority of young pilots in the average American Army unit."[419] McHugh noted in his memorandum: "It was evident at this point that both the Generalissimo and Madame Chiang had expected rather sweeping criticism of the personnel and were surprised at the blanket approval given by the Mission."[420] The discussions were temporarily interrupted by a bombing raid, but later resumed and continued until midnight. The idea of training Chinese pilots in the Philippines was discussed, as well as the idea of extending airline service of CNAC to Manila.[421] Initially, twenty-five Chinese pilots would be trained in flying the heavy bombardment aircraft, along with twenty-five navigators, twenty-five bombardiers, twenty-five armament mechanics, and ten radio engineers.[422]

McHugh apparently believed his first memorandum summarizing the meeting of June 5, 1941, was incomplete. He dictated a second memorandum of June 10, 1941, which essentially reiterated the same points made in his first memorandum, and summarized the conference with the generalissimo and Madame Chiang.[423]

McHugh was not the only author of a report concerning the impressions and findings of the Claggett mission. McQuillen, the assistant naval attaché for air, wrote a nine-page report concerning the status of the Chinese Air Force.[424] While the McQuillen report contained encouraging information about the status of airfields in China, it was less than encouraging in its description of the condition and training of the Chinese Air Force. For example, by the end of 1940, there were only eighty-nine combat planes in the inventory, and half of those were under repair.[425] While the Russians had provided China with seventy-five E-15-3 biplane pursuit planes, seventy-five E-16-3 monoplane pursuit planes, and one hundred SB monoplane light bombers, beginning in January of 1941, the delivery and assembly of those aircraft was not completed until May of 1941. Further, in or during the month of June 1941, thirty-six American P-40 aircraft had arrived in Rangoon, Burma.[426] McQuillen confirmed that the Chinese aspired to have between four- and five-hundred planes in their inventory, and that General Mao (also "Mow") was the director of operations of the Chinese Air Force.[427] The CAF operational headquarters were located in Chengtu.

By American standards, the training progress of the CAF would be considered far from satisfactory. It took two and a half years to complete pilot training, since students could only fly for thirty minutes, three times per week. The flight training school for noncommissioned officers had 124 primary students, 123 basic students, and 114 advanced students. The advanced students were divided into sixty-four bombardment pilots and fifty pursuit pilots. The first group of one hundred noncommissioned officer pilots had graduated in February of 1941.[428]

A description by McQuillen of air combat between the Chinese and Japanese pilots revealed the lack of training, resolve, and initiative of the Chinese pilots. On March 14, 1941, over Chengtu, thirty-one Chinese E-15-3 biplanes engaged twelve Japanese pursuit planes. At the first encounter, the Chinese broke formation, resulting in the Japanese fighter pilots hunting in pairs. For the better part of an hour, Japanese pilots hunted down the Chinese pilots, departing the area only when their fuel supply began to grow low. At the end of the encounter, fifteen Chinese planes had been brought down and eight Chinese pilots had been killed, "without visible damage being inflicted on the Japanese."[429]

Following this disaster, there was a shakeup in the Chinese Air Force that resulted in the elevation of General Mow to the position of director of operations. Several more encounters between Japanese bombers and Chinese fighters took place, resulting, in the first encounter, with the destruction of one Japanese bomber; and in the second encounter, with the destruction of two Japanese bombers.

According to McQuillen's confidential memorandum circa June of 1941, the Japanese sensed there was an infusion of new Russian aircraft into the Chinese Air Force and continued their efforts to reduce and compromise the CAF. There was an air battle between Chinese and Japanese pursuit planes approaching Tienshui, Kansu. While the initial air combat appeared to end in a draw, when the Chinese pursuit planes landed to refuel, the Japanese fighter planes appeared over the field and began strafing the Chinese planes on the ground. "Eighteen planes were damaged on this occasion, many irreparably," according to McQuillen.[430]

Since McQuillen accompanied General Claggett and his entourage on the inspection of airfields throughout free China, McQuillen's discussion of their condition is more detailed than McHugh's. In discussing the Chuchow airfield, McQuillen commented:

> The Chinese hope to eventually use this field as an advanced base from which to launch bombing attacks on Formosa, the Paracel Islands, and even on Japan itself. Unfortunately, the terrain . . . is fairly open, so that it is probable the Japanese would drive inland to capture this field if they found it was being used against them.[431]

McQuillen summarized his findings about the Chinese airfields, explaining that many of them were in excellent condition and were large enough to accommodate medium bombers in considerable numbers. He went on to say, "Each field, though currently seldom used, has a small maintenance and communication force. It should thus be easy to transform these larger fields into operating bases in a relatively short time."[432]

The Chinese strategy for deploying the infusion of American airplanes would take place in three stages. The first stage would involve the concentration of airpower at Yunnan-yi (in Yunnan province) in the form of fighter planes, whose mission would be to protect and keep open the Burma Road. The second and third stages were explained as follows: "As more planes become available and the Airforce [sic] expands, aerial operations will move eastward to cover Kunming, northward to cover Szechuan, and finally the Southeast to harass the Japanese along the Yangtze, in Formosa, in Canton, and on Hainan Island. The northwest is to be left to the Russian-advised section of the Airforce [sic]."[433]

McQuillen recognized that the Chinese-American plan was very ambitious and anticipated the possibility that only the first two stages of the plan might actually be implemented. He recognized there were problems with the prospect of basing considerable numbers of bombers in southeastern China. However, he concluded his report with the following comment:

> The Chinese populace has heard rumors of the arrival of new planes and foreign pilots so is now anxiously scanning the sky for the first appearance of this assistance. There can be no doubt that this extension of American aid has already given a powerful boost to Chinese morale. The results, in the end, can scarcely measure up to the Chinese expectations; nevertheless, this assistance is bound to be very much worthwhile.[434]

If actions speak louder than words, then the cooperation between Washington and Chungking suggested that a de facto alliance existed between America and China. China was sparing no expense in constructing airfields for the operation of Flying Fortresses. In fact, no fewer than twenty-five Chinese pilots were to be trained in the operation and flying of the heavy bomber. The real question was—how much did the Japanese know about this synchronization of action between the American and Chinese governments? Keeping the formation of an American guerrilla air corps a secret would prove to be an impossible goal for Roosevelt and Chiang Kai-shek. The Japanese had their means of acquiring valuable intelligence on the Chinese-American bombing initiative.

Chapter Twelve

JAPAN PREPARES FOR WAR

[W]e cannot rule out the possibility that the enemy would dare to launch an
attack upon our homeland to burn down our capitol and other cities . . .

—Admiral Isoroku Yamamoto, January 7, 1941[435]

The activities of Dr. Soong, Claire Chennault, and their confederates in
Washington were no secret to Tokyo. A Japanese intelligence agent with
close ties to the Nationalist government in Chungking was supplying the
Japanese with information about a "special air unit," and rumors that
China would employ heavy bombers to bomb Tokyo. On May 29, 1941,
the following top secret radio message from Tokyo was transmitted to
Japanese headquarters in Nanking, Shanghai, Peking, and Canton:

> On the 28th, PA [a Japanese intelligence agent] handed a
> member of my staff a strictly secret note which read as follows:
> "A part of the $50,000,000 export loan by the United States
> to China is to be used in purchasing 800 airplanes from the
> United States. These planes, it appears, are of two types, in-
> cluding the Boeing B-17. The United States will under this
> arrangement send pilots and mechanics to manage the planes.
> To affect this deal will require one month."
> In this connection, XYZ [presumably another Japanese
> agent] reports that a Boeing can leave a given base in China, fly
> to Tokyo, raid the city for 2 hours, and then fly back to China.
> Relay to Nanking, Shanghai, Peking, and Canton.[436]

This first Tokyo message was translated by American personnel on June 3, 1941. The American military intelligence community now knew what the Japanese believed to be true about the American bombing initiative.

Tokyo Circular Number 1209 dated June 6, 1941 (concerning message number 282 from Hong Kong, distributed to Japanese offices in Nanking, Shanghai, Peking, and Canton) is further evidence of Tokyo's knowledge about the American Special Air Unit. This circular reads as follows:

Re: My number 267
Intelligence from PA.
"The first party of 100 members of American aviators and technicians dispatched recently has arrived in Rangoon. Gradually they are going to SU. [These parties are apparently being routed through Rangoon.] In the future, too, in continuing this, it is expected that large numbers will be sent out from the United States. However, the number to come has not been made clear.

"Furthermore, according to newspaper information, American aviators are to be utilized in the transportation of bombers to China, the assembly of airplanes, their repair, and a study of actual fighting. However, the results of the matter of the request made by Chungking [is] that it is necessary for them to participate in actual warfare. It seems that about one-third of those sent are to take part in the war.

"Chungking requested that the United States supply some 500 first-class airplanes, and as a result of the contacts made by T. V. Soong (as I told you in my caption message), for the time being, a mere 80 planes had been supplied. Of these, aside from the 9 B-17 Boeing bombers and 18 heavy bombers, all airplanes are of very ordinary types. Furthermore, though I do not know but what there may be early discussions concerning continued supplying of American planes in the future, even though the United States is not avoiding its responsibilities with regard to the Far East, there is a great disparity, I have observed, between Chungking's requests and the amount of actual aid being sent."

In continuing, PA said:

"General . . . , since the request of wireless transmission (see my number 228) has been at outs with the government authorities, but having been made chairman of an investigating committee for the Seventh Zone (covering Canton, Kanshi, and Fukien Provinces) [sic], he has recommended me as his successor. Three times CHIANG KAI-SHEK has wired me to assume that post, but for myself, I have never liked Chungking's policy of doing things, but after some revisions have been made, I am quite prepared to assume that post."[437]

This second message from Tokyo was translated on July 17, 1941. It is apparent from this second message that the Japanese had at least one collaborator in, or close to, the government in Chungking who was feeding information (albeit, not altogether accurate) to Tokyo.

A third significant message from Tokyo was sent to Nanking, Shanghai, Canton, and Peking by way of Tokyo Circular Number 1437, dated July 5, 1941. The following was related:

According to information which HYŌ SI CHŌ got from DAI KŌ HŌ, bombers supplied by the United States (the number of machines is not known but I think they are the 10 Boeing B-17 types and 18 heavy bombers referred to in my message number 282) packed in 300 separate cases and 220 trucks (the Fords mentioned in my number 318) will reach Rangoon sometime between July 15 and 20 on board a steamship belonging to the Ford Company. The bombers are to be sent into the interior as they are. The trucks will be assembled in Rangoon and will leave that city toward the end of July or about the middle of August after being loaded with freight. The Chungking authorities are quite anxious that this war material is shipped safely and have sent MŌ HŌ SHŌ to Singapore to discuss plans with British and American officials. I understand that there are points in this information which coincide with what was confidentially told by PA to a member of this staff. I am sending this for your information.[438]

Not only was a Japanese collaborator tracking the progress of the American guerrilla air corps, but the American press had gotten word of the story. On July 9, 1941, a United Press correspondent filed this dispatch from San Francisco: "Thirty United States airplane mechanics and maintenance men arrived here today from New York, and will go to Rangoon next week *en route* to [China], where they will aid the Chinese Air Force. It was understood that a number of American planes of various types already have arrived in Rangoon and that more were *en route* there."

The Japanese military intelligence community was not the only element in Japan that was concerned about the provision of American military aid to China under the auspices of a "guerrilla air force." A July 1941 report in the Japanese press raised concerns about "large quantities of American war materials, including planes . . . *en route* [emphasis added] to Chungking . . ." The Japanese press noted America could not offer substantial aid to China and declared that Japan must address this military initiative with firmness. In a related story, the Tokyo press declared that America was accelerating plans for a Pacific offensive.

While diplomats and statesmen may have believed there was some hope that negotiations could resolve the crisis between Japan and the United States in the summer of 1941, stories in the Japanese press suggested the prospects for avoiding war were fading as both nations prepared military initiatives, including aerial attacks against the interests of the other.

SPECIAL TRAINING OF JAPANESE AIR UNITS

In the summer of 1941 (at the same time Dr. Currie was urging the provision of bombers to China), Colonel Masanobu Tsuji sent Operation Number 1—a war plan for the Japanese takeover of Southeast Asia and the Pacific—to the General Staff Headquarters in Tokyo. Operation Number 1 considered virtual simultaneous invasions of Malay, Singapore, Burma, the Philippines, Wake Island, Guam, Borneo, and Java.

Genda continued with his planning for an attack on Pearl Harbor through June 1941.[439] He felt, however, that the pilots were only half-trained, since aerial operations were tied to fleet operations (rather than land operations).[440] Finally, acting out of frustration, Genda dispatched a letter to naval staff officer Sasaki of the Japanese Combined Fleet, stating: "Stop this worthless deployed tactic training. Let the area units practice spot-attacking on land. And if the fleet training calls for air units to participate, arrange for it."[441]

By July 1941, the Japanese aircraft units that would attack Pearl Harbor began to train from land bases, giving more time and attention to the training of Japanese pilots and aviation personnel. The Japanese pilots learned to deploy their torpedoes so as not to go below a depth of thirty-three feet (Pearl Harbor having a depth of forty feet). With frequent flights from land bases, Genda writes: "Finally, not only torpedo bombing was practiced but also dive-bombing and low altitude bombing training were carried out in a real way."[442]

For Genda and his comrades, training was going well—until around September, when the Fifth Air Carrier Division (Shokaku and Zuikaku) were assigned to the fleet. This presented a problem, because the squadrons of the Fifth Carrier Division were newly organized and not well trained. Pilots of the Fifth Carrier Division were not keeping up with those of the First and Second Fleets in flight training. The Japanese Naval Personnel Affairs Section, being unaware of training for the Pearl Harbor attack, reassigned pilots and aerial personnel from the Fifth Carrier Division to other units, making Genda's training of pilots all the more difficult.

Genda then went to the Naval Personnel Affairs Section and explained that the fleet had special plans. He was successful in persuading them to assign skilled pilots and aerial personnel to the First and Second Fleets. Not only did Genda finally succeed in collecting the best pilots and aerial personnel for these fleets, but he also got Commander Mitsuo Fuchida appointed as commander of the air unit on the aircraft carrier *Akagi*. By June 1941, bombers of the *Akagi* had on three occasions attacked a very maneuverable target ship, *Settsu*, achieving hits thirty-three times out of one hundred from an attack-out altitude of 10,000 feet. This was a significant improvement in comparison to the earlier experience with the dive-bombers. The *Settsu* and aircraft units from the *Akagi* trained systematically to the point where the *Akagi* pilots ". . . [c]ould attack a navigating fleet with confidence. This type of attack was very good, because it could do the work that the dive-bombing attack could not."[443]

In the midst of training pilots to a high state of readiness, Admiral Nagumo argued that the task force should take the southern route to Hawaii. It was a shorter distance and would not have the rough seas of the northern route. Genda maintained that due to the absence of shipping along the northern route, it should be taken. Only with the intervention of Rear Admiral Yamaguchi, who argued Genda's position to Admiral Yamamoto, was the northern route confirmed, since it presented the best prospects to avoid detection and execute a surprise attack. Genda was summoned in September 1941, along with the chief of staff of the First Air Fleet and assembled leaders, to discuss his plans. It was during this time that Genda was directed ". . . [t]o make the finished plan all by [him]self in the Chief of Staff's room without any outside help."[444] The plan formulated by Genda was substantially similar to the information he had previously provided to Rear Admiral Onishi, the focus being on attacking the American carriers, by surprise, in daylight, with torpedo and dive-bomber attacks and a rendezvous point for the Japanese Combined Fleet from either Atsukeshi Bay or Matsukai Bay. The Japanese Combined Fleet then conducted chart maneuvers (concerning operations in the Hawaiian waters) at the Naval Staff College on September 12 and 13, but the departure point was changed to Hitokappu Bay. There were also combined-fleet chart maneuvers aboard the *Nagato* based on a three-aircraft-carrier attack plan in October 1941.

With invasions planned for, among others, the Philippines, Malaya, Singapore, and the Dutch East Indies, the Japanese military leadership decided it lacked the forces to invade the Hawaiian Islands. The invasion of the Hawaiian Islands no longer being practical, Genda's plan had essentially ten components:

1) The attack would be by six aircraft carriers.

2) The attack would begin at daybreak.

3) The primary targets would be the American aircraft carriers, battleships, and land-based aircraft and other ships.

4) The methods of attack would include torpedo attacks and dive-bombing attacks on ships, as well as strafing and low-level bombing against aircraft.

5) The Japanese would approach from the northern route to gain the advantage of surprise.

6) The assembly point of the Japanese task force would be Hitokappu Bay.

7) Since only two of the Japanese carriers had sufficient fuel supplies for a round-trip mission to Hawaii, Genda had to make plans for refueling at sea.

8) Japanese fighter planes would first attack Hawaii and gain air superiority, followed by bombing and torpedo attacks.

9) There were provisions for a second attack which ultimately was not approved by Admiral Nagumo, the Japanese admiral charged with command of the task force that would strike Hawaii.

10) Japanese floatplanes from escorting Japanese ships would fly over Hawaii in advance of the attacks to ensure the presence of the American fleet before the carrier aircraft were launched.

The training and preparation by the Japanese for the surprise attack on Pearl Harbor was meticulous and thorough in every detail—in sharp contrast to the manner in which American officials worked on the Special Air Unit plan. While Genda was overseeing the training of airmen who would launch the surprise attack, his colleague, Lieutenant Commander Suguru Suzuki, another airman who had been fully briefed on the components of Genda's plan, sailed aboard the Japanese merchant vessel *Taiyo Maru*, on the pretext of being the ship's assistant purser.[445] The vessel took the northern route to Hawaii and was spotted by an American aircraft two hundred miles north of the island of Oahu. Later, American planes made mock attacks on the ship. These events prompted Suzuki to recommend that Japanese aircraft be launched from a distance of at least two hundred miles north of Oahu.

The circumstances under which the *Taiyo Maru* and Suzuki were allowed to enter the territorial waters of Hawaii are especially disturbing. America had placed a total trade embargo on Japan following the Japanese occupation of French Indochina during the summer of 1941. Japanese vessels had no business being near Hawaii in October and November of 1941. However, American authorities gave the *Taiyo Maru* and two other Japanese vessels permission to sail through sanctions to Hawaiian waters. While the *Taiyo Maru* was docked in Honolulu on November 1 and 2, 1941 (slightly more than one month before the surprise attack), Suzuki engaged in surveillance of the harbor from the bridge of the ship with high-powered binoculars. While there, he was met at his ship by the

Japanese consul general, Nagao Kita. Despite the presence of American guards at the gangways, Kita provided Suzuki with sensitive documents, including a list of approximately one hundred questions concerning the location of American ships, where their torpedo nets were located, whether barrage balloons were in place, and similar matters of keen interest to Genda and the Japanese task force. Kita attempted to answer these questions overnight, prior to his return the next day. As the ship sailed on Sunday, November 2, 1941, Suzuki was able to assess the level of activity in the harbor at Honolulu. When Suzuki returned to Japan, he was able to provide fresh information to Genda and other officers who were busy preparing the attack plans.

While the Japanese had experienced difficulty with the accuracy of their horizontal bombing, chief petty officer Akira Watanabe demonstrated that with rigid training and attention to detail, the level of accuracy with the existing bombsights could be raised dramatically.[446] Lieutenant Furukawa was instrumental in administering this strict training to the Japanese horizontal bomber pilots, which ". . . [r]aised the effectiveness of horizontal bombing . . . to a level which never was attained before."[447] Furukawa's training techniques—which included training pilots to the brink of exhaustion and then beyond, to the point known as *kendo*—allowed him to train green pilots in one-third of the time generally allotted.[448]

Lieutenant Commander Shigeharu Murata was instrumental in researching and developing techniques that would ensure the success of the Nakajima Navy Type 97 ("Kate") bombers, which would launch torpedoes during the attack on Pearl Harbor. Murata ". . . [c]ompiled and organized the necessary information as to the topography and depth of Pearl Harbor and finally made the attack on Pearl Harbor a possibility."[449] Murata not only handled all of the initial planning—he also personally commanded the actual attack.

Lieutenant Commander Takashige Egusa was placed in charge of the training of Japanese dive-bomber pilots who would fly the Aichi Navy Type 99 ("Val") dive-bomber.[450] Under Egusa, "The degree of training suddenly went up and the results were amazingly good," according to Genda.[451]

Genda reported that the Japanese believed the American Fleet might be protected by torpedo nets.[452] A torpedo net protects the hull of the ship from an incoming torpedo, in effect, acting as a shield. The Japanese planners never developed a satisfactory solution to dealing with torpedo nets, other than to fly parallel to the ships in the nets and hope to hit the ships with their torpedoes, or to destroy the nets with torpedoes, followed by successive torpedo attacks (through holes blown in the nets).[453] Also, he noted that had barrage balloons been deployed, dive-bombing attacks would have been very difficult.[454] The main purpose of horizontal bombing from an altitude of 10,000 feet was to neutralize anti-aircraft fire and make torpedo and dive-bombing attacks less dangerous. The fighter pilots were led by airmen who had received extensive combat experience in the China Theater.

While Roosevelt and the American leadership focused on the war in Europe and the difficulties presented by diverting supplies of American aircraft from Britain and Russian needs, the Japanese were focused with a singular purpose, to execute a surprise attack on Pearl Harbor. While Chennault and Currie worked feverishly to organize and equip an American guerrilla air force for service in China that could menace Japan and Japanese interests, events in Southeast Asia were overtaking their efforts.

Chapter Thirteen

RANGOON AND BEYOND

*. . . [I]t should be remembered that Chengtu, one of the world's best landing
fields for operation of the heavy military aircraft, was constructed in 99 days.*

—General Clayton Bissell, United States Army Air Forces [455]

*The final cluster of staging fields in Chekiang province was only three to
five hours from the biggest industrial cities in Japan.*

—General Claire Lee Chennault [456]

JAPANESE SPIES CONTINUE TO FORWARD INFORMATION ON THE SPECIAL AIR UNIT TO TOKYO

There was a considerable disparity between the Chinese government's request for aircraft and the willingness of the United States to supply them in light of America's commitment to Great Britain and Russia. While Great Britain and Russia were each slated to receive as much as 40 percent of the aircraft available for export, China would only receive about 10 percent. While General Claggett had led an American military mission to China in May and June of 1941, America needed a more permanent military mission in China if hundreds of American airplanes were going to operate there, ostensibly under the flag of the Chinese Air Force.

Chief of Staff, General George C. Marshall, established the American Military Mission to China (AMMISCA) on July 3, 1941. This mission was headed by Brigadier General John Magruder, who was responsible for coordinating the fulfillment of China's aircraft needs based on America's capabilities.

General Magruder arrived in Chungking on October 9, 1941. His arrival did not go unnoticed by the Japanese. In fact, the Japanese agent in (or close to) the government of Chiang Kai-shek provided information to Tokyo on October 14, 1941. This is confirmed by Tokyo Circular Number 2176 of October 15, 1941, directed simply to the "Net" regarding "Message from Hong Kong #500 on the 14th"[457]:

> MAGRUDER and his party flew to Chungking on the 9th. Taking together information gathered from various sources, I have the following:
>
> The total number of representatives is 30 (of which 13 have already arrived). The advance group arrived about the middle of September and has completed discussion of their itinerary with the Chungking Government. After making an observation tour in many parts of China, the leaders will remain in Chungking, and the others will stay at the various fronts for a considerable length of time. They will keep in close touch with Chungking and at the same time advise their home government of practicable methods of military assistance in keeping with the actual situation. In preparation for a possible crisis, they will also study the arms as well as the tactics used by the Japanese army. It seems that they would also apply themselves to improving airfields, especially those in the southwest.

Besides the Japanese collaborator identified previously as "PA," two other collaborators entered the picture at this stage of the story:

> According to what HYŌ SI CHŪ [sic] heard from TŌ KEN KŌ, who had come as far as Hong Kong to meet the party, representatives will be dispatched to Chungking on September 30, also from Soviet Russia, in order to discuss with MAGRUDER and with the Chungking Government the question of using the Chungking forces in the event Japan attacks Soviet Russia.

At the request of CHIANG KAI-SHEK, Ō SHŌ TEI, accompanied by two military men, went to the Philippines early in October (the story of HO YING-CHIN having gone to the Philippines must be a mistaken telegraphic version of this fact). The purpose of this trip was to discuss with the British and American authorities both the tactics and methods of military cooperation. While the United States is, of course, earnestly hoping that the Japanese-American negotiations would be a success, they are, at the same time, proceeding with fairly frank discussions with the Chungking Government for military cooperation to be effected in case of emergency.[458]

It appears that Ō Shō Tei was the former vice chief of foreign relations for China. Ho Ying-Chin was an official of the Chinese military committee of the Nationalist government and a member of the Central Executive Yuan. As a member of the Central Executive Yuan, Ho Ying-Chin held a cabinet position in the Chinese Nationalist Government. It is certainly possible and perhaps likely that the Japanese informant had connections or contacts with highly placed personnel in the Chinese government.

While the American text of Japanese radio Circular Number 2176 transmitted on October 15, 1941, was decoded on October 18, 1941, there is no explanation of why the message speaks of representatives being dispatched to Chungking on September 30 (in the future tense) unless there was a substantial delay between the formulation and dispatching of the message by the Japanese collaborator. Whatever the case, by the middle of October 1941, the Japanese clearly appreciated that America, China, Russia, and Great Britain were contemplating their military options in relation to Japan "in case of emergency."[459] The word *emergency* must be considered as a euphemism for Japan's contemplated future acts of war against countries such as America, Great Britain, and Holland.

Chennault had spent the first six months of 1941 in the United States acquiring airplanes, engines, armaments, and supplies for America's Special Air Unit. Chennault and Dr. Currie had participated in endless meetings in Washington with top brass in the American armed forces. On July 7, 1941, Chennault made his way to the Mark Hopkins Hotel in San Francisco to meet the second group of volunteers, which consisted primarily of pilots.

The first contingent, under the command of Reverend Paul Frillman, a Lutheran minister, consisted of mechanics and technicians who had sailed from San Francisco in early June of 1941 aboard the *President Pierce*. Frillman was a natural choice to shepherd the first contingent of volunteers to China, since he spoke Chinese and had served as a minister in China when he first met Chennault. While the second ship carrying volunteers, the *Jagersfontein*, would leave San Francisco on July 10, Chennault set out aboard a Pan American Airways clipper on July 8.[460]

The first American Volunteer Group would consist of slightly more than one hundred pilots and two hundred support personnel. Accompanying Chennault on his trip to the Orient would be Owen Lattimore, an American official dispatched to act as a special advisor to the generalissimo. Chennault's volunteers were issued passports by the American government claiming they were musicians, metalworkers, bankers, and clerks. Chennault's passport said he was a farmer.

As the *Jagersfontein* steamed westward in the Pacific, it was escorted by two U.S. Navy cruisers, *Salt Lake City* and *Northampton*. The *Jagersfontein* swung south from the regular shipping lanes to avoid Japanese bases in the Caroline Islands, which are north of New Guinea and Australia and about half of the distance between the Hawaiian Islands and the Philippine Islands. The American cruisers left the *Jagersfontein* off the coast of Australia where escorting duties were assumed by a Dutch cruiser that followed the ship all the way to Singapore. En route, the volunteers on the *Jagersfontein* overheard a radio broadcast from Japan which claimed: "That ship will never reach China [sic]. It will be sunk."[461] Clearly, the Japanese were fully aware of the location and mission of America's Special Air Unit.

Just before Chennault left San Francisco, he received confirmation that the president had approved the formation of the Second American Volunteer Group that would consist of bombers, along with one hundred pilots and 181 gunners and radiomen that would arrive in China by November 1941. An equal number of men were to follow in January 1942.

There can be no doubt about the fact that when Chennault left San Francisco on July 8, 1941, he believed that he would have at his disposal a striking force, including bombers, with which to engage attacks on Japanese interests, and even the Japanese home islands. Anticipating the arrival of American bombers and pilots, China was busily developing airfields within flying distance of Japan. Unhappily, as events unfolded, Chennault would be disappointed—to the deep regret of members of the

Roosevelt cabinet, the American people, and servicemen and -women stationed at or near Pearl Harbor on December 7, 1941.

BRITISH INTRIGUES AND THE LOCKHEED HUDSON BOMBERS

Since his request for Boeing B-17 Flying Fortresses had been denied, Chennault's hopes for bombing the Japanese home islands now depended on receiving a sufficient number of Lockheed Hudson bombers with adequate dispatch to initiate bombing raids by early November of 1941. As noted in Chapter 11, Dr. Currie had discovered the British were not taking delivery of Lockheed Hudson bombers in a timely fashion.

An article appearing in the July 15 issue of *American Aviation Daily*[462] explains how Lockheed Hudson bombers that had been available for delivery to China suddenly became unavailable. An *American Aviation Daily* reporter interviewed British agent Sir Vivian on July 2, 1941, to ask why British demands for Douglas DC-3 transport planes could not be satisfied by converting Lockheed Hudson aircraft to a transport configuration. After all, the Hudson Bomber was nothing more than a modified Model 14 Super Electra airliner. Sir Vivian responded: ". . . we need all the Hudsons we can get as bombers."[463] If Britain was in such dire need of Lockheed Hudson bombers, the reporter asked, why were there 155 of them sitting idly at the Lockheed Air Terminal in Burbank, California? Within a few days of the interview, the Hudson Bombers had been spirited away to Canada.

The British were not about to admit Lockheed was producing more bombers than the Royal Air Force could absorb. However, that was in fact the case in July of 1941. So, when issues arose about the number of Lockheed Hudson bombers sitting idle on the ramp in Burbank, California, the planes had to be sent to Canada. Otherwise, some might be given to the Chinese.

BRITISH-AMERICAN COOPERATION IN BURMA

As Chennault made his way westward in the Pan American clipper (flying boat), he met his old friend, Howard Davidson, the commander of the 19th Fighter Squadron in Hawaii. In Manila, Chennault stayed with Brigadier General Henry B. Claggett and Colonel Harold H. George, both of whom endorsed Chennault's plan for an American Volunteer Group as a method to test men and equipment in China. In fact, Colonel George, the commander of fighters in the Philippines and a World War I ace, wanted to join the AVG, but the War Department had rejected his request. The Air Corps was ramping up for involvement in the war, something that appeared to be inevitable. Men with the experience of Colonel George could not be spared for duty with the Special Air Unit. George had accompanied Claggett on the American air mission to China in May and June of 1941. These men were keenly aware of the enormous job Chennault had undertaken with the formation of a brand-new air force in China.

Chennault arrived in Rangoon, Burma, on July 23, 1941.[464] When he arrived, most of the Curtiss P-40s were still packed in their crates and sitting on the dock.[465] However, a secret telegram from Dr. Currie to the American Embassy in Chungking—dated July 23, 1941, and directed to Madame Chiang—gave encouraging news: "I am happy to be able to report that today the President directed that sixty-six bombers be made available to China this year with twenty-four to be delivered immediately."[466]

Unless Dr. Currie was an avid reader of *American Aviation Daily*, he probably had no idea that the Lockheed Hudson bombers he had promised to China had been flown across the border to Canada.

Chennault set about locating a place to assemble and train his Special Air Unit. He was also desperate to find spare parts for his airplanes, since the American government had not provided any to the AVG. Finally, he had to train his pilots on the tactics that would give them a fighting edge over the Japanese airmen.[467]

The appearance of the American Volunteer Group in Burma presented a very delicate problem for the British government. Neither the British colony of Burma nor the British government had taken a position on the Sino-Japanese War. There was concern among British officials that providing aid and assistance to the American Volunteer Group might give the Japanese further excuses for aggression in Southeast Asia. While in April 1941, the British government had informed Dr. Soong that the AVG might assemble and test-fly planes, there would be no combat training permitted in Burma.

In Rangoon, Chennault conferred with the governor of Burma, Sir Reginald Hugh Dorman-Smith, as well as his senior military commanders, Lieutenant General D. K. McLeod and Group Captain E. R. Manning. Group Captain Manning was concerned about an irregular group of American volunteers operating in Burma who were not under his command.

Arguments were also raised about the political and military status of members of Chennault's Special Air Unit. General Mow argued that since Japan refused to acknowledge there was a *war* with China, members of the AVG could not technically be considered *belligerents*. Eventually, in October 1941, London reversed its position and allowed full combat training for Chennault's Special Air Unit in Burma. The Chinese government was allowed to lease the RAF Kyedaw Airdrome six miles outside the town of Toungoo. Kyedaw featured a 4,000-foot asphalt runway and teakwood barracks. Chennault's volunteers began arriving in Rangoon on July 28, 1941, promptly making their way northward to Kyedaw.

Engaging in shuttle diplomacy, Chennault traveled the Orient and had meetings with Air Chief Marshal Sir Robert Brooke-Popham and also with his aide, Air Vice Marshal Pulford of the Royal Air Force. Brooke-Popham and Pulford were occupied with the task of fortifying the British defenses in the Far East at a time when Japanese aggression in that region was a foregone conclusion. Nevertheless, Brooke-Popham obtained permission for Chennault's pilots to fire their guns at ground targets around Toungoo for strafing practice. Brooke-Popham and Pulford did everything possible to aid the American Volunteer Group, even at the expense of their own meager personnel and equipment. However, it was Chennault's assessment that the Royal Air Force did not have a full appreciation for the danger presented by the Japanese air units they would confront. Like America, Britain underestimated the aircraft and airmen of the Japanese air units.

KINDERGARTEN AT KYEDAW

The pace of flight training at Kyedaw Airfield was intense during the months of September, October, and November of 1941. Many of the pilots had never seen a P-40, much less flown one. Ideally, the men would have received training on how to fly the fighter back in the States, but the pace at which the Special Air Unit had been assembled did not allow time for this activity. The question of survival must have been on the minds of pilots in Chennault's charge. The living conditions were harsh in the jungle, which had the smell of rotting vegetation. The air was filled with insects. Mosquito nets were essential at night if the men were to get any sleep. In addition to physical survival on the ground, the demanding training environment raised questions about the pilots' survival in the harsh flight-training environment, as well as in air combat.

The following section is an attempt to capture the immediacy of what it was like to be a pilot in the Burma jungle, flying over Kyedaw Airdrome, based on interviews with Flying Tiger pilot Tex Hill and firsthand knowledge of the intricacies of formation flying:

In the heat of the Burma jungle, beads of sweat roll down the wingman's forehead and into his eyes as he clicks the parachute buckles around each of his legs and pulls the straps tight. He continues perspiring as he clicks the buckle on his chest for the parachute harness. He then locates his seat belt, which is three inches wide, lays it on his pelvis, and reaches behind his back to find the shoulder harnesses that fit in the buckle, which will clamp his four-point harness into the closed position. He pulls his seat belt tight and then adjusts his shoulder straps. His element leader gives the "start engine" signal.

After the engines of both planes have started, he taxis toward the active runway at Kyedaw. Running through his checklist, he confirms that the aircraft is ready for flight. He gives his element leader a thumbs-up signal, confirming that his pre-takeoff checklist and engine run-up are complete. A glance at the windsock indicates the wind will be from right to left, so his element leader takes the left (downwind) side of the runway to keep his wingman's plane out of his prop wash. Lining up beside and slightly behind his element leader, the wingman runs the power up on his Allison engine, to thirty inches of manifold pressure and 3,000 rpm. His element leader nods his head forward, indicating it is time to go to the full power setting and begin the takeoff roll.

The element leader only goes to forty inches of manifold pressure, giving his wingman six additional inches of additional power to maintain his station on the right side of his aircraft. As the wingman accelerates down the runway, his concentration is focused totally on maintaining his position in relation to his element leader. The wingman makes whatever control inputs and power changes required to stay in position as his aircraft roars down the runway. As he sees daylight under the wheels of his element leader, he too allows his aircraft to become airborne. He pulls the landing-gear selector from the NEUTRAL position to the UP position, and when his element leader nods his head forward, he depresses the button on the control stick that retracts his landing gear. The wingman continues to make small power adjustments on

the throttle to stay glued to the right wing of his element leader. The two pi-
lots retard their respective throttles and propeller controls to the CLIMB
POWER *settings, and streak skyward over the jungles of Burma.*

The wingman is becoming reacquainted with the art of formation flying,
something he learned in the American military. However, the discipline to
remain part of a two-ship element will have a profound effect on his life ex-
pectancy in the months ahead. His failure to fight as a part of a two-ship el-
ement may result in the death of his leader or himself. As he struggles to
keep his aircraft on his element leader's wing, he remembers the saying he
learned in flight school: "Formation flying is a fragile art."

His element leader then rocks his wings to signal "The fight is on." He
turns 90 degrees to the left while the wingman turns 90 degrees to the
right, and the two aircraft separate. Then the element leader reverses course
and the wingman does likewise, converging toward each other at a closing
speed of 600 miles per hour. As the aircraft meet, at the very last moment,
the element leader breaks to his left while his wingman breaks to his right
and then engages in a mock dogfight over Kyedaw Airdrome. This aerial
ballet is observed by their persistent mentor and critic, Claire Chennault,
sitting at his usual spot in the control tower high above the runway at
Kyedaw Airdrome. He carefully notes comments about the performance of
each pilot and debriefs each one after their flying session is over.

The pilots' day began at 6:00 A.M. with lectures by Chennault and
other guests in the pilot briefing room. One of the lecturers was Royal
Air Force Group Captain H. S. "George" Darley,[468] DSO. Darley
demonstrated to the fighter groups the best way to land the P-40 Tomahawk. He and Chennault also drilled the pilots in fighter tactics.[469]

The pilot briefing room was adorned with silhouettes and models of
Japanese fighters and bombers. The pilots were called upon by Chennault to identify the vital spots in the airplanes where the most damage
could be inflicted.[470] Chennault instructed that the Japanese pilots always
maintained rigid air discipline; therefore, the objective was to break up
their formations and use their rigid discipline against them.[471] While the
Japanese fighters had a faster rate of climb, a higher ceiling, and better
maneuverability, the U.S. airplanes were faster in level flight, had a faster
diving speed, and superior firepower. Chennault trained his pilots to use
the attributes of their aircraft to pit their strengths against the weaknesses

of the Japanese fighter planes. Chennault constantly admonished the pilots that they should sharpen their gunnery skills, saying, "Nobody ever gets too good at gunnery."[472] Chennault's fundamental instructions to his pilots included the following:

1) Dive on the enemy airplanes with the sun at your back using superior altitude and airspeed to engage in hit-and-run tactics.

2) Fight in elements of two where the element leader and his wingman protect each other in combat.

3) Never dogfight with the enemy fighter planes.

4) Kill or be killed.

Chennault encouraged his pilots to follow the Japanese airplanes as they departed the area since they would likely be low on gas and ammunition. Just like guerrilla fighters on the ground, Chennault's Special Air Unit was a guerrilla air force, and his pilots were taught to employ hit-and-run tactics. Every pilot who arrived at Kyedaw by September 15, 1941, would receive seventy-two hours of lectures and sixty hours of specialized flying. Chennault was known to be strict with his pilots; anyone who landed beyond a white stripe (one-third down the runway) was fined fifty dollars for this breach of flying etiquette. Otherwise, they were at risk of going off the end of the runway and wrecking their planes. On their off hours, Chennault's pilots were allowed to be boisterous, drink heavily, and run with women (if they could find any). However, there was a form of discipline in the Special Air Unit—and that was the natural ethic imposed by flying. Each man had to be ready to fly when he was scheduled. His squadron mates had to depend on him to be ready to fly and fight effectively. In essence, flight operations of the AVG would resemble those of a civilian airline. At the end of the day, Chennault was all business, and so were his pilots. Tutelage by Chennault offered some of the best flight training in the world.

In the spirit of a friendly challenge, RAF Squadron Leader Brandt flew a Royal Air Force Buffalo fighter plane against a P-40 flown by Eriksen Shilling of the AVG. Brandt, a Battle of Britain veteran, was no pushover. However, Shilling beat him in a mock dogfight over Kyedaw Airdrome.

This photograph of Major General Claire L. Chennault was taken after the end of World War II. Note the command pilot's wings over his left breast pocket and the China-Burma patch on his left shoulder. *(Courtesy of the National Archives and Records Administration.)*

This early model of the B-17 Flying Fortress had a pronounced art deco appearance with its swept vertical fin and rounded rudder. This aircraft would have had the range to stage out of Chuchow in Chekiang Province, fly to and bomb Tokyo, and return. *(Courtesy of Bert Kinzey.)*

This Curtiss-Wright Hawk, Model Number 75H, bears United States Registration NR1276. This is one of the aircraft flown in combat by Chennault over the skies of China. *(Courtesy of* Air Classics Magazine, *published by Challenge Publications, Inc.)*

Chennault appears with Generalissimo Chiang Kai-shek and Madame Chiang in Chungking sometime in 1942 following America's entry into World War II. *(Courtesy of the Flying Tigers Association.)*

Since the pilots in the fighter group of the First AVG had not all received training in the Tomahawk before leaving America, there were training and operational accidents as pilots transitioned to the new aircraft. Here, efforts are being made to salvage or repair a wrecked Tomahawk. *(Courtesy of the Flying Tigers Association.)*

Chinese workers roll and smooth the airfield at Kweilin in 1942. Kweilin was intended to be a fall-back bomber field, since the bombers would stage out of Chuchow for air strikes against Japan. *(Courtesy of the Flying Tigers Association.)*

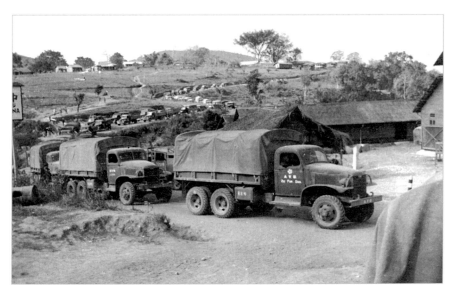

A convoy of the Second Squadron of the First AVG makes its way up the winding Burma Road along the Burma/Chinese border. Under the Joint Board Plan, this route was to provide the supplies necessary to operate America's guerrilla air corps. *(Courtesy of the Flying Tigers Association.)*

A Curtiss Tomahawk Number 68 has its machine guns harmonized. Chennault was adamant about the ability of his pilots to shoot accurately, noting, "Nobody gets too good at gunnery." *(Courtesy of the Flying Tigers Association.)*

A Tomahawk undergoes maintenance in Rangoon, Burma, in 1942, after America's entry into World War II. The conditions under which Chennault's guerrilla air force operated were primitive and demanding on the aircraft, the pilots, and the aircraft mechanics. *(Courtesy of the Flying Tigers Association.)*

LEWIS S. BISHOP
VICE SQUADRON LEADER
3rd PURSUIT SQUARDON "HELL'S ANGELS"

The Third Pursuit Squadron of the First AVG adopted the name "Hell's Angels." The Squadron Leader of the Third Squadron was Arvid "Oley" Olson, and the Vice Squadron Leader was Lewis S. Bishop. *(Courtesy of Shiela Bishop Irwin.)*

A pilot reviews the Airplane and Engine Status Board of the Third Pursuit Squadron, First AVG. *(Courtesy of Shiela Bishop Irwin.)*

Chennault briefs pilots Edward Leibolt, Carl Brown, Third Squadron leader Arvid "Oley" Olson, and First Squadron leader Robert "Sandy" Sandell. *(Courtesy of the Flying Tigers Association.)*

Chennault reviews a map with pilots Carl Brown, Charlie Bond, Edward Liebolt, Arvid "Oley" Olson, and Robert "Sandy" Sandell. *(Courtesy of the Flying Tigers Association.)*

Ace pilot David Lee "Tex" Hill and crew chief James Musick take a moment to smoke. Note the field telephone in the background, which was used to scramble AVG fighters to intercept incoming Japanese planes that were bombing Rangoon. *(Courtesy of the Flying Tigers Association.)*

Chennault would go to great lengths to deceive the Japanese about the number of aircraft at his disposal for flight operations. Here, we see a fake Curtiss-Wright Tomahawk used for this purpose. *(Courtesy of the Flying Tigers Association.)*

The Southwest Yunan University building in Kunming, China, served as the headquarters of the AVG. *(Courtesy of the Flying Tigers Association.)*

The confidence of the AVG pilots soared as a result of this encounter. Chennault was whipping his group into shape.

The P-40 Tomahawks were adorned with Tiger Shark images on their noses. Frequently, the planes were simply referred to as "sharks" by the pilots and ground crew. The pilots in the group went by names like Tex, Moose, Bus, and Rats. The group was composed of three squadrons: The First Squadron (Adam and Eves), The Second Squadron (Panda Bears), and The Third Squadron (Hell's Angels). The wings of the Curtiss Tomahawks were adorned with the emblem of the Chinese Air Force—a white, twelve-pointed star surrounded by a blue disc. The Tomahawks had the "sand-and-spinach" camouflage of the Royal Air Force, since they were diverted from aircraft built for Britain. At this point in history, no one had yet called Chennault or his men "Flying Tigers." They were simply known as the American Volunteer Group, or the AVG.

The flight training at Kyedaw Airfield was not going unnoticed by the Japanese. Sensing the American Volunteer Group might be vulnerable to an air strike by the Japanese Army Air Force (JAAF), Chennault dispatched squadron leaders Robert "Sandy" Sandell, "Scarsdale Jack" Newkirk, and Arvid "Oley" Olson to conduct a reconnaissance flight over Chiang Mai, Thailand, on October 24, 1941.[473] Two days later, a "silver ship" (most probably a Mitsubishi Army Type 100 reconnaissance plane) was observed over Kyedaw. Tomahawk fighters were dispatched to intercept the Japanese intruder, but failed.[474] The following day, silver ships appeared over Kyedaw. In his attempt to intercept the intruders, Erik Shilling reported counting five intruders.[475] No, the air training activities at Kyedaw Airfield were not secret to Japan. However, Japan would not launch a preemptive air raid on a British airfield in Burma. Military action of this nature would give President Roosevelt an excuse to declare war on Japan. It would have been premature at this point to attack the British colony; and besides, military leaders in Japan had more ambitious plans to execute, beginning in early December of 1941.

As American soldiers of fortune patrolled the skies of Burma and Thailand in the fall of 1941, the tension was palpable among the American "volunteers." During briefings, Chennault discussed "Allied" versus "enemy" planes. There was a sense among everyone at Kyedaw of impending war. The pilots wondered when the group might relocate from neutral Burma to China where aerial combat with Japanese pilots was a virtual certainty.

THE STATE DEPARTMENT'S UNREALISTIC EXPECTATIONS OF CHENNAULT

As Jack Samson described in *The Flying Tiger: The True Story of General Claire Chennault and the U.S. 14th Air Force in China:* "The RAF had abandoned Toungoo during the rainy season—May, June, July, and August—because the British felt that Europeans could not survive the jungle monsoons. They were close to being right. It is doubtful that, without the iron will of Chennault, anyone could have driven the young Americans to become a fighting force of any kind. Where mad dogs and Englishmen might have failed, several hundred American youngsters succeeded."[476]

While Chennault suffered with morale problems, supply problems, makeshift airplanes with sport plane radios, and machine guns and ammunition scrounged wherever they could be obtained, Dr. Currie and officials in the State Department expected even more of the intrepid aviator. Consider Currie's telegram to the American Consulate in Rangoon for Chennault, dated November 12, 1941:

> For Chennault.
> It has been suggested that we supply personnel for the reorganization and operation of the whole Chinese Air Force, including the A.V.G. We feel that this is impractical. As an alternative, we suggest the following on which we should like your reaction. We understand that the Chinese have some 200 first-class pilots. Our thought is that you might organize one or possibly two all-Chinese groups with officers and pilots selected by you and under your tactical command. We would undertake to secure more Americans to assist you as staff officers in your larger duties. We believe this is preferable either to turning planes over to Chinese Air Force or to assuming any responsibility for operation of Chinese Air Force. If this experiment is successful, you could organize still another Chinese group as American equipment becomes available, along with the organization of further American groups. We are uncertain as to whether any of the Chinese planes are suitable for your combat purposes. Are facilities available and adequate for the training of both American and Chinese groups in Burma? Whenever couriers are available, I should appreciate

more detail on your progress and problems. Your cable to C.D.S. [China Defense Supplies] just received. Will try to meet your requests.[477]

It takes little imagination to contemplate how Chennault must have felt upon receiving this telegram. He was in the jungle training pilots— many of whom had never seen a P-40 fighter plane—to not only fly the aircraft, but to master it sufficiently to engage in combat with the Japanese. The airplanes came with no spare parts. A number of aircraft had been damaged in training accidents. Only cannibalization and salvage techniques allowed the damaged aircraft to be restored to flight status. The heat and insects were oppressive. He had little time to shape this group of American volunteers into an efficient fighting force. Now, Dr. Currie and the State Department expected him to train two hundred Chinese pilots to operate Russian airplanes in combat. To suggest Chennault would have been frustrated upon receiving this telegram is an understatement.

THE AVG PREPARES TO COMMENCE OPERATIONS IN CHINA

By November 17, 1941, Winston Churchill had dispatched the following message to Chiang Kai-shek, which was forwarded to Dr. Soong, then to Dr. Currie, and finally, to President Roosevelt:

I am very much aware of the serious danger which you have pointed out in your message regarding Japan's impending new drive against China . . . I do realize the gravity of the situation if the Japanese should take Kunming. I am studying special means to help strengthen the International Air Force you have and give immediate support in personnel and material.

Brooke Popham [sic] informs me Colonel Chennault is ready to move into China with three squadrons in ten days' time and is asking Chennault how he can best help.

I will keep in touch with you and I hope to send more [sic] definite statement of what we can do. Needless to say, I am keeping the President informed.[478]

WHERE ARE THE BOMBERS THAT WERE PROMISED TO CHENNAULT AND THEIR CREWS?

By late November 1941, after three months of training, many of the pilots in Chennault's Special Air Unit had been trained to a high level of proficiency. However, the training was not without loss. Jack Armstrong, a navy pilot from Hutchinson, Kansas, was killed in a midair collision while engaged in dogfighting another P-40. Max Hammer of Cairo, Illinois, crashed while attempting to fly through a monsoon. Peter Atkinson of Martinsburg, West Virginia, died when his aircraft suffered a catastrophic structural failure in a power dive.

As noted previously in this text, in advance of the First American Volunteer Group, Brigadier General Claggett, Colonel George, and Commander MacDonald had been dispatched to China as part of the kind of American military mission President Roosevelt alluded to when noting his endorsement to Joint Board 355 on July 23, 1941. The statement the American officers were instructed to give to the press was that they had ". . . [c]ome to China under instructions of our government in response to an invitation of the Chinese Government. The purpose of our visit is to study the Chinese Air Force, its facilities and its operations. *We shall remain as long as is necessary* [emphasis added] to inform ourselves thoroughly on these matters."[479]

By July 22, 1941, Madame Chiang reported in a telegram to Dr. Currie that Chennault planned to start air operations in Kunming by October 15, 1941.[480] With reference to the preemptive strike concept, Madame Chiang wrote, "Will you please try to *expedite bombing planes so necessary in counteroffensive* [*sic*] [emphasis added]. . . . Warm thanks for your efforts on China's behalf."[481]

While Madame Chiang was pleading for delivery of the bombers, Currie was having problems getting the full cooperation of the army and navy in recruiting pilots. Confirming he had "the 66 bombers released by the British,"[482] Currie complained to Roosevelt that the hiring of more army pilots would "not take effect until next January."[483]

Currie, having fought to get sixty-six bombers for China, appeared to be exasperated in a memorandum to the president dated September 18, 1941.[484] Currie told President Roosevelt he was meeting "resistance of the personnel branches of the services."[485] Currie then made the following request: "Would you mind signing the rather mildly worded directive attached? In accordance with my information on the needs and number of personnel in the services, I am suggesting that the Army accept further resignations beginning in October and the Navy in January."

This plaintive request by Currie to dislodge resistance by the army and navy in CAMCO's pilot-recruiting activities resulted in Roosevelt's secret memorandum, dated September 30, 1941, and directed to secretaries Knox and Stimson. The memorandum urged them to take the following actions in January:

> Accept the resignations of additional pilots and ground personnel as care to accept employment in China, up to a limit of 100 pilots and a proportional number of ground personnel. I am directing Mr. Lauchlin Currie to see that representatives of China carry out the hiring program with minimum inconvenience to the [Navy/Army] and also see that no more are hired than are necessary.[486]

On the same day as Roosevelt's secret memorandum, Harry L. Hopkins, President Roosevelt's confidential advisor, spoke with General Hap Arnold, chief of the Air Corps.[487] Of that conversation, Hopkins reported to the president: "He tells me he doesn't believe that many of the men will volunteer. On the other hand, he says he will cooperate fully."[488] Make no mistake—with war looming on the horizon, General Arnold was *not* interested in giving up trained pilots for service in China.

Historian Daniel Ford has written that CAMCO hired 82 pilots and 359 technicians for the Second AVG, which would include thirty-three DB-7 Bostons and thirty-three Lockheed A-28 Hudsons, these being the sixty-six bombers promised to Madame Chiang by early November of 1941.[489] The diversion of these aircraft from Britain to China is established by materials and records in Joint Board 355. Ford further reports that the Douglas Bostons were loaded aboard ships and sent to Africa,[490] where they were to be assembled and then flown to Burma.[491]

Several sources have reported that members of the Second AVG sailed from California on November 21, 1941.[492] Ford wrote that the Second AVG technicians and one pilot sailed aboard *Noordam* and *Bloemfontein*.[493] When the men in the Second AVG sailed on November 21, 1941, the bombers they were to fly and maintain were already en route—or soon to be en route—to Africa (in the case of the Bostons), or Burma (in the case of the Hudsons).

In view of Dr. Currie's declaration (apparently accepted as factual) that as many as one hundred Lockheed Hudsons were awaiting delivery to Britain,[494] it is reasonable to conclude, as Ford apparently did, that the Lockheed Hudsons of the Second AVG were awaiting installation of additional fuel tanks in order to be flown across the Pacific.[495] This is further confirmed by Chennault's letter to Currie dated September 4, 1941, confirming that a senior CNAC pilot could lead a flight of bombers to China in late December of 1941.[496]

Further, on July 16, 2004, the author spoke by phone with Robert Ormsby Jr., a group president of Lockheed Aeronautical Systems, formerly president of Lockheed Georgia Company, and who served on the board of directors for two years of Lockheed Corporation. Mr. Ormsby confirmed that records of Lockheed Hudsons destined for China in 1941 are not "readily available." Chennault was supposed to have had the bombers and the pilots to fly them in Burma by November 21, 1941. It appears that through December 8, 1941, when Chennault first learned of the Japanese preemptive strike on Pearl Harbor,[497] he still expected America to provide him with the bombers promised by Dr. Currie. The twenty-four bombers that Dr. Currie promised Madame Chiang would be "delivered immediately" in the telegram (received at the American Embassy in Chungking on July 23, 1941) were probably the Lockheed Hudsons that were to be flown across the Pacific.

There is evidence suggesting that at least twenty-two Lockheed Hudson bombers were sitting on the ramp in Burbank, California, awaiting delivery to Chennault on December 7, 1941. This appears in a "Summary of Lend-Lease Supplies Furnished to China as of December 31, 1941," signed by Colonel H. W. T. Eglin, chief, Home Office of AMMISCA (American Military Mission to China), which reports: "Twenty-two (22) Lockheed bombers and some Vultee pursuit ships were being held on the West Coast by the freeze order. Their release is being attempted."

Chapter Fourteen

REPORTS IN THE AMERICAN PRESS OF PLANS TO BOMB JAPAN

*B-17s, Chennault's preference, were out of the question; they were too
scarce and too valuable to risk losing. Currie urged that the plan be made
operational by October 31, 1941. The first bombing raids on Japan would
be scheduled for the month of November.*

—Duane Schultz, *The Maverick War:
Chennault and the Flying Tigers*[498]

The morning of Saturday, November 15, 1941, six days before the Second AVG departed from San Francisco and three weeks before the attack on Pearl Harbor, General George C. Marshall is reported to have given a secret briefing to representatives of the *New York Times*, the *New York Tribune*, *Time*, *Newsweek*, the Associated Press, the United Press, and the International News Service.[499] In the briefing, Marshall candidly admitted: "We are preparing an offensive war against Japan."[500] America had thirty-five B-17s in the Philippines and was flying more of the heavy bombers across the Pacific Air Route as rapidly as the bombers could be produced and the crews trained. There were bases in China within flying distance of Japan, and the American aim was to blanket the area with airpower. By December 10, 1941, a large force of American heavy bombers would be positioned for bombing operations. Until then, there was danger that Japan might strike first. If the press kept quiet, war with Japan might be avoided.

Why would Marshall have called a secret press conference? It sounds like an oxymoron. Clearly, Marshall did not act on his own initiative. He must have acted at Roosevelt's direction. If one subscribes to the theory that members of the press can be trusted to keep quiet, then the press conference may be viewed as an attempt by Roosevelt to contain the press for a period of three weeks while America's airpower in Southeast Asia was further strengthened. Those inclined to be less charitable to the press may believe Roosevelt's motives in directing Marshall to conduct the press conference were to guarantee that there *would* be leaks. The press conference would ensure that Japan knew America was planning a bombing initiative to be carried out in the near future.

Regardless of which theory the reader subscribes to, the fact that the press conference was conducted is beyond debate, since General Marshall, on September 21, 1949, wrote Hanson Baldwin, a military correspondent for the *New York Times*, about the event. Marshall was responding to Baldwin's request to confirm the remarks made during the press conference on November 15, 1941.[501]

THE UNITED STATES NEWS

Japan did not require the services of an elaborate spy network in order to appreciate America's intentions. Plans to bomb Japan had been widely circulated in the American press during the fall of 1941. In fact, as early as October 31, 1941, the *United States News* included a two-page illustration entitled BOMBER LANES TO JAPAN—FLYING TIME FROM STRATEGIC POINTS.[502] The illustration featured bases in Chungking, Hong Kong, Singapore, Cavite, Vladivostok, Guam, and Dutch Harbor, from which American bombers could be launched to bomb Japan. A portion of the globe was depicted along with the Japanese home islands. A circle was drawn around the city of Tokyo and silhouettes of bombers were shown closing in on the circle from various points of the bombers' departure. The flying times to Tokyo varied from 1 hour from Vladivostok to 13 hours from Singapore. The flying time from Hong Kong was given as 7 hours, and from Chungking, 8 hours. A caption declared that the illustration assumed the bomber could fly 6,000 miles at 250 miles per hour. In October of 1941, there was no bomber in the inventory capable of that performance. The B-17 had a nominal range of 3,400 miles and could cruise in excess of 200 miles per hour. The performance figures on which the article was based appear to have been very optimistic. Apparently, the article was referencing aircraft such as the Boeing B-29 Superfortress that would one day enter service. The Boeing B-29 Superfortress would eventually be employed in firebombing and nuclear attacks on Japan.

It is noteworthy that the article declared American intentions to provide long-range bombers to China. The words contained in the article were provocative:

> Principal targets for enemy bombers attacking Japan would be the Tokyo-Yokohama area, and the city of Osaka, 240 miles southward. These two areas are the head and the heart of industrial Japan.
>
> Tokyo, city of rice-paper and wood houses, is the center of transportation, government, and commerce.[503]

The *United States News* article declared bombing could cripple Japan's main striking force, the fleet of the Imperial Japanese Navy.[504] America had a tremendous advantage over Japan to the extent American cryptographers were reading, at least, coded Japanese diplomatic messages or "Purple Code." While the American press gave credence to the idea that American bombers could cripple Japan's navy, a Japanese diplomatic dispatch from Tokyo to its consular office in Hawaii (decoded on October 9, 1941, by American cryptographers involved in Operation Magic) raised ominous questions about the security of the American Pacific Fleet anchored at Pearl Harbor. The following message from Tokyo was directed to Japanese spies in Hawaii:

> With regard to warships and aircraft carriers, we would like to have you report on those at anchor (those are not important tied up in wharves, buoys, and in docks). Designate types and classes briefly. If possible, we would like to have you make mention of the fact when there are two or more vessels alongside the same wharf.

A Japanese dispatch decoded and translated in Washington on October 10, 1941, used an elaborate and detailed system of symbols to be employed in designating the location of American vessels in Pearl Harbor. These messages, decoded by Operation Magic personnel during October of

1941, clearly indicated that America was not the *only* country contemplating an air raid on the fleet of a potential adversary. Japan had her own ambitions in such a preemptive initiative.

THE *NEW YORK TIMES*

The *United States News* was not the only American publication that hinted at American plans to initiate bombing operations against Japan. A news story authored by Arthur Krock in the *New York Times* on November 18, 1941, also included an illustration of the flying distances to Tokyo from the Philippines, Vladivostok, Nikolaevsk, and Dutch Harbor.[505] The headline of Mr. Krock's story was: PHILIPPINES AS A FORTRESS—NEW AIR POWER GIVES ISLANDS OFFENSIVE STRENGTH, CHANGING STRATEGY IN PACIFIC.[506]

Like the illustration and story which had appeared earlier in the *United States News*, Krock wrote that while the long-standing American belief had been that bases in the Philippines could not be defended in the event of war with Japan, that belief had since been abandoned. This was because long-range American bombers based in the Philippines (south of Japan) could overfly Japan, drop their deadly cargo, and then land in Vladivostok, Russia, to refuel and rearm. The bombers could then depart Vladivostok, fly south, bomb Japan, and land in the Philippines.

Krock then took aim at Kichisaburō Kurusu, the Japanese ambassador to America who was engaged in peace talks with Cordell Hull, and proudly proclaimed: "Before Mr. Kurusu leaves Washington, he may have been officially acquainted with these new circumstances of warmaking in the Far Pacific area, for official transmission to his government, which is considering the grave question of peace or war."[507]

TIME MAGAZINE

The *United States News* and the *New York Times* were joined in the fall of 1941 by other publications championing America's ability to produce and deploy bombers with great range. The cover of *Time* magazine featured Major Reuben Fleet, the president of Consolidated Aircraft Corporation.[508] Reuben Fleet had learned to fly in the American Air Service during World War I.[509] Following a distinguished career, Fleet left the military and founded Consolidated, which built long-range bombers and naval patrol bombers such as the B-24 Liberator, the PBY Catalina, and the PB2Y Coronado, a four-engine flying boat (or seaplane, in today's parlance).[510]

The story on Fleet related that production at his facility in California was prodigious and featured photographs of large numbers of Catalina flying boats under construction, along with a row of B-24 Liberators decorated with British insignia sitting on the tarmac.[511] Although the article on Major Fleet did not give precise information on the volume of bomber production at his factory, it clearly implied the numbers were large: "In the three big final assembly buildings, they come off the lines at a rate of [military secret] so many a day; no longer as bomber production was once appraised, at so many a month." The import of the *Time* article was that American warplane production was increasing at an extraordinary rate.

Any astute Japanese officer or diplomat would have grasped the significance of these news stories in the fall of 1941. Japan already knew America was establishing a covert air force to attack Japanese interests in China and Southeast Asia. Now, the American press was boasting of plans to bomb Japan. Japan was fully aware of American ambitions to limit Japan's further conquests in Southeast Asia.

THE BRITISH MEMORANDUM

Personnel in the American State Department had been careful to point out that there was no formal alliance between China and America at the time America loaned China funds for the operation of a "guerrilla air force" in China. By the spring of 1941, however, political realities revealed the emergence of a de facto alliance between America, Britain, China, and the Dutch (the "ABCD powers" or "Associated Powers"). How do we know this? One only needs to consider the contents of a secret memorandum from British General Headquarters in the Far East, dated September 19, 1941, entitled: "The Problem of Defeating Japan—Review of the Situation."[512] The "British Memorandum" was delivered to General Douglas MacArthur and is housed in his archives in Norfolk, Virginia.

The British Memorandum confirms that an agreement existed between the Associated Powers, to either coerce Japan into abandoning her ambitions of conquest in Southeast Asia, or to subvert and destroy Japan both economically and militarily. If economic embargoes and the threat of military action failed to force Japan's abandonment of its alliance with

Nazi Germany and Fascist Italy, the Associated Powers would oppose Japanese expansion by one or more of the following means (some of the more pertinent information about the designs of the Associated Powers appears in the British Memorandum starting at paragraph 14):

14.   (a) Common statements of policy by the associated powers to convince Japan that any move of hers will result in war.

(b) The Chinese army and air force (including the I.A.F.) to increase pressure on Japanese forces throughout China, and particularly in the Shanghai and Canton areas along the French Indo-China frontier.

(c) Improvement of the Burma Road (including doubling), and the organization for moving war material into China.

(d) Great expansion of 204 Mission. At least trebling is required in the first instance.

(e) Expansion of our organization for operating our air forces in China as far East as possible.

(f) Arrangements for the closest liaison with Russian forces in the Far East.

(g) Subversive organizations in the China coast ports, and in French Indo-China. Those must commence operation as soon as possible concentrating on propaganda, terrorism, and the sabotage of Japanese communications and military installations, creating discontent amongst the population, culminating in open rebellion.

(h) Subversive organization in Thailand. For the present the organization must spread its tentacles, so that it is ready to act immediately should the Japanese attempt to enter the country. Assassination of individual Japanese should also be considered.

(i) Reinforcement of the American garrison of the Philippines, particularly in air force and submarines.

(j) Propaganda to emphasize our strength, the increasing weakness of Japan; and the fact that Hitler has no longer any hope of winning the war.

15. Our ultimate object is to force Japan to eschew the Axis and embrace the Democracies. Should we fail by political methods, we must be prepared to fight Japan. In order that we may be in a position to act when the time comes, our plans must be decided and our preparations made without delay, and in concert with those of the associated powers.

The British Memorandum referred to the IAF, or International Air Force. This was Churchill's name for the American Volunteer Group. Interestingly, not only was the AVG meant to put pressure on the Japanese, but air operations, including bombing, by the RAF were contemplated in China "as far east as possible." The farther east bombers were based, the shorter would be the trip to the Japanese home islands. The buildup of heavy bomber strength in the Philippines did not portend good things for Japan, either. Furthermore, bases in eastern China were being stocked for bomber operations. The British Memorandum confirms the ambitions of the Associated Powers to encircle and reduce Japan and her military-industrial complex with airpower:

> . . . To the north, within air range of her vitals, is Russia, with air and submarine bases in the Vladivostok area. To the west there is China, where [there] are bases [that] are already being prepared and stocked, and there are large but at present, ill-equipped and led, Chinese armies. To the south there is Luzon in the Philippine Islands, within easy air range of Hainan, Formosa, and Canton, and extreme range of Southern Japan . . .

Obviously, American and British war planners were considering action against Japan. But as October passed and November emerged, what were the Japanese doing? The fact that Britain was also involved in plans for bombing initiatives against Japan is telling. She was fighting for her survival with Germany. Nevertheless, she did not wish to surrender Hong Kong, Malaya, Singapore, nor Burma to the Japanese. It appears Churchill saw the wisdom in moving to preempt Japanese ambitions directed at British interests.

JAPANESE DIPLOMATIC DISPATCHES DECODED BY THE UNITED STATES

Clearly, there were war clouds on the horizon, evident in the following Japanese diplomatic dispatch from the Foreign Ministry in Tokyo to the Japanese ambassador in Washington (decoded and translated on November 5, 1941):

> Because of various circumstances, it is absolutely necessary that all arrangements for the signing of this agreement be completed by the 25th of this month. I realize that this is a difficult order, but under the circumstances it is an unavoidable one. Please understand this thoroughly and tackle the problem of saving the Japanese-United States relations from falling into a chaotic condition. Do this with great determination and with unstinted effort, I beg of you. This information is to be kept strictly to yourself alone.

In a Japanese dispatch from the Foreign Ministry in Tokyo to the Japanese ambassador in Washington, decoded and translated in the Navy Department on November 12, 1941, the following appeared:

> Judging from the progress of the conversations, there seem to be indications that the United States is still not fully aware of the exceedingly critical-ness of the situation here. The fact remains that the date set forth in my message #736 is absolutely immovable under present conditions. It is a definite deadline and therefore it is essential that a settlement be reached by that time. The session of Parliament opens on the 15th . . . The government must have a clear picture of things to come in presenting its case to the Session. You can see, therefore, that the situation is nearing a climax . . . Please, therefore,

make the United States see the light, so as to make possible the signing of the agreement by that date.

The agreement referred to in this message concerned a termination of America's trade embargo against Japan. America was demanding Japan's withdrawal from China, Manchuria, and French Indochina—but Japan remained reluctant to abandon her conquests.

A Japanese dispatch of November 15, 1941, from Tokyo to its consul in Hawaii, decoded and translated on December 3, 1941, reported: "As relations between Japan and the United States are most critical, make your 'ships in harbor' report irregular, but at the rate of twice a week. Although you already are no doubt aware, please take extra care to maintain secrecy."

American cryptographers decoded this message on December 3. The meaning of this signal is very clear. Japan was tracking American naval vessels, and they did not want America to know it.

In a Japanese dispatch from the foreign minister in Tokyo to the Japanese ambassador in Washington (decoded in Washington on November 17, 1941), the following appeared:

For Your Honor's own information.

1. I have read your #1090 and you may be sure that you have all my gratitude for the efforts you have put forth, *but the fate of our Empire hangs by the slender thread of a few days*, [emphasis added] so please fight harder than you ever did before.

2. In your opinion, we ought to wait and see what turn the war takes and remain patient. However, I am awfully sorry to say that the situation renders this out of the question. I set the deadline for the solution of these negotiations in my #736 and there will be no change. Please try to understand that. You see how short the time is; therefore, do not allow the United States to sidetrack us and delay the negotiations any further. Press them for a solution on the basis of our proposals and do your best to bring about an immediate solution.

The Japanese diplomatic (Purple Code) messages that were being decoded by army and navy cryptographers in November of 1941 clearly revealed that relations between Japan and America had reached the boiling point. A satisfactory solution to the crisis had to be found by November 25,

1941, since Japan's fate hung by the slender thread of these few days. While the message was metaphorical, no intelligence officer reading these dispatches could have reached any conclusion other than the fact war between Japan and America was imminent if an agreement was not reached to lift the American trade embargo.

In a Japanese dispatch of November 18, 1941, from Tokyo to its consul in Hawaii (decoded and translated in Washington on December 5, 1941), the following appeared: "Please report on the following areas as to vessels anchored therein: Area N. Pearl Harbor, Mamala Bay (Honolulu), and the areas adjacent thereto (make your investigation with great secrecy)."

The deadline of November 25, 1941, was extended by four days until November 29, 1941, as revealed in a Japanese dispatch from Tokyo to Ambassador Kurusu in Washington, decoded and translated on November 22, 1941, which provided:

> It was awfully hard for us to consider changing the date we set in my #736. You should know this, however; I know you are working hard. Stick to our fixed policy and do your very best. Spare no efforts and try to bring about the solution we desire. There are reasons beyond your ability to guess why we wanted to settle Japanese-American relations by the 25th, but if within the next three or four days you can finish your conversations with the Americans; if the signing can be completed by the 29th (let me write it out for you—twenty-ninth); if the pertinent notes can be exchanged; if we can get an understanding with Great Britain and the Netherlands; and in short, if everything can be finished, we have decided to wait until that date. *This time we mean it, that the deadline absolutely cannot be changed. After that, things are automatically going to happen* [emphasis added]. Please take this into your careful consideration and work harder than you ever have before. This, for the present, is for the information of you two Ambassadors alone.

Clearly, the Japanese Foreign Ministry had given Nomura and Kurusu until November 29 to resolve the trade embargo crisis with America. American military intelligence officers knew in late November of 1941, that failing a solution to the crisis, things were automatically going to happen. The portent of this message was clearly ominous.

On November 24, 1941, Ambassador Nomura and Special Envoy Saburo Kurusu were instructed that the November 29, 1941, date for resolving the trade embargo crisis with America was set in Tokyo time (it would be November 28, 1941, in America).

On November 24, a secret message was dispatched from Washington to General Short in Hawaii, declaring that negotiations with Japan appeared to have terminated, and that America desired Japan to commit the first overt act. Short was cautioned to take reconnaissance and other measures, but not to alarm the civil population.

On November 26, 1941, after America received word that a Japanese fleet of troopships was sailing south from the mouth of the Yangtze River with as many as 50,000 troops, Cordell Hull met with Japanese Ambassador Nomura and Special Envoy Kurusu in his apartment. Hull gave Japan an ultimatum: If Japan wished the U.S. to lift her trade embargo, then Japan would have to get out of China and French Indochina. Hull's ultimatum was a disappointment to the Japanese, as confirmed by a Japanese diplomatic dispatch decoded and translated on November 28, 1941, which provided:

> Well, you two Ambassadors have exerted superhuman efforts but, in spite of this, the United States has gone ahead and presented this humiliating proposal. This was quite unexpected and extremely regrettable. The Imperial Government can by no means use it as a basis for negotiations. Therefore, with a report of the views of the Imperial Government on this American proposal which I send you in two or three days, the negotiations will be *de facto* ruptured. This is inevitable.

AMERICA'S WAR WARNING DISPATCH

A secret message released by Admiral Royal E. Ingersoll in Washington on November 27, to Admiral Kimmel in command of the Pacific Fleet in Hawaii, and to Admiral Thomas Hart in command of the Asiatic Fleet in the Philippines, was ominous in its portent:

> This dispatch is to be considered a war warning. Negotiations with Japan looking toward stabilization of conditions in the Pacific have ceased and an aggressive move by Japan is expected

within the next few days. The number and equipment of Japanese troops and the organization of naval task forces indicates an amphibious expedition against either the Philippines, Thai, or Kra Peninsula or possibly Borneo. Execute an appropriate defensive deployment preparatory to carrying out the tasks assigned in WPL46. Inform district and army authorities. A similar warning is being sent by War Department. Spenavo inform British continental districts, Guam, Samoa directed take appropriate measures against sabotage.

This war warning to commanders of the American fleets in the Pacific suggests the principal concern for America was the prospect of Japanese invasions in the Philippines, Malaya, or Guam. No mention was made of anticipated action against Pearl Harbor. To Admiral Kimmel in Hawaii, this may have suggested the areas of concern were in Southeast Asia and the Western Pacific, not in Hawaiian waters. Hawaiian military installations were instrumental as a fuel stop for bombers flying from America to the Philippines, and as a staging and training area for the forces of the American army and navy. The mind-set at Pearl Harbor, viewed as a training base, may have been to preserve resources rather than expend them. This mentality may have been a factor in the decision to not have significant numbers of American twin-engine patrol bombers airborne and searching for hostile forces on the morning of December 7.

Another comment about the war warning message of November 27 is in order. Since it was directed both to Hart in the Philippines and to Kimmel in Hawaii, this seems to suggest the authorities believed Hart's forces in the Philippines were in more danger than Kimmel's forces in Hawaii. After all, the Philippines were south of Japan, not halfway across the Pacific Ocean like Hawaii.

JAPANESE DISPATCHES OF DECEPTION

A Japanese dispatch of November 28, 1941, provided the following:

> . . . I do not wish you to give the impression that the negotiations are broken off. Merely say to them that you are awaiting instructions and that, although the opinions of your govern-

ment are not yet clear to you, to your own way of thinking, the Imperial Government has always made just claims and has borne great sacrifices for the sake of peace in the Pacific . . .

In a dispatch from the Foreign Ministry of Tokyo to the Japanese Embassy in Washington of December 1, 1941, the following appeared: ". . . [T]o prevent the United States from becoming unduly suspicious, we have been advising the press and others that though there are some wide differences between Japan and the United States, the negotiations are continuing . . ." On the same day, Tokyo advised Nomura and Kurusu: "The date set in my message #812 has come and gone, and the situation continues to be increasingly critical."

FIRST BLOOD IN THE PACIFIC

Japanese army pilots drew the first blood of the Pacific War on December 6 (Tokyo time) when a Royal Australian Air Force Lockheed Hudson pilot spied a Japanese task force sailing off the coast of Malaya. The Australian pilot managed to radio the position of the Japanese task force before being downed by Japanese fighters and crashing into the Gulf of Siam.[513]

By 3:00 P.M. on December 6, 1941, thirteen parts of the fourteen-part message from Tokyo to Nomura and Kurusu had been received. Tokyo was waiting to sever diplomatic relations until Sunday, December 7, in Washington. The American decoding was completed by 9:00 P.M. There was no need for translating, since the message was in English. By midnight, the first thirteen parts of the Japanese message had been distributed to President Roosevelt, members of his cabinet, and senior military personnel. When the message was delivered to the president at around 9:00 P.M., he turned to Harry Hopkins and said, "This means war."

It has been reported that the president was having dinner on the evening of December 6, 1941, and told his guests that war would begin with Japan on the next day. It has further been reported that President Roosevelt stayed awake part of the night surrounded by his advisors, contemplating the events that would befall America on December 7, 1941. If the president understood on the evening of December 6, 1941, that war would begin the next day, one is left to wonder why this information was not rapidly conveyed to Admiral Kimmel and General Short.

MAGIC INTERCEPTS AND THE IMPENDING ATTACK

Operation Magic intercepts included Japanese diplomatic traffic, which included spy information. The following message was transmitted by the Japanese consul general in Honolulu, to Tokyo on December 6, 1941:

> On the American continent in October, the Army began train-ing barrage balloon troops at Camp Davis, North Carolina. Not only have they ordered four or five hundred balloons, but it is understood that they are considering the use of these bal-loons in the defense of Hawaii and Panama. Insofar as Hawaii is concerned, though investigations have been made in the neighborhood of Pearl Harbor, they have not set up mooring equipment, nor have they selected troops to man them. Fur-thermore, there is no indication that any training for the maintenance of balloons is being undertaken. At the present time, there are no signs of barrage balloon equipment. In ad-dition, it is difficult to imagine that they actually have any. However, even though they have actually made preparations, because they must control the air over the water and land run-ways of the airports in the vicinity of Pearl Harbor, Hickam, Ford, and Ewa, there are limits to the balloon defense of Pearl Harbor. *I imagine that in all probability there is considerable opportunity left to take advantage for a surprise attack against these places.* [Emphasis added.]

Barrage balloons carried steel cables aloft, making flying below or near them hazardous for aircraft. The absence of barrage balloons boded well for the Japanese airmen who would attack Pearl Harbor.

CHURCHILL'S DRAFT TELEGRAM TO ROOSEVELT

In London on December 7, 1941, Churchill was concerned about the Japanese task force that had been spotted by the Hudson pilot off the coast of Malaya. It spurred him to action, prompting him to compose a draft telegram for the new British ambassador to America, Lord Halifax, to inquire of Roosevelt if "we should be justified in attacking at sea any

Japanese expedition sailing in the direction of Thailand or Malaya (and presumably East Indies). We ourselves should desire to have this latitude."[514] As revealed by Churchill's telegram, Great Britain was contemplating a preemptive strike against the Japanese task force approaching Malaya—although in the end, the Japanese would commence landing operations before Britain could preempt the invasion of Malaya.

While Chennault and his Special Air Unit composed of fighter planes were standing by in Burma, ready to commence operations, a Japanese task force including six aircraft carriers and 465 airplanes had departed Japan, sailing toward the Hawaiian Islands. In light of the fact that an American guerrilla air force was operating in Burma, and declarations had been made in the American press about America's plans to firebomb key industrial centers in Japan, it is not surprising that Japan elected to launch a preemptive strike against American military bases in Hawaii. After all, as Bywater had noted in his novel, *The Great Pacific War*: "Moreover, at a time of national crisis, any scheme which promises to achieve major results at small costs must inevitably make a strong appeal to political leaders . . ." To Emperor Hirohito, General Tojo, and Admiral Yamamoto, an attack on Pearl Harbor appeared to be just such an opportunity.

Japan chose Hawaii because it was the base for the American Pacific Fleet, which posed a direct threat to Japan's eastern flank as she moved south into Malaya, the Philippines, and the Dutch East Indies. Destroying—or at least, crippling—the American Pacific Fleet in Pearl Harbor would minimize Japan's exposure to attacks from America as Japan moved south in her conquests.

Japanese planning for a preemptive strike had begun in February of 1941 and proceeded methodically and with meticulous attention to every detail. They would take a northern route to Hawaii. Shallow draft torpedoes were perfected. The location of American ships was recorded in a plot-and-grid method.

In contrast, America's movement toward a preemptive strike, or offensive initiative, appears to have been poorly coordinated, poorly planned, and ultimately, was never executed. After a year of planning and preparation for what should have been an American preemptive strike on Japan, Chennault must have felt a pronounced form of rage toward those who prevented his acquisition of the men and equipment that would have taken the war to Japan first.

Reports in the American press about U.S. military plans to bomb Japan in the months preceding the Japanese attack on Pearl Harbor were not without basis. On November 21, 1941, a secret bombing offensive memorandum was prepared for Secretary of War Stimson concerning an "Air Offensive against Japan."[515] To gather facts for such an undertaking, General Marshall had "directed that information be obtained referring to an air offensive against the Japanese Empire."[516] General Marshall wanted answers to four questions:

1) What General MacArthur would attack in Japan (from bases in the Vladivostok area) if war were declared December 1, 1941;

2) What data we have assembled in Washington on the subject;

3) What appears to us to be profitable systems of objectives; and

4) How much of our data was presented to and was taken to the Philippines by General Brereton.[517]

What came out of this discussion was the bombing offensive memorandum, which showed military leaders were concerned that the American strategy for the two groups of heavy bombers assembled in the Philippines had primarily been defensive in nature. The plan of operation for American bombers in the Philippines had been to attack Japanese lines of communication and Japanese shipping in the China Seas. There had also been consideration given to attacking Japanese naval bases in the islands off Formosa, even though there were no specific details provided about those bases. General Brereton—who commanded what was referred to as the Philippine Air Force—had, prior to his departure for the Philippines, taken with him air staff studies on the steel and petroleum industries and the electric power establishments in Japan. These materials would be essential to Brereton's execution of a bombing offensive directed toward Japan from the Philippines.

After General Brereton's arrival in the Philippines, military intelligence (G-2) received requests from him for "data on objectives in Japan."[518] In response, "a series of maps showing the location of approximately 600 industrial objectives in Japan proper" had been mailed to General MacArthur.[519] MacArthur was also told that an objectives folder to support those maps was in preparation and would be forwarded to him "at the earliest possible date."[520] The bombing offensive memorandum in MacArthur's possession concluded: "The present status of this project (now under way in the Chief of Air Corps branch office at Bolling Field) indicates that about one-third of the total projected number of objective folders may be completed and prepared for shipment to the Philippines."[521]

Accompanying the bombing offensive memorandum was a map of the Western Pacific, depicting the bombing radii of operation for B-17 Flying Fortresses, B-24 Liberators, and Douglas B-18A bombing aircraft. Due to the increased fuel capacity, the radius of action for the B-17 and the radius of action for the B-24 were considerably greater than for the Douglas B-18A aircraft. The center of two radii (one for the B-17 and one for the B-24) appears to be Vladivostok, which placed Tokyo and other Japanese cities within easy flying distance for those American heavy bombardment aircraft. Radii of action for the American heavy bombers were also centered with projected bases of operation in the Philippines, Australia, New Guinea, New Britain, and Sumatra.[522]

The bombing offensive memorandum leaves little doubt that in the closing days of November 1941, American military planners were engaged in "target selection" of key Japanese cities. The American War Department was clearly contemplating bombing raids on Japan. It had to appreciate that the Japanese troop convoy that sailed south from the Yangtze River on November 25, 1941, would likely strike colonies of the Associated Powers in Southeast Asia.

The assumption that Russia would allow American heavy bombers to fly from Vladivostok appears to have been misguided, especially in light of the Japanese-Russian non-aggression pact signed on April 13, 1941. Why did American military planners decide that preemptive air strikes on targets in and around Tokyo should originate from the Philippines, then proceed to bomb Tokyo, land and refuel in Vladivostok, and then, on a return flight to the Philippines, bomb Tokyo again, as opposed to simply mounting bombing raids on Japan from Chuchow in southeastern China?

More importantly, as American military planners were anticipating that war would be declared on December 1, 1941, why didn't the military take some of the American bombers based in the Philippines and move them to Chuchow, to place them within easy flying distance of Tokyo? A B-17 flying from the Philippines would be near the limit of its radius of action flying to targets in southern Japan. Tokyo was beyond the range of B-17s if they were to return to bases in the Philippines.

Perhaps American military planners distrusted Chennault and Chiang Kai-shek. After all, Chiang Kai-shek's Kuomintang-led Nationalist government suffered from corruption. Chennault, with his abrasive personality and his theories on fighter tactics running counter to Air Corps dogma, had offended and angered a number of his colleagues. But with the outbreak of war appearing to be a certainty, why weren't some American heavy bombers relocated to China? Perhaps American war planners were concerned there were insufficient fuel supplies in China to support the Flying Fortresses. Whatever the case, the expensive bomber bases in China were not destined to fulfill their purpose before the Japanese attack on Pearl Harbor.

AMERICAN PLANS FOR MASSIVE HEAVY BOMBER STRENGTH IN THE PHILIPPINES

Recognizing that Chennault was not destined to have B-17 Flying Fortresses at his disposal, how many heavy bombers were available to attack Japan from American bases in the Philippines? What plans did America have to increase the number of heavy bombers in the Philippines in support of a strategic bombing offensive against Japan? Finally, if the American aircraft carriers *Enterprise*, *Lexington*, and *Saratoga* were not at Pearl Harbor on December 7, 1941, where were they, and what functions had they been performing?

As reported by Lieutenant General Lewis H. Brereton, commander of Army Air Forces in the Philippines, the Philippine air strength stood at thirty-five Flying Fortresses, two squadrons of Douglas B-18 bombers, seventy-two P-40s, and twenty-eight P-35 fighters, along with two squadrons of fighters in the Philippine Air Force.[523] However, another B-17 squadron en route to the Philippines landed on Oahu during the Japanese attack. At the time of the Japanese attack, America was in the process of flying forty-eight Flying Fortresses across the Pacific from America to the Philippines.[524] In fact, Brereton confirms ". . . the 7th Bomb Group was to depart from the States for the Philippines the first week of December, and would push through as rapidly as possible."[525] Further, beginning November 26, 1941, B-24 Liberator bombers were ready to fly westward via Midway and Wake Islands to carry out reconnaissance missions of the Gilbert and Marshall Islands in the Western Pacific.[526] The United States anticipated having as many as one hundred heavy bombers in the Philippines by April of 1942. In fact, Brereton, in a meeting with Lieutenant General Hap Arnold and other senior air force officers of October 6, 1941, was told of far more ambitious plans for expanding American airpower in the Philippines.[527] There would be 272 heavy bombers (B-17s and B-24s) in four groups.[528] There would be 260 fighter planes in two groups and 52 dive-bombers.[529] The air defenses of the Philippines would be supported with appropriate radar and personnel to operate that equipment.[530]

However, convoys of American heavy bombers could not fly across the Pacific to the Philippines if their safety could not be assured during fuel stops at Midway and Wake Islands. Because it would take too long to transport Air Corps fighters to Midway and Wake Islands, it was determined to be more expedient to transport navy fighter squadrons to those islands via aircraft carriers.

This explains why the American aircraft carriers *Lexington* and *Enterprise* were not at Pearl Harbor on December 7, 1941. They had been deployed to deliver fighter planes to Midway and Wake Island, the refueling stops of the American heavy bombers being flown to the Philippines. The aircraft carrier *Saratoga* had been dispatched to California. America's decision to increase its heavy bomber strength in the Philippines was complemented by Great Britain's dispatching the battleship *Prince of Wales* and the heavy cruiser *Repulse* to the Western Pacific in late 1941. This Anglo-American cooperation was then believed to be capable of deterring Japanese aggression in the Pacific, and it has been argued that this strategy played a major role in Japan's decision to strike first in the Pacific.[531]

CHENNAULT AND CURRIE'S PLANS FOR THE SECOND AVG IN LATE 1941

Chennault's thoughts in the late summer and fall of 1941 were not merely focused on the training of the fighter pilots in the first AVG. Correspondence between Chennault and Currie clearly indicates plans were under way to transport bombers to China and provide pilots to fly them. What is surprising is to learn that the British were considering, in effect, a reverse Lend-Lease by providing Hawker Hurricane fighter planes for operations in China, along with Bristol Blenheim bombers. In fact, the ever-imaginative Pawley was engaged in discussions with the British Air Ministry so that the United Kingdom could dispatch its own volunteer air force to China.

Currie dispatched a telegram to Madame Chiang to be relayed to Chennault with an intriguing question: WOULD YOU BE INTERESTED IN HURRI-CANES IN 1942 WITH PERFORMANCE AS FOLLOWS: THREE THREE NINE MPH AT TWENTY-ONE THOUSAND FEET, CEILING THIRTY-THOUSAND FEET, TWELVE GUNS 303 OR FOUR CANNON, TWENTY MM. IMMEDIATE ANSWER.[532] Currie went on to relate: HOPE TO GET SOM B-25S EARLY IN 1942.[533]

A telegram from Currie to Madame Chiang for delivery to Chennault, dated August 26, 1941, clearly indicated that British involvement in China was contemplated. Dr. Currie cabled: GOOD PROSPECTS OF OBTAINING FOUR HUNDRED HURRICANES WITH AUXILIARY TANKS. STILL NEGOTIATING WITH BRITISH FOR BOMBERS. AM WORKING ON YOUR SUGGESTIONS CONCERNING OTHER PURSUIT SHIPS.[534]

While telegrams from Dr. Currie in Washington to Madame Chiang presented the prospect of Britain providing fighter planes for operations in China in 1942, General Magruder (in charge of America's second air mission to China) dispatched an extensive message to Secretary of War Stimson and Chief of Staff Marshall on November 8, 1941. Magruder, who was more honest than the leaders of the first American mission had been in assessing the capabilities of a Chinese air force, related:

> The 30th of October I had a talk with the Generalissimo, who frankly stated that his Chinese force that is the Air Corps has become a complete washout. That he was afraid of its combat efficiency. He then urgently asked that the mission would assume this organization, take it over, and reorganize same; also, reorganize its training. He asked about our sending an Air Corps officer of high rank to take over and command his force. He insisted to the fact that full and absolute authority, free from any and all existing Air Corps interference or politics.[535]

Magruder was careful to point out that his comments were directed only at the Chinese Air Force, which was differentiated from the American Volunteer Group.[536] Magruder's message confirms the political reality in China: the Chinese were trying to challenge American authority, since the generalissimo had "[a]ssured that all our efforts are not negatived by the Chinese, whose tendencies are to try to undermine the authority that may be set up by U.S."[537]

The generalissimo's proposal to Magruder envisioned that this American general officer would have full command authority, including "immediate command of the A.V.G."[538] In time, the Chinese personnel would be integrated with the American Air Corps personnel, and the American general officer should have a staff of at least five officers.[539] The Magruder radiogram confirmed that the plan was still in place for operation of a force of five hundred planes in China.[540]

Magruder dispatched a second radiogram on November 9, 1941, revealing the problems encountered by training a combat unit in the field: FUTURE VOLUNTEERS FOR THE A.V.G. BE ASSEMBLED AT ONE OF OUR AIR STATIONS THERE IN THE U.S. AND PRIOR TO RELEASE FROM THE AMERICAN MILITARY SERVICE BE TRAINED AS SQUADRONS WHICH HAVE BEEN ORGANIZED AND ALL THEIR TRAINING BE ON THE TYPE OF PLANES AND EQUIPMENT THAT HAS BEEN RELEASED TO THE CHINESE GOVERNMENT.[541] Magruder's comments were appropriate. Chennault's hastily assembled fighter group had lost a number of planes in training accidents. A makeshift airfield in the jungles of Burma was hardly an ideal training environment.

CHENNAULT'S PLAN TO HAVE THE BOMBERS FLOWN TO CHINA

While Magruder was assessing the condition of the Chinese Air Force and relaying the generalissimo's request for an American general officer to take charge of the CAF and the AVG, Chennault dispatched a letter to Dr. Soong on September 4, 1941, concerning transporting long-range bombers to China. Chennault explained to Soong:

> One of the older CNAC pilots, who has been your personal pilot on a number of flights, is scheduled to return to the U.S.A. on leave about Dec. 1, 1941. He has stated to me that

he will be available to lead a formation of bombers back along the Pan American route or north over the Alaska-Siberia route to any designated point in China, about the end of December, 1941. He also states that he would be willing to accept command of the bombardment Group for subsequent tactical operations. Since this pilot is a very skillful navigator and is acquainted with most of the Chinese Airdromes, his services would be of great value to us.

It is proposed that a number of long-range bombers, say ten to twenty, be held at the factory and that crews of volunteer personnel be employed to fly the bombers from the factory to China. The bombers should be fully equipped with bombsights, radio direction finders, navigating instruments, oxygen apparatus, and bomb racks. Guns, ammunition and bombs should not be carried, but should be shipped to China in advance of the flight.

Permission to make the flight via Honolulu, Wake, Guam, and Manila would have to be obtained from the U.S. government. It is not believed that a stop at Midway Island would be necessary. It would also be necessary to obtain information as to whether the runways at Wake and Guam will be available, say by Dec. 31, 1941.

From Manila, these bombers could be flown at night so as to arrive at any designated airdrome in China just before dawn. If this plan is approved, I will instruct the CNAC pilot to call upon you for instructions after his arrival in the States.[542]

In addition to training a fighter group and preparing it for operations in China, Chennault was working to get bombers delivered to complete the inventory of his growing air force.

THE ORGANIZATION OF THE SECOND AVG

Besides transporting heavy bombers to China, Chennault had been in discussions with Madame Chiang and others about the operation and command of the Second American Volunteer Group, composed of bombers. In Chennault's letter to Dr. Soong of September 23, 1941, he offered two options to the Chinese government regarding the manning and operating of the Hudson bombers. As his first choice, Chennault noted: ". . . I would choose to have *all* trained personnel employed in America. Under this plan, all of the pilots, co-pilots, mechanics, radio, armament, clerical, and administrative personnel would be volunteers from the U.S. services."[543] If, due to economic or other considerations the first plan was not acceptable, then:

> Under the second plan, only key personnel are volunteers and the majority of the members of the group are to be furnished by the Chinese—an organization similar to that of the first American Volunteer Group (Pursuit). The Commission on Aeronautical Affairs assures me that well-trained Chinese personnel are available for assignment to this group in order to complete the full required strength . . .
>
> If it is desired that I exercise general supervision and command of the new bombardment group as well as the First American Volunteer Group (Pursuit), it will be necessary to organize a staff for a composite Wing. This will require the employment of a small number of additional personnel. Some of the personnel who will serve on the Wing staff are already employed on the First A.V.G. staff.[544]

Chennault was clearly walking a tightrope, trying to please both the American military and the Chinese. As a retired American officer employed by the Bank of China, he was a consultant to the Chinese Aeronautical Commission, in charge of setting up both fighter and bomber squadrons in China. Chennault's telegram to Currie of October 22, 1941, reveals how he was trying to satisfy his Chinese employers, while not giving offense to the American military mission in China. Chennault's telegram to Currie advised:

COLONEL HOYT AIR MEMBER MAGRUDER MISSION JUST HERE SHOWED PROMISING EVIDENCES DESIRE HELP GROUP STOP GAVE HIM COMPLETE HISTORY STATUS REPORT INCLUDING ALL PRESENT NEEDS WITH PRIORITIES REOPENING MANY DEAD QUESTIONS SUCH AS SPARE PARTS VULTEE TURBOSUPERCHARGERS PEE THIRTYNINES STOP AIRMAILING YOU SOONG COPIES STOP TRUST CLOSE LIAISON EXISTS OR ARRANGEABLE BETWEEN YOU AND MISSION IN GROUP WORK STOP MISSION EXPECTS OUR COOPERATION

STOP BYPASSING IT DANGEROUS BUT ABOVE ALL ANXIOUS DO
NOTHING YOU DISAPPROVE STOP KNOW YOU WILL UNDERSTAND
POSITION HOPE STEPS TAKEN AGREEABLE YOU STOP PLEASE AD-
VISE BEST COURSE FOR FUTURE STOP[545]

The cryptic words in Chennault's telegram to Currie indicate they
were trying to satisfy the expectations of both the Americans and the
Chinese, in terms of providing cooperation without giving offense. The
telegram further suggests that Chennault hoped to fulfill his need for
spare parts, and there were discussions about the provision of P-39 Bell
Air Cobra fighter planes for service in China.

Even before combat operations began, the first AVG was suffering
from shortages of spare parts. This is confirmed by a letter from Currie
to Chennault dated November 22, 1941, where Currie wrote:

> Your cable of November 12 came to us as a bombshell. None
> of us had any idea of the status of your equipment until that
> time. Nothing at all had come in from the Magruder mission
> except a cable on solenoids and bomb racks, and one contain-
> ing certain proposals that the Army deemed impractical. I am
> hopeful that one result of all this will be that a supply officer
> will be sent out to strengthen the air arm of the mission.[546]

Currie explained to Chennault: "Your whole supply problem for next
year is now being worked on. In the meantime, we are doing all we can
to expedite the delivery of the remaining parts and of the P-66s, P-43s,
DB-7s, and the Lockheed Hudsons."[547]

The shortage of spare parts, problems with getting the bombers to
China, and the operational losses and damage to fighter planes during
transition training provided to the fighter pilots of the First AVG were
clearly taking their toll on Chennault. Currie, in trying to give Chennault
emotional support, concluded with the following comment:

> I know you have had a most discouraging time. I hope you will
> derive some encouragement from the fact that so far as I can
> judge, your standing with the Air Corps is higher than ever
> before and there is general praise for the way you have con-

ducted yourself throughout. Moreover, I am certain that you will get much more support than you have up to now.[548]

While Chennault was confronting a host of logistical and political obstacles in China, William Pawley had approached the British Air Ministry about the idea of providing United Kingdom "volunteers" to serve in China with British airplanes. In fact, this concept was discussed on November 20, 1941.[549] Pawley's discussions with representatives of the British Royal Air Force concerned payments to pilots and other personnel who would be released from the British Air Ministry Service (with the RAF) for service in China as employees of CAMCO. This was, in effect, "reverse" Lend-Lease, since British airmen and aircraft would be employed alongside American aircrews in China. Pawley discussed with the British officials the pay scale for United Kingdom volunteers serving in China, as well as provisions for their survivors in the event they were killed or disabled. Three pages of draft notes dealing with the initiative of United Kingdom air crews serving in China were made in connection with the meeting of November 20, 1941.

According to the draft notes which accompany the note on that meeting, the British military initiative in China was to have the following elements:

1) The British Air Ministry would agree to loan such aircraft and equipment as may be released by the Commander-in-Chief of British forces in the Far East or the air officer commanding;

2) The Air Ministry to release such personnel as may be decided by the Air Officer Commanding for employment by the Company and the Company shall enter into an agreement with each individually and severally to employ such personnel under the conditions set forth in their agreements;[550]

3) The date and place of delivery of aircraft and equipment to be designated by the Air Officer Commanding. The date and place of release and commencement of engagement of personnel to be designated by the Air Officer Commanding;[551]

4) CAMCO could terminate engagements and release personnel at the request of the British Commanding Air Officer;

5) There were provisions for the exercise of discipline over the United Kingdom personnel;

6) CAMCO could only terminate the United Kingdom personnel for specific reasons;

7) CAMCO would pay or cause to be paid monies to relatives or dependents of the United Kingdom volunteers;

8) CAMCO agreed to accept the financial responsibility arising for widows and orphans and the like as may hereafter be determined and agreed-upon by the Company and the Air Officer Commanding jointly;[552]

9) The Company agrees to notify the Air Officer Commanding and to such other person being the legal representative of the employee such casualties or occurrences to the employee such as death, wounds, dangerous sickness, and the like as the Air Officer may request.[553]

Pawley's discussions with the British Air Ministry explain why Prime Minister Churchill referred to the Special Air Unit in China as the "International Air Force." It also indicates that the United Kingdom, like America, was contemplating military initiatives in China while operating under the auspices of the Chinese government.

Chapter Fifteen

PEARL HARBOR ATTACKED

Surprise, therefore, becomes the means to gain superiority, but because of its psychological effect, it should also be considered as an independent element. Whenever it is achieved on a grand scale, it confuses the enemy and lowers his morale . . .

—Carl von Clausewitz, *On War*[554]

While the American Special Air Unit was training in Burma for combat in the Sino-Japanese War, and rumors flourished in Japanese radio communications and the American press about American ambitions to bomb Japan, the Japanese were assembling a carrier task force in Hitokappu Bay. After the attack force was assembled, the pilots studied models of Oahu Island and Pearl Harbor each day while on the *Akagi*. Each airman studied his route to the target, along with the approach path to execute his attack. One pilot from the *Akagi* said that his thorough study of the models enabled him to easily orient himself with respect to his location on the island.

On November 5, 1941, Admiral Yamamoto issued Task Force Secret Order Number One to the Japanese task force destined for Hawaii. On November 26, the Japanese task force set out from Hitokappu Bay for the attack on Pearl Harbor. On December 3, 1941, as the Japanese task force approached the halfway mark in its journey, the Japanese consulate in Hawaii dispatched a long message to Tokyo, including a list of warships in the harbor and their positions.[555] Although American navy and army cryptographers were capable of deciphering the Japanese diplomatic code, the volume of work and relative low priority attributed to this kind of message resulted in a delay in deciphering this extremely revealing message until

December 11, 1941, four days after the Japanese preemptive strike. While the magnitude of the danger is readily apparent after translation, the volume of diplomatic messages being translated at the time apparently prevented it being afforded an earlier decryption and translation.

The coded message from the Japanese consulate in Hawaii of December 3, 1941, was the handiwork of the Japanese spy, ensign Takeo Yoshikawa, alias Tadashi Morimura. A graduate of the Japanese naval academy, Eta Jima, Yoshikawa's presence in Hawaii aroused the suspicions of special agent Robert Shivers of the FBI. Rear Admiral Anderson—who had previously been in the Office of Naval Intelligence in Washington when Leighton made his pitch to Major Rodney Boone—was now in command of the American battleships at Pearl Harbor. Rear Admiral Anderson told Special Agent Shivers that the navy, not the FBI, would undertake surveillance of the espionage activities that were under the auspices of the Japanese consulate. Yoshikawa's appearance aroused suspicion because he had no previous diplomatic posting, and he was not listed in the official Japanese Diplomatic Registry.

Yoshikawa had busied himself with spying on American military installations in Hawaii, with particular attention directed to the American Pacific Fleet. Yoshikawa found a confederate in the form of Richard Kotoshirodo, who held dual (American and Japanese) citizenship and was a clerk in the Japanese consulate.

In keeping with directions from Tokyo, Pearl Harbor had been broken down into various grids, with the locations of battleships and other warships relayed to Tokyo from a Japanese consulate's office in Hawaii. Yoshikawa befriended Teisaku Eto, a Japanese alien who had a soft drink stand directly across from the naval air station at Ford Island. Yoshikawa was soon comfortably ensconced at this stand, finding it to be the ideal vantage point from which to observe the schedule and activities of the American Pacific Fleet. There was no need for Yoshikawa to take photographs of the area, since color postcards picturing military bases and maps by the United States Geographic Survey were readily available from local merchants.

After the Japanese carrier task force sailed from Hitokappu Bay on November 26, 1941, a Japanese courier plane was brought down in China. The Japanese aircraft contained a plain text (message) relaying the following: "Japan, under the necessity of her self-preservation and self-defense, has reached a position to declare war on the United States of America." It is inconceivable that China came into possession of this information and did not share it with the Americans and the British. It is more than probable that Chiang Kai-shek would have shared such a message with Roosevelt and Churchill.

On December 1, 1941, President Roosevelt was considering a decoded diplomatic intercept from Japanese prime minister Togo to the Japanese ambassador in Berlin. The ambassador was directed to tell the Nazi government that war between Japan and the Anglo-Saxon nations "may come quicker than anyone dreams." Accordingly, Roosevelt told Secretary Hull and Admiral Stark (Chief of American Naval Operations) that he would take command of all diplomatic and military news concerning Japan.

On December 2, 1941, Admiral Yamamoto dispatched a coded message to the Japanese carrier task force that read CLIMB MOUNT NIITAKA. This was the coded message for the Japanese task force to attack Pearl Harbor. Also, on December 2, 1941, Captain Johann Ranneft, a Dutch naval attaché, was gazing at a map on the wall in the Office of Naval Intelligence. Depicted on the map was an orange formation of ships proceeding eastward from the Japanese home islands toward Hawaii. In querying an American naval officer as to the meaning of that depiction, the response was that it was the Japanese task force proceeding east.

At a cabinet meeting on December 5, 1941, Naval Secretary Knox intimated that the United States Navy knew the location of the Japanese fleet. Perturbed, Roosevelt interrupted Knox, saying, "We haven't got anything like perfect information as to their apparent destination."

As alluded to in Chapter 14, at about 9:30 P.M. on December 6, 1941, American navy lieutenant Lester Schultz appeared in President Roosevelt's study at the White House, where the president was in conversation with his closest aide and confidant, Harry Hopkins. The president read the first thirteen parts of a Japanese diplomatic message from Tokyo to Ambassador Nomura and Special Envoy Kurusu, after which Roosevelt said, "This means war." Hopkins responded by saying "It's too bad we can't strike the first blow and prevent any sort of surprise." Roosevelt's response was: "No, we can't do that. We are a democracy and a peaceful people. But we have a good record."

While accounts vary, it has been reported that Roosevelt met into the early morning hours with Navy Secretary Knox, his aide, Captain Frank Beatty (who had worked with Chennault in the organization of the American Volunteer Group), Secretary of War Stimson, Admiral Harold "Betty" Stark (chief of naval operations), General George C. Marshall (army chief of staff), and Harry Hopkins. While some historians maintain that no such meeting occurred, it does seem likely that Roosevelt, knowing war with Japan was imminent, would have called together his closest military and political advisors.

On Sunday morning, December 7, 1941, at 9:30 A.M., Admiral Stark was surrounded by naval officers, including Commander Alvin Kramer of OP-20G, the naval facility charged with intelligence in the Far East. Staff at this facility had decoded the first thirteen parts of the message from Tokyo, sent to its ambassador and special envoy in Washington. Stark, presented with two supplements to the thirteen-part message of the day before, had before him clear evidence of Japanese intentions to terminate diplomatic relations with the United States, effective by 1:00 P.M. Washington time on December 7. Despite being provided with this information, Stark did not share it with Admiral Kimmel, commander of the American Pacific Fleet in Hawaii. Rather, Stark dismissed his officers, declaring that he first wanted to speak with President Roosevelt. The fact that 1:00 P.M. in Washington would be 8:00 A.M. in Hawaii was a fact that clearly could not have been lost upon American naval officers addressing Admiral Stark.

While Admiral Stark was pondering his options on the morning of December 7, 1941, the Japanese naval officer who would lead the attack on Pearl Harbor, Commander Mitsuo Fuchida, was engaged in last-minute preparations aboard the Japanese aircraft carrier *Akagi*. Japanese aircraft were not to attack until 8:00 A.M. local time, because that would be 1:00 P.M. in Washington, the time by which Japanese diplomats were supposed to have delivered a message to Secretary Hull terminating diplomatic relations with the United States. If Fuchida fired a single black dragon rocket, then the fighter planes would attack the airfields first. If two rockets were fired, then the dive-bombers would attack first.

At 11:15 A.M. in Washington on December 7, 1941, Captain Frank Beatty delivered a report to Navy Secretary Knox from the Office of Naval Intelligence, which had interpreted the two supplements to the thirteen-part message from the Japanese government in Tokyo. In reading the report's conclusion, Beatty told Knox: "This means a sunrise attack on Pearl Harbor today." While Admiral Stark in Washington pondered whether or not to notify the commanders of army and navy forces in Hawaii, the Japanese aircraft were taking off from the aircraft carriers, approximately 220 miles north of Hawaii. Admiral Stark's decision not to notify Admiral Kimmel in Hawaii remains a mystery to this day.

At 11:25 A.M. in Washington, Colonel Rufus Bratton of Army G-2 (Military Intelligence) was waiting in the office of General George C. Marshall, the army chief of staff. Upon General Marshall's arrival, he was briefed on the contents of the two supplemental parts of the thirteen-part message, decoded the previous evening. Apparently, General Marshall pondered the document for nearly one hour before finally authorizing Colonel Bratton to send a message via army radio to General Walter C. Short, the commander of American army forces in Hawaii. Although General Marshall could have telephoned Hawaii via the "scrambler" (a direct telephone line to Hawaii, which was thought to be secure from Japanese wiretapping), General Marshall elected not to do so. The decision to dispatch the message to General Short via radio had onerous results, since atmospheric conditions prevented direct radio contact between Washington and Hawaii. Consequently, General Marshall's warning had to be dispatched to the army commander in Hawaii via Western Union telegram. Precisely why Marshall refused to use the scrambler remains a mystery.

Shortly before 8:00 A.M. on December 7, 1941, Commander Fuchida fired a single black dragon rocket. This meant that the Japanese Zero fighters were to attack the American airfields before the Japanese Aichi Navy Type 99 ("Val") bombers commenced dive-bombing. However, the pilots in the Japanese Zeros did not see the first black dragon rocket. In desperation, Fuchida fired a second black dragon rocket. The pilots in the Aichi dive-bombers, having seen both black dragon rockets, began departing the formation and accelerating for the attack on the American airfields. As church bells were ringing and the Aloha Clock Tower said 7:55 A.M., the Japanese Aichi dive-bombers began their bombing attack on Wheeler Field.

THE AFTERMATH OF THE JAPANESE PREEMPTIVE STRIKE

It is sufficient to say that the attack on Pearl Harbor—without a formal declaration of war by Japan—was, and still is, viewed as a savage, barbarous violation of international law, and even murder. America suffered 2,403 casualties, and 1,178 were wounded. The battleship *Arizona* was catastrophically destroyed with the deaths of sailors from forty-eight states. The battleship *California* was sunk but later raised. The battleships *Maryland* and *Nevada* were damaged but later repaired. The battleship *Oklahoma* was capsized, and later, raised and scrapped. The battleship *Pennsylvania* was damaged but repaired, along with the *Tennessee*. The battleship *West Virginia* was sunk but later raised.

Helena and *Raleigh* were heavily damaged but repaired. *Honolulu* suffered collateral damage but was repaired. *Shaw* had its bow blown off in an explosion. *Cassin* and *Downs* were heavily damaged and rebuilt. *Helm* was damaged but continued duty. *Oglala* was sunk, raised, and repaired. *Curtis* was damaged and repaired. *Sotoyomo* was sunk, raised, and repaired. *Utah* capsized and was left at the bottom. *Vestel* was damaged, grounded, and repaired. *YFD-2* was sunk, raised, and repaired.

Ten aircraft were destroyed at Bellows Field. Thirty-three aircraft were destroyed at Ewa Marine Corps Naval Air Station. Twenty-six naval aircraft were destroyed at Ford Island. Eighteen army aircraft were destroyed at Hickam Field. Thirteen aircraft were destroyed at Kaneohe Naval Air Station. Forty army aircraft were destroyed at Wheeler Field, and five aircraft from the aircraft carrier *Enterprise* were destroyed. Ironically, a flight of B-17s bound for the Philippines, four of which were destroyed, were landing to refuel in Hawaii at the time of the attack.[556]

ATTACKS TO THE SOUTH

Across the International Date Line, it was December 8, 1941. The Japanese invaded Malaya and began air attacks on the Philippine Islands. They landed troops on Bataan Island in the north Philippines. Air raids were conducted over Singapore (Britain's fortress of the Pacific), Wake Island (the American Alamo), and Hong Kong.[557] A great number of America's precious Flying Fortresses that had not been delivered to China for offensive operations over Japan were destroyed on the ground in the Philippines. To declare that the Associated Powers (America, Britain, China, and Holland) had suffered a "bloody shambles" at the hands of the Japanese was no understatement.[558]

After learning of the attack on Pearl Harbor, beginning at 5:00 A.M. on December 8, General Lewis Brereton (the Air Corps commander in the Philippines) appeared in the office of General Douglas MacArthur. When he was denied access to the general, Brereton requested that in light of Japan's attack on Hawaii, B-17 Flying Fortresses in the Philippines should be allowed to attack Japanese air bases on Formosa. Although Major General Richard Sutherland had refused Brereton's request to meet with MacArthur, he did agree with Brereton's plan to prepare for bombing operations against Japanese airfields at Takao Harbor on Formosa. All available B-17s at Clark Field in the Philippines were to be prepared, and B-17s based at Del Monte Field were to be flown north to Clark for refueling and bomb loading. However, Brereton was directed to not take any offensive action until ordered.

Brereton returned at 7:14 A.M., again requesting an audience with MacArthur, which Sutherland again denied. Sutherland told Brereton that MacArthur was too busy to see him.

While Brereton's pleas to launch the B-17s on bombing raids against Japanese airfields on Formosa were stalled, an armada of Japanese bombers and fighters destined to attack the Philippines were grounded in fog. As the fog began to lift, the Japanese planes winged their way toward Clark Field to deliver their deadly cargo.

With fifty-four American planes in the air and reports of Japanese airplanes over Luzon, Brereton phoned Sutherland after 9:30 A.M. and advised that if American bombers at Clark Field were attacked successfully, it would be impossible to carry out offensive action. At about 10:10 A.M., Sutherland advised that MacArthur had decided to send reconnaissance missions to Formosa.

In the midst of confusion about which air operations were actually authorized, Major David Gibbs—operations officer of the 19th Bombardment Group and the senior officer then present at Clark Field—had ordered all B-17s aloft, without bombs. The Flying Fortresses were milling about the skies of the Philippines in the belief that they were less at risk airborne than they would be sitting on the ground. However, they would eventually have to land and refuel.

By midday, a number of B-17s were still on the ground at Clark Field. Suddenly, the Japanese bombers and fighters appeared overhead. In minutes, out of the force of thirty-five B-17s, twelve had been destroyed and two had been damaged. Prior to the Japanese attack on the Philippines, Brereton had placed a phone call to MacArthur's office. Despite his third request, he still did not receive permission to launch the B-17s on offensive operations.

After learning about the Japanese attacks on Pearl Harbor and in the Philippines, MacArthur speculated that the pilots must have been white mercenaries, evidence that some American military commanders believed the Japanese were not capable of executing such devastating attacks. As America had suffered humiliation at the hands of the Japanese, so did the British on December 10, 1941, when the battleship *Prince of Wales* and cruiser *Repulse* were sunk by Japanese aircraft off the coast of Malaya.[559] The Japanese conducted a second major air raid on the Philippine Islands on December 10, and began landing additional troops at Vigan and Appri, north of Luzon in the Philippines.

Although U.S. Marine troops and civilians repulsed an attempted invasion by the Japanese of Wake Island on December 11, Wake (the Alamo of the Pacific) would finally fall on December 23. By December 12, British forces were in retreat in Hong Kong, and Japanese forces had landed at Legaspi in southern Luzon in the Philippines. By December 16, the Japanese had landed on Miri, Sarawak. As December 1941 became January of 1942, the Japanese conquest in the Western Pacific continued, to the point where they controlled a geographic territory three times larger than that conquered by Nazi Germany.

One of the few bright notes in this Japanese blitzkrieg of success in Southeast Asia was a group of mercenary pilots under the command of Claire Chennault. They were reported to have shot down nine out of ten Japanese bombers on December 20, 1941, in an attempted bombing raid on Kunming. By December 23 and again on December 25, 1941, there were massive air battles over Rangoon, Burma, where the AVG and Number 67 Squadron of the Royal Air Force inflicted substantial damage on Japanese bomber and fighter aircraft. The numbers of pilots and planes at the disposal of Chennault were minimal. Nevertheless, they were inflicting stunning blows to the Japanese during America's darkest hour.

When the American Volunteer Group, America's Special Air Unit in China, was disbanded on July 4, 1942, they were officially credited with destroying 296 Japanese aircraft with the loss of four American pilots in aerial combat. If the claims of Chennault's Flying Tigers are accepted, it is a combat record unequalled in history. But what use did America make of this phenomenal military resource when it eventually undertook to absorb the remains of the American Volunteer Group into the United States Armed Forces? Only five American pilots who had volunteered for service in China accepted induction into the 23rd Fighter Group of the China Air Task Force. America bungled an opportunity to maintain a cadre of experienced fighter pilots in China at a critical juncture in the war.

This, of course, raises a substantial question: What would have happened if Chennault had been given an adequate force of bombers with sufficient time to mount bombing strikes against the Japanese home islands *before* the attack on Pearl Harbor? This question is answered in Chapter 17.

Chapter Sixteen

AMERICA'S REACTION TO JAPAN'S PREEMPTIVE STRIKE

Sorrow . . . Pain of mind from loss of or disappointment in the expectation of good; grief; regret; sadness . . . [560]

Anger . . . A violent, revengeful passion or emotion, excited by a real or supposed injury to one's self or others; passion; ire; . . . rage; wrath . . .

—*The New Webster Encyclopedic Dictionary of the English Language* [561]

PRESIDENT ROOSEVELT'S ADDRESS OF DECEMBER 8, 1941

Millions of stunned and shocked Americans listened intently to the radio broadcast of President Roosevelt's address before a joint session of Congress at 12:30 P.M. on Monday, December 8, 1941. Standing before members of America's government was a man who had been waging a personal war with poliomyelitis for twenty years, his legs essentially paralyzed. President Roosevelt's upper body was well-developed from years of moving himself about, and his powerful hands now gripped the podium as he prepared to address the members of Congress and the American people.

As he stood there, his legs made rigid by steel braces, Roosevelt's face revealed the strain of serving in the office of President of the United States for nine years. Despite his best efforts to rescue America from the Great Depression, unemployment was still at 17 percent. Ten million Americans were out of work, and many survived on as little as a thousand dollars a year. With the country facing such economic despair, Roosevelt must have understood why many Americans were attracted to the America First movement and its message of isolationism. A poll taken in the summer of 1940 indicated that Americans believed Germany would defeat Britain and Russia and dominate Europe. How could America, which ranked *fourteenth* in global military power in 1940, expect to defeat Japan?

Roosevelt had served as assistant secretary of the navy during World War I, when the keel was laid to America's thirty-ninth battleship, the USS *Arizona*. Roosevelt had desired to leave his civilian duties and obtain a commission as an officer in the navy, for which he had a deep and abiding attachment. During World War I, he had been involved in the growth of the United States Navy as a powerful military force. That Roosevelt had a profound affection for the Navy is without question. His shock and despair upon learning of the Japanese preemptive strike cannot be overstated.

The Japanese surprise attack on Pearl Harbor was the darkest hour for Americans in the twentieth century. With the fortitude and determination of a man who had been successfully engaged in his own personal struggle for survival; a man who anticipated the inevitability of war with the Axis Powers; a man who had been preparing, in secret, for the war he saw looming on the horizon—President Roosevelt would firmly declare:

> Yesterday, December 7, 1941—a date which will live in infamy—the United States of America was suddenly and deliberately attacked by naval and air forces of the Empire of Japan.
>
> The United States was at peace with that nation and, at the solicitation of Japan, was still in conversation with its government and its Emperor looking toward the maintenance of peace in the Pacific. Indeed, one hour after Japanese air squadrons had commenced bombing in the American island of Oahu, the Japanese Ambassador to the United States and his colleague delivered to our Secretary of State a formal reply to a recent American message. And while this reply stated that it seemed useless to continue the existing diplomatic negotiations, it contained no threat or hint of war or of armed attack.
>
> It will be recorded that the distance of Hawaii from Japan makes it obvious that the attack was deliberately planned many days or even weeks ago. During the intervening time the

Japanese Government has deliberately sought to deceive the United States by false statements and expressions of hope for continued peace. . . .

As Commander-in-Chief of the Army and Navy, I have directed that all measures be taken for our defense.

But always will our whole Nation remember the character of the onslaught against us. No matter how long it may take us to overcome this premeditated invasion, the American people in their righteous might will win through to absolute victory. . . .

Hostilities exist. There is no blinking at the fact that our people, our territory, and our interests are in grave danger.

With confidence in our armed forces—with the unbounding determination of our people—we will gain the inevitable triumph—so help us God.

I ask that Congress declare that since the unprovoked and dastardly attack by Japan on Sunday, December 7, 1941, a state of war has existed between the United States and the Japanese Empire.[562]

In view of the ominous threat to America's security, President Roosevelt's remarks focused on the "dastardly attack" of the Japanese government. However, there was no disclosure by our president of plans to sponsor the firebombing of Japan by American bombers; nor was there any discussion of an American Special Air Unit operating in Burma; and there certainly was no mention of a de facto alliance between the ABCD powers to curtail Japanese expansion in Southeast Asia. Finally, President Roosevelt did not disclose that the Japanese were aware of American and Chinese initiatives to bomb Japan.

Members of Congress erupted into applause with the conclusion of the president's remarks. Roosevelt had correctly interpreted the will of the American people. By 4:10 P.M. on the date of his address, a joint resolution had been passed by Congress that authorized the president "to carry on war against the Imperial Government of Japan and to bring the conflict to a successful conclusion . . ."[563] Three days later, America would be at war with Germany and Italy, Japan's partners in the Tripartite Pact.[564]

On the same day as the president's address, Lindbergh wrote to the America First Committee, declaring, "We have been stepping closer to war for many months . . . Now it has come and we must meet it as united

Americans regardless of our attitude in the past toward the policy our government has followed. Whether or not that policy has been wise, our country has been attacked by force of arms, and by force of arms we must *retaliate* [emphasis added]."[565]

What was Claire Chennault thinking on December 8, 1941, while all of this was developing? Chennault, Lauchlin Currie, and Madame Chiang had been engaged in a race against time. When Chennault's plans for a bombing initiative had been rebuffed by General Marshall in December of 1940, the plan was put on hold—until Dr. Currie resurrected Chennault's plan in the form of Joint Board 355 in May of 1941. In time, a plan Marshall had opposed would become part of America's official war strategy, championed by Secretary of War Stimson, who insisted on a massive buildup of American heavy bomber strength in the Philippines.

On the day he learned of the attack on Pearl Harbor, Chennault must have been thinking about all of his efforts to develop a Special Air Unit in China. His level of frustration with war planners and military bureaucracy must have been beyond description. America had the military resources to have provided China with 350 fighters and 150 bombers by October 31, 1941, as provided in the Joint Board timetable, which the war planners— subscribing to a "Europe first" policy—elected not to meet.

With outcries of "Remember Pearl Harbor!" ringing throughout America and around the globe, the focus would now be on a *retaliatory* strike. However, Chennault was a pragmatist. His first thoughts after coming down from the control tower at Kyedaw Airfield on December 8, 1941, were for the protection and security of his pilots and planes. Unlike General MacArthur in the Philippines, Chennault had no intention of getting ambushed on the ground.

RESURRECTION OF THE CHINA OPTION

What are we to imagine of the conversations between Roosevelt and the Plus Four (Morgenthau, Hall, Knox, and Stimson) in the days and weeks following the Japanese preemptive strike? Thoughts of using Chiang Kai-shek's airfields did not leave the president's mind. Is it too much to suggest that as he left the halls of Congress in his wheelchair on December 8, 1941, his mind hearkened back to one year earlier, when he had entertained the generalissimo's plan to engage in preemptive bombing raids on Japan? In a private moment, is it possible that Roosevelt might have had regrets that he had not given Chennault the bombers he'd requested a year ago?

It is quite likely the president may have remembered the words he uttered to Henry Morgenthau one year earlier: "It would be a nice thing if China bombed Japan." Evidence that Roosevelt had not forgotten the plan to bomb Japan from China is found in the question he posed to General Hap Arnold on January 28, 1942, which prompted the general to write a memorandum, declaring, "I feel that the plan which is now in progress, for carrying out an attack upon the Japanese enemy's center of gravity, by making use of facilities for which the Chinese Government can guarantee us a reasonable degree of security on the Eastern Asiatic mainland, is the logical and most effective plan."[566]

No, the president had *not* forgotten about the air bases in China from which America might bomb Japan, as evidenced by General Robert L. Scott's report of his piloting a B-17 in the spring of 1942 (as part of Operation Aquila): "We were to fly thirteen four-engine bombers—one B-24 and twelve B-17Es—to Asia. There we were to 'bomb up' the ships to bomb objectives in Japan. Our orders read that we were to coordinate our attack from the West with another attack coming from the East."[567] Operation Aquila was part of a program to provide fighters, bombers, and a supply chain to Chennault's Flying Tigers.

Unfortunately, the force of B-17s with which Robert L. Scott was flying did not bomb Japan. However, Scott, a fighter pilot at heart, flew as a "guest" of the Flying Tigers on one or more missions. When some of the remaining personnel and the equipment of the AVG/Flying Tigers were "absorbed" into the 23rd Fighter Group of the Army Air Force, Scott would serve as the Group's commander, reporting to Chennault, beginning July 4, 1942.

The force attacking from the east that was mentioned in Scott's report would be made up of B-25 Mitchell bombers, taking off from the carrier *Hornet*. This mission was led by Lieutenant Colonel James Doolittle, an aeronautical engineer, a great pilot, and a risk taker.[568] This force of sixteen B-25s departed on April 18, 1942, and was to recover in Chekiang province in eastern China, in what some people regarded as a "suicide mission." Only volunteers participated in this mission, in which Tokyo and other Japanese cities were bombed, causing a loss of face to the military leadership of Japan.

Historian Craig Nelson describes the Doolittle Raid as "the turning point in the war against Japan."[569] While it may have been the turning point in the Pacific Theater from a psychological perspective, the Battle of Midway was the defining moment from a strategic standpoint. In the Battle of Midway, three American carriers succeeded in destroying four Japanese carriers. Although America herself lost a carrier in the engagement, it signaled the beginning of the end of Japanese naval superiority in the Pacific.

All of the planes participating in the Doolittle Raid were lost. A number of the crewmen from the Mitchell bombers were captured by the Japanese and tried as war criminals. Several were executed. Doolittle would initially consider the raid a failure upon hearing of the loss of the aircraft. However, Roosevelt recognized that while he had been denied a preemptive strike, Doolittle had given America a successful retaliatory strike. For this feat, Doolittle received the Congressional Medal of Honor.

In reality, there were three bombing initiatives for Japan planned after the attack on Pearl Harbor: 1) The Doolittle Raid, consisting of B-25 Mitchell bombers launched from a carrier; 2) Operation Aquila, involving one B-24 Liberator and thirteen B-17 Flying Fortresses under the command of Colonel Caleb Haynes; and 3) HALPRO, involving twenty-three B-24 Liberators under the command of Colonel Halverson. While the Doolittle Raid went forward, the HALPRO mission failed because Liberators being flown to India—and, ultimately, China—were diverted to Palestine, as German forces under the command of General Irwin Rommel were pushing hard on Egypt. These aircraft became the nucleus of the 9th Air Force. Operation Aquila did not go forward, despite the fact that the bombers reached India. By April of 1942, the Japanese had begun bombing airfields in southeastern China, including Chuchow. Because there were concerns about defending and repairing these airfields, Operation Aquila was canceled.

According to field orders issued by Chennault on December 8, 1941, news of the Japanese attack on Pearl Harbor reached him at 7:00 A.M. on December 8. Chennault issued orders that the Third Pursuit Squadron of the American Volunteer Group would act as the assault echelon, the Second Pursuit Squadron as the support echelon, and the First Pursuit Squadron as the reserve echelon. All members of the American Volunteer Group were authorized to wear firearms, and all leaves were cancelled. An air raid system was implemented, and a constant watch was maintained for enemy parachute troops.

Typical of the kind of deception Chennault would use on the Japanese, the airfield at Kyedaw was blacked out, while an auxiliary field four miles north was illuminated at night with red lights marking the runways and white lights marking the boundaries of the airfield. Obviously, Chennault was hoping that in the event of an enemy air attack, the Japanese would bomb the wrong field. The fighter planes in the group were fully armed and loaded in preparation for combat against the Japanese.

While the exploits of the AVG or Flying Tigers have gone down in the annals of history as a remarkable achievement, historians are prone to forget that the Flying Tigers were part of a much larger initiative. As Chennault wrote in his memoirs:

> Out of all the plans, the First American Volunteer Group of fighter pilots and fighter planes was the only salvage. Chinese orders were placed for the Republic P-43s and Lockheed Hudsons, but only a few of each were delivered before the Japanese attack turned off the spigot of supplies to the Orient. The fighter group was China's most urgent need-first, to smash the Japanese over Chungking and then to protect the trickle of supplies winding up the Burma Road.

With the Japanese attack on Pearl Harbor, Chennault found himself in command of only a fighter group. The bombers Chennault and Currie had feverishly worked for in the service of China failed to arrive in time to inflict any damage upon the Japanese before Pearl Harbor.

Chapter Seventeen

A POSTMORTEM ON CHENNAULT'S PLAN FOR A PREEMPTIVE STRIKE ON JAPAN

Between December, 1940, and July, 1941, agents and agencies of the United States did conspire with private military entrepreneurs and the Chinese Nationalists to develop a program for secret air warfare. This appears to have set a major precedent for U.S. military and political planning . . .

—Michael Schaller, *The U.S. Crusade in China, 1938–1945* [570]

The facts revealed in America's planning for bombing raids on Japan before the attack on Pearl Harbor are bizarre. Few Hollywood screenwriters employing all of their imagination and talents could have created such an intriguing story. An Air Corps captain forced into early retirement found employment with a foreign warlord, flew combat missions in an undeclared war, and enlisted assistance from the cabinet members of an American president to establish a guerrilla air corps with money laundered through a series of dummy or "front" corporations. The guerrilla air corps would be manned by American pilots who would fly in combat without the protection of the Geneva Convention, and the ultimate objective was to bomb Tokyo and other Japanese cities.

Equally intriguing is the subplot of the Japanese military initiatives, designed to beat America to the preemptive-strike punch, including the actions of a collaborator in Chiang Kai-shek's government who shared information with the Japanese about the formation and objectives of this Special Air Unit. Britain, an ally of America and China, spirits away hundreds of Lockheed Hudson bombers just as Dr. Currie is promising the delivery of bombers to Madame Chiang. And finally, we see still another subplot: Roosevelt's ostensibly loyal deputy, Dr. Currie, was feeding secret information to the Russians. It sounds too bizarre to be true, but it is. The story becomes even more compelling when one considers how many warnings the American government received about an imminent attack on Pearl Harbor, and how they went unheeded. While the account is certainly fascinating, several questions come to mind.

First, what would have been the effect on the outbreak of war between Japan and America if Chennault *had* received 350 fighters and 150 bombers in a timely fashion, as proposed in the Joint Board Plan? An air force of that strength, although outnumbered by three times that amount of Japanese aircraft, would have posed a real problem for Japan.

The Special Air Unit, as Chiang Kai-shek suggested, would have operated behind interior lines. If the Japanese had wanted to destroy the American planes and airmen, they would have been required to fly into enemy territory where Chennault had assembled his radio and telephone warning net. In light of the kill ratio enjoyed by the AVG in fighting the Japanese pilots *after* the attack on Pearl Harbor, it is reasonable to conclude that Japan would have suffered heavy casualties if they had mounted attacks on Chennault's Special Air Unit.

In addition, the operations facilities and quarters at Kweilin were designed to be bombproof. Japan may have been frustrated in her efforts to destroy the American bombers unless she could have ambushed them in the air, since Chennault would not have left these aircraft at a forward airfield and subject to attack. Rather, following an attack, they would have been withdrawn to Kweilin or the bomber field near Chengtu. While still possible, with the bombers operating at night, and with Japan having no effective radar system, interception of the bombers could have presented a challenge to the Japanese pilots.

If China and America had assembled a substantial force of bombers in China, and if Japanese air attacks had resulted in significant losses of Japanese pilots, then the other option for Japan would have been to redouble her efforts in the Sino-Japanese War and attempt to conquer greater areas in China. This option would have involved pushing the

Special Air Unit's bomber bases farther from the Japanese home islands. Committing more troops and resources to the war with China is precisely what Japan did *not* want to do in 1941, when her army was planning offensive operations in Malaya, Burma, the Dutch East Indies, and the Philippines.

Certainly, Japanese war planners had an appreciation for the problems that were presented to their plans of conquest in Southeast Asia by an efficient guerrilla air corps operating in China. More disturbing for Japan was the reality that greater numbers of American planes would be reaching China in 1942. These would include Lockheed Hudson bombers with adequate range to bomb southern areas of the Japanese home islands. Chuchow, Kweilin, and Chengtu airfields had been specifically designed by China to serve as bases of operations for American Flying Fortresses.

In addition, American bureaucrats were engaged in an economic war against Japan and were assisting the U.S. military in locating and selecting "bombing objectives" in Japan. Not only was there open concert of action between America and China, but a de facto alliance emerged between America, Britain, China, and the Dutch (the "Associated Powers") to combat Japan's imperialistic ventures in Southeast Asia. China was receiving an infusion of American planes, pilots, and support personnel in 1941. Japanese war planners clearly appreciated that the time to strike America (as well as the British and the Dutch) was *sooner* rather than *later*.

Second, how effective would bombers under Chennault's command have been in attacking Japan or Japanese interests? If the objective was to bring Japan to her knees by bombing the Japanese home islands, then a force of 150 bombers would not have been successful. However, when Chennault, as commander of the American 14th Air Force, finally obtained consolidated B-24 Liberators (four-engine heavy bombers), his focus was on Japanese shipping, supply lines, and resources vital to the production of the Japanese war economy. If one can draw upon what Chennault did with a modest number of American heavy bombers later in the war as an indication of how he would have conducted operations in 1941, it is reasonable to assume he would have deployed his bombers, as he did his fighters, in hit-and-run attacks, keeping the odds in his favor and keeping the Japanese off balance.

While Chennault has a reputation as a maverick, he was anything but a gambler. He schemed to keep the odds in favor of his men where combat was involved. Bombers under Chennault's command would have slashed Japanese supply lines and staging areas vital to Japan's interests. For example, imagine what would have taken place on November 25, 1941, when a Japanese task force that had assembled on the mouth of the Yangtze River sailed south to attack Malaya, Singapore, the Dutch East Indies, and the Philippines. Can there be any doubt that if Chennault had been provided American bombers—and American pilots to fly them—he would have bombed the task force before it left the coast of China? In fact, this was anticipated in the Joint Board Plan, since the plan's third strategic objective called for "Destruction of Japanese supplies and supply ships in order to handicap operations of an expeditionary force to the south of Indo-China."[571] The Joint Board Plan was intended to be *preemptive*, since American bombers attacking a Japanese task force that was destined for colonies and possessions of the Associated Powers could have preempted this Japanese military operation.

In pondering the relationship between the Joint Board Plan and the Japanese attack on Pearl Harbor, a number of thoughts come to mind. The Plan called for Chennault to have 350 fighters and 150 bombers by October 31, 1941. If bomber operations had commenced against Japan in November of 1941, several things would have happened. First, America's intentions toward Japan—albeit under the auspices of the Chinese Air Force—would have been obvious. The gauntlet would have been thrown down. The significance of armed conflict between American pilots and the Japanese would not have been lost on American commanders in Hawaii. With a high alert status in Hawaii, would Japan have succeeded in sailing a task force *undetected* to Hawaii? Second, the timely execution of the Joint Board Plan held the promise, not only to curtail Japanese aggression in Southeast Asia and the Western Pacific, but also in Hawaii. One may also ponder whether the task force would have sailed for Hawaii if the Japanese home islands had experienced nightly bombing raids. Perhaps the Japanese admirals would have turned their interests toward the Special Air Unit operating in China as opposed to Pearl Harbor.

Third, why did Chennault's plan fail to materialize? There are several reasons Chennault did not receive American bombers in a timely fashion. First and foremost was Roosevelt's Europe-first policy. According to an issue of *American Aviation Daily* magazine, dated August 1, 1941, one thousand Lockheed Hudson bombers had been delivered to Great Britain by July 17, 1941.[572] While Currie's telegram to Madame Chiang of July 23, 1941, promised China sixty-six bombers "with twenty-four to be delivered immediately," America failed to keep her promise to China. Even with her limited production capacity before Pearl Harbor, fighter plane production for the Army Air Corps was 1,422 aircraft in 1940, and 3,784 aircraft in 1941.[573] Light bomber production was 891 in 1940 and 2,396 aircraft in 1941.[574] Medium bomber production was 62 in 1940 and 460 aircraft in 1941.[575]

In 1940 and 1941, the Royal Air Force received 1,180 Curtiss Tomahawk P-40 fighters, with one hundred being diverted to China and two hundred being diverted to Russia.[576] If American priorities had been different, there would have been plenty of American fighter planes to supply the Special Air Unit in China. Not only were there ample supplies of Lockheed Hudson bombers and Curtiss P-40 fighters, but the French had also taken possession of one hundred Douglas DB-7 bombers.[577] Although the DB-7 lacked the range to bomb Japan and return to China, it could have attacked Japanese ships off the coast of China, as well as Japanese airfields and troop concentrations in China and French Indochina.

According to historians Charles Romanus and Riley Sunderland in their work, *China-Burma-India Theater: Stilwell's Mission to China (United States Army in World War II)*, there was concern the Chinese would deploy the B-17s "without fighter cover or antiaircraft support."[578] However, this criticism of the Joint Board Plan is without foundation. Chinese air operations of the AVG were to move forward in three phases: 1) provide air cover over southwest China and the Burma Road; 2) commence air operations from central China, including Kweilin; and 3) position bombers at Chuchow for raids on Japan. In fact, Chennault, the AVG's taskmaster, would whip the American fighter pilots into shape in an accelerated training program.

If there were any shortcomings in Chinese anti-aircraft support, they would have been overcome with the radio and telephone warning net, along with AVG fighters engaged in interceptions and combat air patrols over the bomber bases. In reality, in late March of 1942, when runways were extended and ammunition and fuel were being accumulated at Chusien, Lishui, and Yushan, the Japanese reported: "This work was protected by fighters that flew almost daily from Hengyang and Kweilin."[579]

The Japanese realized "that the airfields in the *Chekiang* area could be used to advantage by the enemy as terminals in raids against Japan."[580]

Even when the Japanese succeeded in bombing the forward air bases, they reported that "each time, the enemy succeeded in rebuilding the field."[581] The suggestion that Chennault would have staged B-17s at forward air bases for attacks on Japan without air cover does not warrant further comment.

Others who would contest the plan's viability for lack of fuel supplies should ponder the contents of a memorandum dated July 26, 1942, from General Clayton Bissell, U.S. Army Air Forces, to General Joseph Stilwell, who was in charge of the American military mission to China. It confirmed that the Chinese had 1,500,000 gallons of 100-octane aviation fuel, and 1,300,000 gallons of 87-, 91-, and 92-octane aviation fuel. Besides United States aviation fuel, the British had 375,000 gallons of 100-octane fuel. The memorandum also confirmed that the Chinese had plenty of bombs. It is not likely that the Chinese added substantially to their fuel supplies after December of 1941. The quantity of fuel stores in China suggests there was sufficient 100-octane gasoline in China in late 1941 for a number of B-17 raids on Japan, if not a major campaign.

However, the War Department and General Marshall would not permit the B-17s to be flown to China by American aviators because trained American crews were as scarce as B-17s. Permitting them to volunteer would have greatly handicapped the Army Air Corps' expansion program. Moreover, because it was so difficult to ship spare parts to airfields within bombing range of Japan, maintenance problems for the B-17s would have been insoluble.[582]

Perhaps another factor in the mix was Chennault's reputation with the Air Corps as a maverick. The last thing air force chief General Hap Arnold had on his mind was sending Boeing B-17 Flying Fortresses to operate under Chennault's command in China. As America was recovering from the throes of the Great Depression, there were only 114 late-model B-17s in service.[583] According to U.S. Air Force Historical Study No. 6, "Development of the Heavy Bomber 1918–1944," citing a letter from the Chief of Air Staff to the Assistant Secretary of War dated October 17, 1941, there were eighty-three B-17s in the United States and thirty-one overseas. The total number of B-17 Flying Fortresses produced (including prototypes) through the end of 1941, was 235, the majority of which had been delivered to the U.S. Army Air Forces, and twenty having been delivered to the Royal Air Force.[584]

While China was not favored with the provision of American heavy bombers like the Boeing B-17 Flying Fortress and the Consolidated B-24 Liberator, Great Britain, after a few bombing missions over Europe, relegated these aircraft to patrols over the North Atlantic in search of Nazi submarines. If the British exaggerations of their needs for American aircraft had not been taken so seriously, there would have been plenty of fighters and bombers for China.

What became of American planes allotted to China under the Joint Board Plan? Eventually, China did receive a number of these aircraft. For example, 104 Vultee Vanguard fighter planes arrived in Karachi, India, in May of 1942.[585] The Lockheed Hudson bombers began arriving in China in August of 1942.[586] China received a total of twenty-six Lockheed Hudson bombers. Rather than being flown in combat by American pilots, it appears the Vanguards and Hudsons were flown primarily by Chinese pilots. Of 108 Republic P-43 Lancers allotted to China on April 1, 1942, China received about forty-one of these Lancer fighter planes in 1942.[587]

Fourth, was the American Volunteer Group legal? There are two elements to explore in responding to this question. Did Americans volunteering for service in China risk losing their citizenship? And, if captured by the Japanese, what was the status of a member of the American Volunteer Group under international law?

The American State Department was careful not to allow recruiting by Chinese agents in the United States. It could not sanction a blatant violation of criminal law. However, even with the charade in place—having American agents recruit United States military personnel to sign employment contracts with CAMCO—some volunteers raised the question of whether service in China in her war with Japan could result in loss of citizenship. Chennault is reported to have assured the men that their citizenship would remain intact, so long as they fought for a country that professed democratic faith.[588] However, the words *profession of democratic faith* did not ring true for the Nationalist government of China, which was no model of democracy by Western standards. While ostensibly a republic with the overthrow of her last Chinese emperor, concentrations of political power resided with the warlords who controlled various regions.

While Chiang Kai-shek had emerged as generalissimo, his Kuomintang government had been engaged in open warfare with the Communists, led by Mao Tse-tung and Chou En-lai. Japan's attack on Chinese interests in 1937 led to a rise in Chinese nationalism and a quasi armistice between the Communists and the Kuomintang government. However, Chiang Kai-shek's government was plagued with graft and corruption. While Chiang Kai-shek may have professed a belief in democratic principles, China was no bastion of democracy in 1940–41.

Regardless of the shortcomings of the Kuomintang regime in China, its survival was viewed as serving American interests. No, the volunteer's citizenship would not be placed at risk by serving the government of China. But what would happen to volunteers captured by the Japanese? Would they be executed as war criminals?

In his excellent monograph, "Chennault and the Flying Tigers—Heroes, But Were They Legal?", former U.S. Air Force Judge Advocate General (JAG) officer Richard Dunn analyzes the legality of the AVG. According to Dunn, lawful combatants are privileged to engage in combat under the Laws of War. A lawful combatant, if captured, is entitled to prisoner-of-war status. Combatants who take up arms unlawfully are not entitled to prisoner-of-war status.

The AVG (or Flying Tigers) were not members of the Chinese Air Force or of the American armed forces. The only legal basis for arguing that they were lawful combatants would be if they met the four requirements of a "volunteer corps." While they 1) had a fixed and distinctive emblem, 2) carried arms openly, and 3) conducted operations in accordance with the laws of war, they were 4) "commanded by a person responsible for his subordinates." After all, the pilots and technicians were employed by CAMCO, and Chennault had been employed since 1937 as a consultant paid by the Bank of China, *not* by CAMCO.

According to Dunn, if Chennault were viewed as having a direct relationship with AVG personnel, it would have been based on contract. The International Committee of the Red Cross (which administers the Geneva Convention) does not view such a contractor as being responsible for his employees in the sense required by the Convention.

Stated simply, the Flying Tigers were mercenaries—soldiers of fortune in the service of a foreign power—who engaged in acts of war *without* the protections of the Geneva Convention. It is questionable whether such a fighting force would or could be assembled today in America's politically correct and legalistic environment. To characterize the members of the AVG as mercenaries is not intended to be disrespectful of their motives, but is merely a recognition of their legal status as it was understood at the time.

PREEMPTIVE VERSUS RETALIATORY STRIKES

What was the posture of the American military forces in the Pacific—and the forces positioned in China—in the summer and fall of 1941? Was America focused on executing preemptive strikes against Japan? Or, was she focused instead on post-preemptive/retaliatory strikes?

The evidence indicates that through the fall of 1941, the American government was planning preemptive military action against Japan. These plans were consistent with the Action Memorandum authored by Lieutenant Commander McCollum of the Office of Naval Intelligence, Far Eastern Section, dated October 7, 1940 (the "McCollum Memorandum"). As suggested by McCollum, America had taken a number of provocative, if not preemptive, initiatives against Japan, including a total trade embargo and the provision of substantial economic and military aid to China. Evidence of American preemptive military initiatives against Japan is confirmed not only by the presence of the American Volunteer Group training in Burma and by promises to the government of Chiang Kai-shek for the provision of American bombers, but it is also found in the British Memorandum relayed to General MacArthur in September of 1941:

> Commence operations as soon as possible, concentrating on propaganda, terrorism, and sabotage of Japanese communications and military installations . . . Assassination of individual Japanese should be considered . . . We must base mobile forces as near Japan as practicable . . . To the west there is China, where air bases are already prepared and stocked . . .

The content of the British Memorandum provides evidence that as late as September of 1941, the positioning of American B-17s in China was still being considered by the Roosevelt administration. In addition, bomber bases were being built in China at a prolific rate. According to General Bissell's memorandum to General Stilwell of July 26, 1942, ". . . it should be remembered that Chengtu, one of the world's best landing fields for the operation of heavy military aircraft, was constructed in

99 days." Not only were bomber bases being built in China, but fuel stores were also being augmented to support an American, Chinese, and even British initiative against Japan.

We cannot forget that General Brereton, prior to his departure from Washington for the Philippines, underwent substantial military briefings and was provided with a detailed quantity of documents from the air staff of the U.S. Army Air Forces. Brereton departed from Washington bound for the Philippines on or about October 17, 1941.[589] Because Secretary of War Stimson believed the American B-17s should function as "the big stick" in the Pacific—bombing Japan and preventing the Philippines from falling to hostile enemy forces—a massive buildup of heavy bomber strength in the Philippines was under way in the latter part of 1941.

A military confrontation between Japan and America became inevitable after the Japanese task force sailed southward from the Yangtze River on November 25, 1941. President Roosevelt had Lindbergh and the America First Movement to contend with, as well as American public opinion polls that showed Americans were opposed to entering into World War II. Ever the astute politician, Roosevelt altered his position with the "war warning" message from Admiral Ingersoll to Admiral Kimmel of November 27, 1941, declaring that Japan must commit "the first overt act." From that date forward, the American military posture in the Pacific changed from one of *preemptive action* to one of *retaliatory action*. Unhappily, even after the attack on Pearl Harbor and General Brereton's request to attack Takao Harbor on Japanese-controlled Formosa, General MacArthur's refusal to give Brereton permission to launch the B-17s on these missions prevented the execution of American plans for retaliatory strikes. Curiously, the change in the American military posture from preemptive to defensive or retaliatory action was, in part, a result of the Hull ultimatum conveyed to Nomura and Kurusu on November 26, 1941—for Japan to get out of China and French Indochina. If there had been any hope of averting war, it was lost at that point.

CONCLUSION

The American plan to bomb Japan under the auspices of a guerrilla air corps flying in the service of China, along with Secretary of War Stimson's initiatives to base large numbers of Boeing B-17s in the Philippines, must be viewed as a lost opportunity in American history to preempt Japanese military aggression in Southeast Asia. While timely implementation of the Joint Board Plan may not have prevented war between the United States and Japan, there is reason to believe that the Joint Board Plan was viewed ominously by the Japanese government. The Japanese knew America and her allies were preparing to encircle and reduce Japan with airpower.

It does appear that timely execution of the Joint Board Plan offered America and the Associated Powers the means to force Japan to expend further resources in China, and may well have prevented the Japanese attack on Pearl Harbor.

If the Chinese-American bombing initiative had begun in early November of 1941, American forces in Hawaii would have been on a very high-alert status. Increased vigilance in the form of sea and air patrols would very likely have eliminated the element of surprise enjoyed by the Japanese forces on December 7, 1941.

The Joint Board Plan, denied the men and material necessary for preemptive action against Japan, languished in obscurity for decades following the attack on Pearl Harbor. Today, it is a footnote to history, an unusual and unorthodox American military initiative that was not implemented in a timely or effective fashion. However, in the summer and fall of 1941, the Joint Board Plan was alive and, to the Japanese, moving forward at an alarming pace. The facts revealed in this text should place the clash of power between Japan and the United States on December 7, 1941, in a more complete and accurate historical perspective.

The political climate in which the Joint Board Plan was conceived illustrates an American president effectively planning and engaging in military initiatives in support of a combatant, at a time when America was not openly at war. If the full extent of the Joint Board Plan had been known to the American people in the summer of 1941, President Roosevelt may have risked impeachment. To suggest that the Joint Board Plan would have been unpopular with most Americans in 1941 would be an understatement.

However, it is worth mentioning that Japan possessed "weapons of mass destruction." It employed anthrax and bubonic plague in its war of extermination against the Chinese. It even aspired to develop nuclear weapons. Would Americans have been more tolerant of the Joint Board Plan if they appreciated the dangers presented with Japan's ascendancy to power in Southeast Asia?

Some of the most talented and gifted members of the Roosevelt administration, along with key military personnel, saw Chennault's preemptive-strike plan as an effective way to keep Japan bogged down in war with China. However, they were ultimately unwilling to allocate the resources necessary to successfully execute the plan.

Before the formation of the United Nations at the conclusion of World War II, international law authorized preemptive military action if a nation was responding to an imminent *and* immediate danger of attack. It was akin to the law of self-defense, allowing an individual to utilize deadly force against an aggressor threatening an individual or others with the prospect of death or serious bodily injury. The Joint Board Plan was not that kind of preemptive strike. While war with Japan was "imminent," the danger to American interests was not "immediate" when the bombing initiative was first discussed in the fall of 1940. However, the danger to American lives and interests became both imminent *and* immediate when Japanese troop convoys sailed from the Yangtze River on November 25, 1941, and when the Japanese carrier task force sailed for Hawaii on November 26, 1941. While there was still hope for peace during the fall of 1941, the actions of the Japanese military did not bode well for a nonviolent solution.

To what extent is the arguable justification of preemptive military action going to be expanded or liberalized in the wake of America's military intervention in Iraq, beginning in 2003? It is difficult to answer that question. However, applying the historical (pre–United Nations) standard for preemptive action—imminent and immediate danger of attack—not everyone agrees that President Bush presented the American people, nor the jury of world opinion, with sufficient evidence that the government of Iraq possessed weapons of mass destruction, thereby justifying a preemptive military initiative. However, others would argue that the government in Iraq was connected to the attacks on United States soil of September 11, 2001. Under this analysis, Iraq was part of an "axis of evil," and deserving of an American retaliatory—if not preemptive—strike.

Looking back to December 7, 1941, it does appear that after the attack on Pearl Harbor, America became more inclined to act preemptively. America's involvement in Korea and Vietnam was designed to preempt the proliferation of communist regimes in Southeast Asia.

Recognizing the harsh and inescapable reality that there are forces driven by suicidal ambitions to kill and injure innocent people, the historical test for an imminent and immediate threat may be relaxed to arguably justify a preemptive initiative, even if the threat is more than moments away. If it is a certainty that an attack by national, supranational, or religious forces is imminent, civilized societies may become more tolerant of the use of preemptive force, even if the danger is not *immediate*.

In light of suicide attacks by Islamic extremists in America, Spain, Great Britain, and elsewhere, the people of civilized nations have real and palpable concerns for their peace and security. While this climate may lead to a greater tolerance for preemptive military initiatives, it should not cause world leaders to relax their sense of diligence and responsibility in avoiding unnecessary human suffering.

EPILOGUE

With the outbreak of World War II, Claire Chennault's American Volunteer Group became known as the "Flying Tigers." According to their official history, they are credited with the destruction of 296 Japanese planes with the loss of four American pilots during six months of aerial combat. The Flying Tigers achieved the highest kill ratio of any American fighter group in history.

Re-inducted into the U.S. Army Air Force as a brigadier general, Chennault commanded the China Air Task Force and eventually the 14th Air Force. Chennault ultimately rose to the rank of major general, but he was relieved of his command shortly before the Japanese surrendered in August of 1945. In keeping with the American military establishment's rejection of Chennault, he was not invited to attend the surrender ceremonies on the battleship USS *Missouri*. Ironically, those ceremonies were conducted by General Douglas MacArthur, the commander who had suffered devastating losses of American B-17 Flying Fortresses in the Philippines upon America's entry into World War II.

After the war, Chennault was not anxious to lead a conventional life in the United States, so he formed an airline that would operate in China called Civil Air Transport (CAT). CAT flew supplies to Generalissimo Chiang Kai-shek during the Chinese Civil War. With the exile of Chiang Kai-shek from China to Taiwan, CAT flew missions for the Central Intelligence Agency (CIA). In time, the CIA bought CAT and renamed it Air America. During the Vietnam War, Air America was engaged in clandestine operations in Laos and Cambodia.

Charles Lindbergh, the Lone Eagle, found his way into air combat over the skies of the Pacific theater as a civilian pilot. He wore a naval officer's uniform without rank or insignia. Had he been captured, he would have been a man without a country. He flew combat missions as a "technical consultant," flying both the F4U Corsair and the Lockheed P-38 Lightning. He shot down a Mitsubishi Army Type 99 "Sonia" on July 28,

1944, while flying with the 433rd Fighter Squadron. Lindbergh's opposition to Roosevelt's policies precluded his service as a member of the Army Air Force, so he found alternative means to satisfy his patriotic duty. Ironically, like Chennault and the Flying Tigers, Lindbergh flew in air combat as a civilian.

Dr. Lauchlin Currie, President Roosevelt's trusted aide who administered the China Project as the Joint Board Plan was developed, fled the United States for Latin America and renounced his American citizenship.

Mitsuo Fuchida, who led the attack on Pearl Harbor, converted to Christianity and became an evangelist. Among his friends was the Reverend Billy Graham.

Cordell Hull won the Nobel Peace Prize for his work in founding the United Nations.

After World War II, William Pawley became an American ambassador in Brazil, and later, in Peru. Pawley was an active member of the Republican Party and a close friend of CIA director Allen W. Dulles. Pawley played a role in the coup d'état that overthrew Jacobo Arbenz's Guatemalan government in 1954, following the nationalization of the United Fruit Company. The owner of an airline and bus company in Cuba, Pawley helped keep Fulgencio Batista in power. In fact, Pawley pressured President Dwight D. Eisenhower to provide military and financial help to anti-Castro Cubans based in the United States after Batista's fall from power. In June of 1963, Pawley and a number of other men secretly arrived in Cuba in an attempt to find Soviet officers in that country. One of the men who accompanied Pawley, Eddie Bayo, remained behind. There were rumors that Bayo had been captured and executed. Pawley died of gunshot wounds in January of 1977. It was officially classified as a suicide, but Pawley's clandestine activities present the possibility that this conclusion is incorrect.

Emperor Hirohito, who oversaw the extermination of millions of Chinese, who sanctioned experiments on live prisoners, who presided over Japan during the Rape of Nanking and the attack on Pearl Harbor, escaped trial as a war criminal, though this was sought in a joint resolution of Congress in September of 1945.

Admiral Isoroku Yamamoto, who conceived the Pearl Harbor attack, died when his Mitsubishi G4M "Betty" bomber was shot down by Lieutenant Rex T. Barber on April 18, 1943.

General Hideki Tojo, Japan's Prime Minister at the time of the Pearl Harbor attack, following a trial conducted by the International Military Tribunal of the Far East, was hanged after he was convicted of war crimes.

Beginning in December of 1940, Claire Lee Chennault undertook the pursuit of an unorthodox military initiative that offered the potential of curtailing Japanese aggression directed toward the Chinese, the Americans, the British, and the Dutch. His ambitions would ultimately be sanctioned by an American president and his cabinet. He surrounded himself with men of action who were not afraid to take risks. He engaged and combined in a conspiracy to organize a covert air force that would attack Japan. Although all of his ambitions were never fully realized, he is held in honor and high esteem by the people of China. To the people of China, Chennault and all the men and women who served under him are heroes. Their efforts prevented the collapse of China to Japan during World War II. Chennault died in 1958 with the honorary grade of lieutenant general. He is buried at Arlington National Cemetery.

APPENDIX 1

Index of Documents Found in Henry Morgenthau Jr.
Diary 342-A, China: Bombers, December 3–22, 1940

Exhibit	Description of Documents
1.	Cover sheet to Diary Book 342-A, entitled "China: Bombers December 3–22, 1940."
2.	Index to Diary Book 342-A.
3.	Memorandum from Henry Morgenthau Jr. dictated December 3, 1940, regarding a meeting with British Ambassador Lothian on December 2, 1940.
4.	Memorandum from Secretary Morgenthau of December 7, 1940, concerning a call to British Ambassador Lothian; and memorandum discussing conversation with T. V. Soong on Sunday, December 8, 1940, regarding 500 planes for China.
5.	Memorandum from Generalissimo Chiang Kai-shek, requesting 500 airplanes for operation in China, November 30, 1940.
6.	Handwritten letter from T. V. Soong to Secretary Morgenthau, December 9, 1940, enclosing maps showing secret air bases in China.
7.	Map of secret air bases in China.
8.	Second map of secret air bases in China.
9.	Memorandum from Morgenthau to the file concerning his conversation with Secretary of State Cordell Hull, December 10, 1940.
10.	Memorandum from Morgenthau dated December 18, 1940, concerning a telephone conversation with President Roosevelt, wherein the president said he had been waiting for four years for the Chinese to indicate a willingness to attack Japan.
11.	Memorandum from Morgenthau to the file, concerning telephone conversation with T. V. Soong, December 18, 1940, indicating Chiang Kai-shek was in agreement that Boeing bombers with escort planes could operate from China and bomb Japan; the generalissimo requested that he be allowed to send a personal message to President Roosevelt.

Exhibit	Description of Documents
12.	A second memorandum from Morgenthau, dated December 18, 1940, concerning a conversation with T. V. Soong in which Morgenthau related to Soong that Secretary of State Hull (a) not only approved of the plan to bomb Japan, but (b) Hull also agreed that the planes could be flown from the West Coast of the United States to Hawaii, then to Wake Island, then to the Philippines, and then directly to China.
13.	Telegram from Generalissimo Chiang Kai-shek to President Roosevelt, December 12, 1940, thanking the president for a substantial loan to China and expressing interest in an air force for China to prevent the spreading of the war to southern Asia.
14.	Telegram from Generalissimo Chiang Kai-shek to Morgenthau, December 16, 1940, relating: ". . . I am most anxious to acquire as many of your latest Flying Fortresses as you can spare, which from our air bases could effectively bomb all vital centers of Japan, and harass their fleet and transports."
15.	Notation to the file that Secretary Morgenthau had given Secretary of State Hull the two telegrams from Chiang Kai-shek identified as Appendices 13 and 14.
16.	Memorandum concerning the substance of conversations between Morgenthau and T. V. Soong on December 20, 1940, at 4:00 P.M.
17.	Transcript of telephone conversation between Secretary of the Navy Frank Knox and Morgenthau of December 20, 1940, at 5:13 P.M.
18.	Notes on conference at home of the Secretary (Morgenthau), 5:00 P.M., Saturday, December 21, 1940, the persons in attendance being: (a) Morgenthau (b) Soong (c) General Mow (d) Col. Chennault and (e) Phillip Young.
19.	Memorandum from Secretary Morgenthau of December 22, 1940, concerning a meeting with Secretary Knox and General Marshall at Secretary of War Stimson's house in which it was discussed that General Marshall had two meetings with Soong, General Mow, and Col. Chennault, and General Marshall: ". . . questioned the advisability of simply letting them have the bombers."
20.	Confidential memorandum from Mr. Young to Secretary Morgenthau, December 22, 1940, discussing the aircraft available for China and the production and delivery schedules of these aircraft for December 1940 and January, February, and March of 1941.

APPENDIX 2

Index of Documents Found in U.S. Navy American Volunteer Group Papers, Record Group 4.9, Emil Buehler Naval Aviation Library, National Museum of Naval Aviation, Accession Number 1997.269 ("The Pensacola Papers")

Exhibit Number	Document Summary and Description	Date of Document
1	Statement of Mr. Bruce Leighton concerning the Central Aircraft Manufacturing Company, circa early 1941, and including the following information:	
	a) The Chinese government sent a special mission to Washington in early 1941 to arrange for loans and other assistance to develop the Chinese Air Force.	
	b) Arrangements were made for a $100 million loan to China from the United States and for the release of one hundred Curtiss P-40 pursuit planes from the then-current British allocations.	
	c) That because of the complex nature of the high-performance aircraft being provided to China, American military personnel were required to fly and maintain the aircraft.	
	d) ". . . for obvious reasons, individuals engaged in operations of the nature contemplated in China must have no connection with the U.S. Government Services . . ."	
	e) Intercontinent Corporation is a concern with long experience in China, which has provided aircraft to the Chinese government through its subsidiary corporation, the Central Aircraft Manufacturing Company (CAMCO).	
	f) CAMCO trained Chinese mechanics and established repair and maintenance facilities in China since the beginning of hostilities in Shanghai in 1937.	
	g) CAMCO maintains offices in New York, Chungking, Rangoon, and Hong Kong. Also, CAMCO operates a factory and repair base adjacent to the Burma route.	

h) CAMCO's president is William D. Pawley, and its vice president is Lt. Cdr. B. G. Leighton, a naval officer with twelve years' active service, and on inactive duty with the U.S. Navy at the time the statement was prepared.

i) CAMCO personnel offered to provide their company as a vehicle whereby pilots and ground personnel could be recruited and "would be under contract, ostensibly as civilian employees . . ."

j) CAMCO's expenses would be reimbursed by the Chinese government, there being a formal agreement between the Chinese Embassy and CAMCO to that effect. (A copy of the formal agreement referenced in this statement was not appended to the statement.)

k) All activities in relation to the formulation of this project with the United States government were "handled orally" with no file record of any nature.

l) CAMCO's representatives were given letters of introduction by the Secretary of the Navy's offices and by the offices of the Chief of the Air Corps to commanding officers of naval and military installations.

m) After clearing with the commanding officer of the military station, CAMCO employees made contact with individual reserve officers and enlisted men receiving applications for employment.

n) The military agreed that resignations or discharges from the service to accept employment with CAMCO would be approved.

o) "Although they completely sever their official connections with the United States military service, it is the intent of the War and Navy Departments that upon completion of their employment with CAM Co. [sic] and to the extent granted by the broad discretionary powers of the Secretaries of War and Navy in relation to Reserve personnel that they will be accepted for re-commission or re-enlistment in the active Reserve in such rank or grade and under such conditions as will give them the same seniority and other benefits, including disability benefits, as they would have enjoyed had they remained on active duty in the Army or Navy Reserve."

	p) Successful applicants would be processed by CAMCO representatives who would submit the resignations of the volunteers to the army or navy as appropriate, and who would also submit a passport application to the passport division of the State Department which would obtain the required visas from the British and Chinese embassies.	
	q) The CAMCO personnel would arrange transportation of the volunteers to China.	
	r) The CAMCO personnel would instruct the volunteers with respect to where and when to report.	
	s) CAMCO agreed to provide weekly summaries of this project to the Secretary of the Navy and to the Special Chinese Affairs desk of the State Department.	
	t) Interested offices in Washington would be kept constantly informed of the progress of this project.	
	u) In addition to the one hundred Curtiss P-40 aircraft, substantial additional numbers of aircraft were anticipated as an extension of the original project, along with plans for the supply of bomber-type planes to China.	
2	Confidential Memorandum for the Secretary of the Navy from W. L. Keys, February 3, 1941, which includes the following information:	
	a) That William Pawley and Col. Chennault indicated on February 3, 1941, that an agreement had been reached between Curtiss Wright Aircraft Corporation and Intercontinent Corporation and the Chinese government for the provision of one hundred P-40 aircraft for China.	
	b) That the personnel requirements were 100 pilots and 150 ground crewmen.	
	c) "They realize the necessity for keeping the thing quiet and will take due precautions."	
	d) Volunteers resigning from the service would do so "without detriment to their future status in the service in order to accept employment with the Central Aircraft Corporation [sic]."	

	e) Note: "BuNav is ready to do this, but it will have to be taken up with the Army, and I understand that Gen. Arnold has not yet been informed by Sec. Stimson. I suggest that you personally take this up with Sec. Stimson, and also with Adm. Towers, who is not very enthusiastic about this idea, I believe."	
	f) The volunteers would be deferred from the draft.	
	g) Passports would be issued for employment in China by the State Department to individuals as bona fide employees of Central Aircraft [sic].	
	h) William Pawley, Bruce Leighton, and Chennault would all require letters of passage from the War and Navy Departments authorizing them to visit various air stations.	
	i) "It was pointed out to me that this considerable organization would hardly be worth sending out and establishing unless there were excellent prospects for further release of planes to carry on the work. They will have to start more or less from scratch in Burma and work their way in against probable opposition."	
3	Memorandum for Commanding Officer, Naval Air Station Jacksonville, from Capt. Frank E. Beatty, aide to the Secretary of the Navy, introducing Mr. C. L. Chennault, April 14, 1941.	**April 14, 1941**
4	Memorandum for Commanding Officer, Naval Air Station San Diego, from Capt. Frank E. Beatty, aide to the Secretary of the Navy, introducing Rutledge Irvine, April 14, 1941.	**April 14, 1941**
5	Memorandum for Capt. James M. Shoemaker, Commanding Officer, U. S. Naval Air Station, Pearl Harbor, Hawaii from Capt. Frank E. Beatty, aide to the Secretary of the Navy, introducing Lt. C. B. Adair, August 4, 1941, this memorandum stating, in part: "It has been the policy of our government for some time to facilitate the hiring by the Chinese government of pilots and mechanics from our Services. The above-mentioned officer is a representative of the Intercontinent Company, which company is doing the hiring for the Chinese government. The cooperation of the Commanding	**August 4, 1941**

	Officer is requested in permitting this representative to interview pilots on your station, to see if they are interested in being hired by the Intercontinent Company for service in China."	
6	Secret Memorandum for Adm. Nimitz from Cdr. J. B. Lynch of the Navy Department Bureau of Navigation, August 7, 1941, concerning releases of naval personnel to accept employment in China with the Central Aircraft Manufacturing Company in which the following points are made:	**August 7, 1941**
	a) During the month of May 1941, Cdr. Lynch had heard about the possibility of the navy being required to release from active duty a considerable number of officers and enlisted personnel for the purpose of employment in China with the Central Aircraft Manufacturing Company.	
	b) The source of this information to Cdr. Lynch was Capt. Shafroth who indicated "that the Department would be reluctant to lose the services of this much-needed personnel"	
7	Confidential letter from Aubrey W. Fitch, Cdr. Carrier Div. One, San Diego Naval Air Station to the Chief of the Bureau of Aeronautics concerning pilot resignation for employment by CAMCO, indicating the following:	
	a) That thirty-eight navy pilots had resigned for employment by CAMCO.	
	b) "It is also understood that a program of 266 additional Navy and Air Corps pilots will be initiated in the future."	
	c) Because of the loss of pilots under the program, the Bureau of Aeronautics was requested to "immediately fulfill shortages in compliments which had been caused by the resignations of pilots . . ."	
8	Secret Memorandum for the Chief of the Bureau of Navigation, from Capt. H. M. Briggs, regarding enlisted personnel—discharged for China, August 8, 1941, confirming the following:	**August 8, 1941,**

	a) Capt. Briggs attended a conference in May of 1941 in which other persons in attendance were Capt. Shafroth, Capt. Good, Cdr. Lynch, Mr. Leighton (a graduate of the United States Naval Academy in 1913), and one or two other civilians (ex-Army).	
	b) With regard to enlisted personnel who elected to resign from the navy to serve in China: if they were killed in China, their families would receive no benefits. Men who returned and desired to reenlist would be allowed to reenlist regardless of their physical condition, and they would be allowed to serve until they had sufficient time in the service to retire.	
	c) "All requests for discharge would state that the men desired to take employment with the Central Aircraft Manufacturing Co., which would signify that they were going to China."	
	d) "The matter was secret."	
	e) Effective August 8, 1941, forty-five men had been discharged for that project.	
9	Handwritten Memorandum for Adm. Dunfield from H. G. Hopwood, August 14, 1941, indicating the following:	**August 14, 1941**
	a) That of the 100 pilots and 150 enlisted ground crew required from the army and navy, 33 pilots and 50 ground crew were to come from the navy, with the rest coming from the army;	
	b) That through August 14, 1941, 56 navy pilots had been provided to the program as well as 45 enlisted ground crewmen.	
10	Confidential Memorandum from Capt. F. E. Beatty, aide to the Secretary of the Navy to Frank Knox, Secretary of the Navy, August 15, 1941, outlining the following facts:	**August 15, 1941**
	a) With the approval of the Secretary of the Navy, the aide to the Secretary has assisted representatives of the Central Aircraft Manufacturing Company to obtain the acceptance of resignations of certain volunteering	

	naval personnel for the purpose of accepting employment with CAMCO, the idea being to permit this personnel [sic] to ultimately accept employment under the Chinese government for the purpose of operating a number of P-40 planes to operate against the Japanese over China. Reference (D) is the operating memorandum. *This has been carried on in a secret manner.* [Emphasis added]	
	b) The pay scales for CAMCO employees were shown in Reference E to the Confidential Memorandum.	
	c) While two-thirds of the pilots of the volunteers were to come from the army and one-third from the navy, that ratio was not maintained, particularly in regard to pilots.	
	d) "Although recruiting continues both in the Army and Navy, there may be considerable difficulty in reaching the total of 100 pilots set. Commanders of Stations and Units are naturally loathe to let trained pilots resign. Although it is felt that the present set-up will suffice to accomplish the recruiting of the first 100 pilots mentioned above, Mr. Currie is setting up a far more extensive program projected into the future, which envisions sending a far larger number of pilots to China, as well as the training of Chinese pilots in this country. Brigadier Gen. Lewis B. Hershey, Deputy Dir., Selective Service System, has been advised of the names of all men accepting employment with CAMCO."	
	e) "Due to the extent of expansion of the project as well as the change of status from its formerly secret classification, it is recommended that the entire project be transferred to the Office of the Chief of Naval Operations."	
11	Handwritten notes by Adm. Chester W. Nimitz, August 18, 1941, confirming a meeting on that date with a number of naval officers, including Capt. Beatty and Mr. Lauchlin Currie, Mr. Currie having agreed with Cdr. Lynch that if the navy released a total of sixty-three officers, Mr. Currie would be satisfied for the present.	**August 18, 1941**

12	Secret Memorandum for the Secretary of the Navy from Adm. Chester W. Nimitz, August 15, 1941, concerning release of naval personnel for ultimate employment by the Chinese government in which the following points are confirmed:	**August 15, 1941**
	a) There had been informal conferences between the aide to the Secretary of the Navy, representatives of the Navy Bureau of Navigation, and representatives of CAMCO about naval personnel accepting "civilian employment with the Central Aircraft Manufacturing Company for ultimate employment by the Chinese government."	
	b) "Because of the nature of the project, all matters have been considered as *secret* and any promises made to those releases are effected have been or will be made *orally* [emphasis added]."	
	c) That of the 100 pilots and 150 enlisted personnel required for the project, approximately one-third would be recruited from naval personnel.	
	d) Prior to accepting employment with CAMCO, naval personnel must first be separated from the service by way of resignation or discharge.	
	e) That naval officers who participated in the program and who returned to the navy for active service would be entitled to return to the navy "with the identical seniority in the grade held at the time of separation."	
	f) Naval officers who participated in the program would not be entitled to receive a bonus for continuous service with the navy.	
	g) That enlisted personnel would be allowed to reenlist regardless of their physical condition at the time of making re-application for enlistment.	
	h) That personnel applying for reenlistment would be ineligible if they were "known to be guilty of a charge involving moral turpitude."	
	i) That families of personnel killed in the line of duty would not be entitled to any benefits from the United States government.	

	j) That the personnel records of individuals who elected to separate from the navy or service in China as civilian employees of CAMCO would have appropriate entries made in their personnel records to that effect.	
	k) This memorandum bears the inscription in the bottom left-hand corner, *OK—Knox*.	
13	Confidential Memorandum from Cdr. J. B. Lynch to Adm. Chester Nimitz, August 19, 1941, concerning releases and resignations to accept employment with the Central Aircraft Manufacturing Company, confirming the following: "At a meeting of August 19, 1941, between Adm. Nimitz, Lauchlin Currie, and Cdr. Lynch, it was determined that the navy would accept the resignations of sixty-three aviators as a quota for the program. Adm. Nimitz would be notified with respect to the names, stations, and dates of release of the aviators as they were released from the Navy."	**August 19, 1941**
14	Letter from H. V. Sterling, director of finance, Veterans Administration, to Mrs. Blanche Knight, September 4, 1941, concerning a change of address for Noel Richard Bacon.	**September 4, 1941**
15	Secret Memorandum for the Secretary of the Navy from President Franklin D. Roosevelt confirming the following: a) That the Chinese government had hired 100 pilots and 181 ground personnel to man and service 100 P-40 aircraft. b) "In the next few months we are delivering [to] China 269 pursuit planes and 66 bombers. The Chinese pilot training program here will not begin to turn out well-trained pilots until next summer. In the interim, therefore, I think we should facilitate the hiring by the Chinese government of further volunteer pilots here. I suggest, therefore, that beginning in January, you should accept the resignations of additional pilots and ground personnel as care to accept employment in China, up to a limit of 100 pilots and a proportional	

	number of ground personnel. I am directing Mr. Lauchlin Currie to see that representatives of China carry out the hiring program with the minimum of in-convenience to the Navy and also to see that no more are hired than are necessary."	
16	Letter from Harry C. Claiborne of the Central Aircraft Manufacturing Company to Adm. Chester W. Nimitz, October 4, 1941, reciting as follows: "On September 30, 1941, we received a note from Capt. Beatty advising us that you were taking over the details of the foreign project. We have been sending out a confidential 'weekly progress letter' to those closely associated with the project of which this is the current issue."	**October 4, 1941**
17	Memorandum of CAMCO to Mr. Lauchlin Currie, aide to President Roosevelt, October 4, 1942, providing a list of seven officers and one enlisted man who resigned from the project, and two men who deserted from the project, with the recommendation that upon their return to the United States, they be drafted as enlisted men and stationed either in Iceland or Newfoundland, a copy of this letter going to Adm. Chester Nimitz.	**October 4, 1941**
18	Confidential Memorandum for Adm. Nimitz from Capt. V. D. Chapline, dated October 8, 1941, dealing with the requirements of the navy for trained pilots by January 1, and February 1, 1942, along with a handwritten notation in the bottom left corner suggesting that resignations be limited to graduates of training centers within three months of graduation and prior to beginning fleet training.	**October 8, 1941**
19	Letter from Frank Knox, Secretary of the Navy, to Lauchlin Currie, aide to President Roosevelt, November 7, 1941, requesting that pilots recruited for this special program be limited to naval aviators who were recent graduates of Naval Flight Training Centers and that the recruitment take place within three months of their designation as a naval aviator.	**November 7, 1941**
20	Letter from Lauchlin Currie, aide to President Roosevelt, November 8, 1941, to Frank Knox, Secretary of the Navy, agreeing to the suggestion that naval aviators recruited for service in China be recruited within three months of their graduation after completion of flight training.	**November 8, 1941**

21	Memorandum of Frank Knox, Secretary of the Navy, to Adm. Nimitz, November 10, 1941, enclosing Lauchlin Currie's letter of November 8, 1941, with notations at the body of the memorandum by Adm. Nimitz, indicating that the agreement between Currie and Knox to restrict recruitment of naval aviators to within three months of graduating from a primary flight center were okay with Adm. Tower, okay with Adm. Nimitz, and Nimitz would prepare a reply.	**November 10, 1941**
22	Letter from Lauchlin Currie, aide to President Roosevelt, to Adm. Chester Nimitz, December 4, 1941, indicating that Mr. Currie had been advised by T. V. Soong, the chairman of China Defense Supplies, that Richard Aldworth, H. C. Claiborne, and F. L. Brown were persons authorized to contact pilots and enlisted men about "the possibilities of securing employment with the Volunteer Air Group in China."	**December 4, 1941**
23	Secret Memorandum from Col. H. W. T. Eglin to Lt. Col. H. P. Chrisman, January 13, 1942, confirming the following: a) It is our understanding that Gen. Magruder has recently been given authority to accept this volunteer group into either the army or the navy, as they may prefer, in commissioned grades held by them prior to their being decommissioned to go to China. This authorization was given by both the Secretary of War and the Secretary of the Navy. b) The memorandum questions whether the army can pay navy fliers from army funds while receiving reimbursement from the navy.	**January 13, 1942**
24	Secret Memorandum from Lt. Col. W. T. Johnson to Col. H. W. T. Eglin concerning the American Volunteer Group, dated January 15, 1942, and indicating that while it would be preferable to have navy officers paid by the navy, they could be paid by an army finance officer, and the army could obtain reimbursement from the navy.	**January 15, 1942**
25	Secret Message from the War Department to the Navy Department concerning the induction of the AVG into the 23rd Pursuit Group at their former grade in the navy, or in a corresponding grade in the army as they may elect.	

26	Secret Message from the Secretary of the Navy to the Chief of the U.S. Military Commission in China, January 28, 1942, confirming that former naval and marine personnel serving in the American Volunteer Group may be inducted into the army for the time being, with payment to those individuals being made by the army and reimbursement by the navy. Request was also made that the individuals execute the oath of office and that the navy be notified of the names of the individuals so inducted, the date of execution of the oath of office, and their date of reporting for active duty.	**January 28, 1942**
27	Special Order No. 36 from the Headquarters of the American Volunteer Group, February 14, 1942, granting Noel R. Bacon ninety days' leave from the 2nd Pursuit Squadron and directing that McMillan, Older, Haywood, Smith, Green, and Laughlin proceed by air transport to Cairo, Egypt, and report to the Com. Gen. of the United States Air Force Middle East for instructions.	**February 14, 1942**
28	Letter from H. V. Sterling, director of finance, the Veterans Administration, to Mr. Noel Richard Bacon, March 7, 1942.	**March 7, 1942**
29	Telegram from the naval attaché in Chungking, China, to the Bureau of Navigation, April 3, 1942, requesting information with respect to the rank and rating of navy and marine corps personnel prior to being discharged to join the American Volunteer Group. The information being characterized as being essential to induction.	**April 3, 1942**
30	Secret Telegram from the Secretary of the Navy to the Com. Gen. of the U.S. Military Mission in China, confirming that ex-naval and marine corps personnel serving with the American Volunteer Group are authorized for induction into the naval service and are authorized to engage in assignments involving flying.	
31	Secret Message from Gen. Joseph Stilwell to AGWAR for AMMISCA, April 11, 1941, including the following text: "More than half of present AVG pilots are ex-navy or marine officers. Policy furnished naval attaché Chungking apparently confirmed your 430 April 9 discriminates against ex-navy and marine officers if	**April 11, 1942**

	they elect induction into naval service and attachment to 23rd Pursuit Group. They may be inducted only in grade previously held and are ineligible for temporary promotion authorized for AVG ex-Army pilot [sic]. This policy also appears to penalize ex-navy officers to an extent that their former naval contemporaries may have been promoted since these officers joined AVG. In view of adverse effect of this policy on success of induction and on effectiveness of 23rd Group, as well as fairness to these outstanding pilots, information is requested if the apparent discrimination is intended."	
32	Secret Draft of radio message to General Stilwell, Chungking, China (date unknown): "Attn Stilwell. Number AVG who are ex-naval and marine corps personnel may elect induction in AUS [Army, U.S.] or naval service. Those electing induction in AUS may be appointed to suitable and appropriate grades to include that of colonel. If all elect induction in AUS, there is no discrimination. Navy Department advises that those ex-naval and marine corps reserve officers electing induction in naval service will be inducted in grade previously held as reserve officers and upon report to Navy Department by Naval Attaché Chungking such officers will be promoted to grades held by their former contemporaries, and thereafter their promotion will be covered by Navy Department policies for all personnel. This in answer to your 5/3; Navy has no appointment comparable to AUS."	**(date unknown)**
33	Secret Telegram from ALUSNA Chungking, China, to Secretary of the Navy, dated April 12, 1942, stating in part: ". . . must be inducted into former grade . . . Appropriate promotion for later after repeat after induction is essential to avoid discrimination and is paramount consideration in success of project. . . . General Stilwell . . . in name of president to make such naval promotions within the group as may be merited and in consonance with similar advancements given to Army personnel. Majority of former navy people do not repeat do not want to join army. Military mission desires that induction proposal shall be equally fair in all respects to	**April 12, 1942**

	naval personnel. Fighting efficiency of this unit whose record continues outstanding and whose further operations are vital to morale of Chinese hinges on above."	
34	Message from the War Department to Gen. Stilwell, April 13, 1942, providing: "Immediately upon induction in grade previously held by ex-naval and marine corps personnel and upon report to Navy Dept. by Naval Attaché Chungking such personnel will be promoted to grades held by their former contemporaries. This in answer to your 5/3. Navy has no appointment comparable to AUS. Thereafter permanent or temporary promotion of ex-naval and marine corps personnel will be governed by Navy Dept. policies for all personnel."	**April 13, 1942**
35	Secret Telegram from Secretary of Navy to ALUSNA Chungking, China, April 14, 1942, in part: ". . . After induction authority further granted to temporarily promote individuals to appropriate ranks not above Lieutenant in Naval Reserve and Captain in Marine Corps Reserve."	**April 14, 1942**
36	Letter from Richard Aldworth of CAMCO to N. R. Bacon, AVG, acknowledging receipt of his letter with letters from Chennault enclosed, inviting Bacon to New York or Washington for interview.	**April 22, 1942**
37	Letter from Aldworth to Bacon sending $1,000 bonus from CAMCO and reporting a future bonus will be sent of $750.	**May 4, 1942**
38	Letter from R. G. Malone, CAMCO, to Bacon, May 23, 1942, requesting Bacon contact Chennault if Bacon does not intend to return to Orient.	**May 23, 1942**
39	Telegram from Chennault to CAMCO regarding Bacon.	**May 26, 1942**
40	Telegram from CAMCO to Chennault concerning Noel Bacon, who is requesting reinstatement in the Naval Reserve.	**May 27, 1942**

41	Restricted Telegram May 28, 1942, from Naval Attaché Chungking, China, to Dept. of the Navy inquiring if former navy personnel now serving with AVG who may accept induction into army be eligible to resume former naval status after the war? Will service in Army Air Force count toward longevity and retirement?	**May 28, 1942**
42	Telegram from Naval Attaché Chungking, China, May 28, 1942, to Naval Operations, asking "Is Navy making appointments to permanent commissions from selected applicants? If so, under what conditions? Request same for Marine Corps. Can members of AVG be made eligible for above?"	**May 28, 1942**
43	Telegram from Gen. Chennault to Central Aircraft in New York, May 29, 1942, advising that if Noel Bacon is not in Chungking by July 4, he will be given a dishonorable discharge.	**May 29, 1942**
44	Confidential routing slip from Naval Attaché Chungking, China, to Van Norden.	**June 4, 1942**
45	Telegram from attaché in Chungking, China, to Capt. L. E. Denfield: "Your 260910 former naval personnel now serving with AVG who desire reappointment in the naval service must be inducted immediately upon termination of AVG status in accordance with previous directives."	**June 1, 1942**
46	Letter from CAMCO, A. H. Leonard to Noel Bacon.	**June 2, 1942**
47	Secret Telegram to Stilwell, relating in part: "ACTIVATE TWENTY THIRD PURSUIT GROUP ACCORDING TO PREVIOUS INSTRUCTIONS ISSUED YOU AND MAGRUDER period YOUR PLAN IN YOUR FOUR FORTY TWO IS APPROVED period OFFER EVERY REASONABLE INDUCEMENT TO ENCOURAGE INDUCTION OF MEMBERS AVG comma RECOGNIZE PREVIOUS MERITORIOUS SERVICE BY SUITABLE AND APPROPRIATE GRADE IN AUS TO INCLUDE GRADE OF COLONEL REGARDLESS OF TABLE OF ORGANIZATION VACANCIES period EX NAVY AND MARINE PERSONNEL MAY ELECT INDUCTION IN AUS OR NAVAL SERVICE period NAVAL AND MARINE PERSONNEL	**No date**

ELECTING INDUCTION IN NAVAL SERVICE MUST BE
INDUCTED IN GRADE PREVIOUSLY HELD IN THAT SERVICE
ACCORDING TO INSTRUCTIONS DISPATCHED NAVAL
ATTACHE CHUNGKING FEBRUARY SECOND period
SECRETARY OF WAR DIRECTS THAT ORIGINAL
AERONAUTICAL RATING OF U S PILOTS INDUCTED IN AUS
BE REINSTATED AND LOCAL ORDERS ISSUE [sic] TO PLACE
INDIVIDUALS ON DUTY REQUIRING PARTICIPATION IN
FREQUENT AERIAL FLIGHTS period INSTRUCTIONS FOR
FLIGHT STATUS OF NAVAL AND MARINE PERSONNEL WILL
BE SENT TO NAVAL ATTACHE CHUNGKING BY NAVY
DEPARTMENT period IN YOUR NEGOTIATIONS IT IS
DESIRABLE TO TRANSFER ALL AIRPLANES ASSIGNED TO
OR INTENDED FOR AVG AS CONDITIONS WILL NOT
PERMIT EARLY REPLACEMENT IF CHINESE GOVERNMENT
RETAINS SUCH AIRCRAFT FOR THEIR AIR UNITS period
DIVERSION OF LEND LEASE EQUIPMENT WILL BE SUBJECT
TO APPROVAL OF GENERALISSIMO PURSUANT OUR THREE
FOUR MARCH TWENTY SIXTH period DETACHMENT OF
THREE OFFICERS TWO HUNDRED FIFTEEN ENLISTED
MEN TO PROVIDE HEADQUARTERS AND ADMINISTRATIVE
PERSONNEL FOR TWENTY THIRD PURSUIT GROUP NOW
EN ROUTE INDIA TO ARRIVE ABOUT JUNE FIRST period
THIRTY THREE PURSUIT PILOTS TO PROCEED INDIA IN A
dash TWENTY NINES [sic] SHOULD ARRIVE BY JUNE
period ADDITIONAL TWENTY TWO PURSUIT PILOTS WILL
BE SENT FROM U S BY FIRST AVAILABLE TRANSPORTATION
period IN NAME OF PRESIDENT CALL UPON AVG TO
CONTINUE IN PRESENT GENERAL ASSIGNMENT UNTIL
CONDITIONS PERMIT OPPORTUNITY FOR LEAVE period
U S DECORATION FOR MERITORIOUS SERVICE PERFORMED
PRIOR TO ENTRY IN AUS OR NAVAL SERVICE NOT
AUTHORIZED UNDER EXISTING LAW period U S CITIZENS
MEMBERS OF AMERICAN VOLUNTEER GROUP WHO
DECLINE INDUCTION AND ELECT TO RETURN TO U S
WILL BE SUBJECT TO SELECTIVE SERVICE semi-colon
FORMER RESERVE OFFICERS MAY BE REINSTATED AND
CALLED TO ACTIVE DUTY end"

| 48 | Telegram from ALUSNA Chungking, China, to OPNAV regarding procedures to be followed in processing applicants. | **June 3, 1942** |

49	Confidential Telegram from American Military Mission in Chungking, China, to Secretary of Navy concerning induction of enlisted navy and marine personnel and whether their AVG service will count toward their twenty years of military service for retirement and longevity.	**June 11, 1942**
50	Confidential Telegram from Secretary of Navy, June 16, 1942, in part stating that directives are amended to direct that ex-regular officers may be inducted only in reserve in former rank, eligible for temporary promotion and service with AVG would not by law count toward twenty-year retirement.	**June 16, 1942**
51	Confidential Telegram from Secretary of the Navy to Attaché in Chungking, China, June 16, 1942, stating in part that accepting word of applicants as to their former status would be subject to correction by department after report of induction.	**June 16, 1942**
52	Letter to Rear Adm. Randall Jacobs, from Mrs. Alice H. Leonard of W. D. Pawley's office, enclosing roster of inductees and locations of personnel.	**July 31, 1942**
53	Letter to Jacobs from Mrs. Leonard, August 21, 1942, correcting rosters.	**August 21, 1942**
54	Letter to Jacobs from Mrs. Leonard, September 18, 1942, enclosing rosters and locations of personnel.	**September 18, 1942**
55	Secret Extracts of radiograms re: AVG from the American Military Mission in Chungking, China, i.e., a) No. 136—Appoint board to supervise induction. Permission to commission former naval personnel in former grades and attach to army. b) No. 140—Transfer of AVG from CAMCO to U.S. government. Induct into U.S. armed forces. c) No. 159—Waive physical defects on anything else necessary. d) No. 161—Assurance the AVG will continue to protect Chinese interests.	**No date**

APPENDIX 3

Index of Documents Found in Franklin D. Roosevelt Library:
Small Collections: FDR Library: Misc.: Joint Board 355

Exhibit No.	Document Summary and Description
1.	Memorandum for the Commander-in-Chief from Captain W. R. Purnell, May 13, 1941, Subject: Certain Strategic Considerations in Connection with an Orange War—Rainbow No. Three.
2.	Letter from the Commander-in-Chief of the United States Asiatic Fleet to the Chief of Naval Operations, May 13, 1941, concerning a Memorandum prepared by Captain W. R. Purnell.
3.	Memorandum from the Special Committee for Scheduling of Transport Aircraft for South America and Other Programs to the Joint Aircraft Committee—Subcommittee on the Allocation of Deliveries, May 24, 1941, regarding Case No. 725.
4.	Report of a meeting of the Joint Aircraft Committee on May 27,1941, approving Case No. 725 with the proviso that the Allocation Subcommittee is "instructed to explore possibilities of increased production to Hudson and/or Loadstar types."
5.	Report of interview from R. A. Boone to the Office of the Chief of Naval Operations, January 17, 1940, concerning report of interview with Lieutenant-Commander Bruce G. Leighton, USNR.
6.	Single-page document consisting of six numbered paragraphs appearing to be a memorandum from Lieutenant-Commander Bruce G. Leighton with no date and no addressee.
7.	Memorandum for the Chief of Naval Operations from W. S. Anderson, January 17, 1940, enclosing a memorandum prepared by Mr. Bruce G. Leighton, formerly of the U.S. Navy, and now vice president of Intercontinent Corporation.
8.	J.B. No. 355 (Serial 691), May 29, 1941, regarding a Short-Term Aircraft Program for China.
9.	Letter from Lauchlin Currie, administrative assistant to the president, to Honorable Frank Knox, Secretary to the Navy, May 28, 1941.

10.	Letter from Frank Knox, Secretary of the Navy, to the Joint Board, dated May 29, 1941, forwarding the letter from Lauchlin Currie of May 28, 1941.
11.	J.B. No. 355 (Serial 691) captioned "Strategic Estimate" outlining the provision of aircraft to China in three stages, outlining both strategic and tactical objectives and giving the distances from bases in China to Nagasaki, Kobe, Osaka, and Tokyo.
12.	Memorandum from Lieutenant Colonel E. E. MacMorland to Colonel Orlando Ward, May 12, 1941, concerning Chinese aircraft requirements.
13.	Letter from Lauchlin Currie, administrative assistant to the president, to General George C. Marshall, Chief of Staff, May 19, 1941.
14.	Confidential Memorandum from Lieutenant Colonel W. P. Scobey of the Joint Board to the Joint Planning Committee, May 26, 1941, concerning aircraft requirements of the Chinese government.
15.	Letter from Henry H. Arnold, Major General, U.S. Army, to the Secretary of War, May 10, 1941, concerning aircraft requirements of the Chinese government.
16.	Confidential Memorandum from Henry L. Stimson, Secretary of War, to the Joint Army/Navy Board, May 13, 1941, concerning air craft requirements of the Chinese government.
17.	Secret Memorandum for the Chief of Staff from Brigadier General L. T. Gerow, May 29, 1941, concerning airplanes for China.
18.	Secret radiogram from Grunert in Manila to the War Department, June 14, 1941, at 10:00 P.M.
19.	Secret Memorandum for the Chief of Staff from Brigadier General L.T. Gerow, June [the date is missing] 1941, concerning training facilities for Chinese pilots in the Philippine Department.
20.	Douglas DC-3 Recommended Delivery Schedule, Joint Aircraft Committee, Subcommittee on the Allocation of Deliveries, Case No. 725, Exhibit B, May 23, 1941.
21.	Letter from W. L. Bond to Lauchlin Currie, June 6, 1941.
22.	Letter from Lauchlin Currie, administrative assistant to the president, to Henry L. Stimson, Secretary of War, June 7, 1941.
23.	Lockheed Loadstar Recommended Delivery Schedule, Joint Aircraft Committee, Subcommittee on the Allocation of Deliveries, Case No. 725, Exhibit A, May 23, 1941.

24.	Confidential Memorandum to the Joint Aircraft Committee, from the Special Committee for Scheduling of Transport Aircraft for South America and Other Programs, May 24, 1941, Case No. 725.
25.	Report of meeting of the Joint Aircraft Committee, May 27, 1941, concerning Case No. 725, with the notation "Enclosure (C)" in the bottom right-hand corner.
26.	Confidential Memorandum of the Joint Aircraft Committee, Subcommittee on the Allocation of Deliveries, June 3, 1941, concerning Case No. 704, Addendum I, P.N.R. No. [none], 125 Republic P-43 aircraft for China.
27.	Another copy of a Secret Memorandum from W. R. Purnell, to the Commander-in-Chief concerning certain Strategic Considerations in Connection with an Orange War—Rainbow No. 3, May 13, 1941, with the notation "Enclosure (B)" in the bottom right-hand corner of the document (this having been previously identified as Exhibit 1).
28.	Secret Memorandum from the Commander-in-Chief, United States Asiatic Fleet, to the Chief of Naval Operations, May 13, 1941, forwarding Captain Purnell's memorandum of May 13, 1941 (this exhibit being a duplicate of Exhibit 2).
29.	A second copy of the Report of Interview with Lieutenant-Commander Bruce G. Leighton from R. A. Boone, dated January 17, 1940, with the additional inscription "Enclosure (B)" in the bottom right-hand corner of the document.
30.	A second copy of the document believed to be Commander Bruce G. Leighton's memorandum presented on or about January 17, 1940, to R. A. Boone.
31.	A second copy of a Confidential Memorandum from W. S. Anderson to the Chief of Naval Operations, January 17, 1940, referencing a memorandum prepared by Mr. Bruce G. Leighton.
32.	J.B. No. 355 (Serial 691), May 29, 1941, entitled "A Short-Term Aircraft Program for China."
33.	Letter from Lauchlin Currie, administrative assistant to the president, to Honorable Frank Knox, Secretary of the Navy, May 28, 1941.
34.	Letter from Frank Knox, Secretary of the Navy, to the Joint Board, May 29, 1941, concerning an Aircraft Program for China with the notation "First Endorsement."
35.	Memorandum from Major General E. S. Adams to the Secretary of the Joint Board concerning aircraft requirements of the Chinese government with the notation "For Action in Connection with

	Memorandum from the Joint Aircraft Committee, May 10, 1941, which was transmitted by First Endorsement, this office, May 16, 1941 . . ."
36.	Another copy of the document entitled "J.B. No. 355 (Serial 691) (Strategic Estimate)."
37.	Another copy of a letter from Lieutenant Colonel E. E. MacMorland to Colonel Orlando Ward concerning Chinese aircraft requirements, with the notation "For the information of General Marshall, I am attaching a strategic estimate which I obtained from Mr. Currie, indicating the interest which the British should have in a strong Chinese Air Force on the flank of any attack on Singapore. I make this remark because I have heard that the British will be invited to attend the Joint Board meeting, and if diversions are seriously discussed, it would be very desirable to emphasize the importance of a Chinese Air Force to them."
38.	Letter from Lauchlin Currie, administrative assistant to the president, to General G. C. Marshall, Chief of Staff, May 12, 1941.
39.	Note from Lieutenant Colonel W. P. Scobey on behalf of the Joint Army/Navy Board to the Joint Planning Committee, forwarding enclosures (a) and (b) for consideration with reference to (a), previously transmitted."
40.	Memorandum to the Secretary of War from Major General Henry H. Arnold, May 10, 1941, concerning aircraft requirements of the Chinese government.
41.	Confidential Memorandum from Henry L. Stimson, Secretary of War, to the Joint Army/Navy Board, May 13, 1941, identical to an earlier version of this document, except there is a notation "Enclosure (A)" on the bottom of the document.
42.	Memorandum for Mr. Lovett from H. H. Arnold, Major General, Deputy Chief of Staff (air), June 11, 1941, concerning status of Chinese requests for aid.
43.	Secret Memorandum from the Joint Planning Committee from the Joint Army/Navy Board, July 9, 1941, concerning aircraft requirements for the Chinese government.
44.	Secret Memorandum from the Joint Army/Navy Board to the Secretary of War, July 14, 1941, recommending that the subject report be approved and forwarded to the president.
45.	Letter from Acting Secretary of War and the Secretary of the Navy to President Roosevelt, July 18, 1941, recommending for the President's approval the Joint Planning Committee Report of July 9, 1941, J.B.

	No. 355 (Serial 691), with the notation in the bottom left-hand corner: "July 23, 1941 OK—but restudy military mission versus the attaché method."
46.	Handwritten note from Admiral Turner to Lieutenant Colonel Scobey.
47.	Confidential Memorandum from Admiral H. R. Stark, to the Joint Board of July 14, 1941, recommending that the provision of aircraft to the Chinese government be approved by the board and then forwarded to the president for his consideration.
48.	Secret Memorandum from McDowell, Secretary, War Plans Division, July 16, 1941, concerning approval of Joint Board paper indicating that J.B. No. 355 (Serial 691)—Aircraft Requirements of Chinese Government—was approved by the Secretary of the Navy, Frank Knox, on July 15, 1941.
49.	Secret Memorandum for the Chief of Staff, July 16, 1941, from Lieutenant Colonel W. P. Scobey, concerning approval of Joint Board Serial by the Secretary of the Navy.
50.	Confidential Memorandum for Lauchlin Currie from Lieutenant Colonel W. P. Scobey, July 18, 1941, concerning aircraft requirements for the Chinese government, with the following comment: "This report has been approved by the Joint Board and the Secretaries of War and the Navy. It was transmitted to the White House for the President's consideration July 18, 1941 [sic]."
51.	Letter from Colonel Orlando Ward to the Secretary of the Joint Board, July 18, 1941, relating: ". . . joint letter to the President was signed by the Acting Secretary of War and Secretary of the Navy dated July 18 and was given to the Secretary of the Joint Board for transmission to the President . . ."
52.	Confidential Memorandum for the Chief of Naval Operations from Lieutenant Colonel W. P. Scobey, July 19, 1941, relating: ". . . You are advised that the following Joint Board Serial was approved July 18, 1941 [sic] by the Acting Secretary of War, Mr. Patterson: J.B. No. 355 (Serial 691)—Aircraft Requirements of the Chinese Government."
53.	Letter from Lieutenant Colonel W. P. Scobey to the Chief of Naval Operations, July 23, 1941, relating: ". . . The President approved the subject study on July 23, 1941, by endorsing on the Letter of Transmittal . . ."
54.	Secret Memorandum from Lieutenant Colonel W. P. Scobey to the Chief of Staff, July 23, 1941, concerning aircraft requirements of the Chinese government, relating: ". . . The President approved the study subject on July 23, 1941 by [sic] endorsing on the Letter of Transmittal . . ."

55.	Confidential Memorandum for Admiral Turner from Lieutenant Colonel W. P. Scobey, August 28, 1941, with the following closing paragraph: "May I say in this connection that my records of this case indicate that my action as Secretary in connection with this paper was complete. I feel that a failure on the part of either the War or Navy Department to implement approved recommendations is no fault of mine."
56.	Page bearing the following notations: "Reproduced from the holdings at the Franklin D. Roosevelt Library . . . small collections . . . Joint Board No. 355—Aircraft Requirements of the Chinese Govern ment . . . 98 pp."
57.	Single page bearing the following inscriptions: "Reproduced at the National Archives—J.B. No. 355 (Serial 691) AIRCRAFT REQUIREMENTS OF THE CHINESE GOVERNMENT . . . "

APPENDIX 4

A Clash of Power between America and Japan in 1940–1941

Factors Encouraging Japan's Expansion in Southeast Asia	Factors Encouraging a Preemptive Strike by America Against Japan
1. There was a vacuum in military power in Southeast Asia in 1940–41, since France and Holland had fallen to Germany, and Britain was fighting for her survival.	1. Japan signed the Tripartite Pact with Germany and Italy on September 27, 1940.
2. Japan signed a non-aggression pact with Russia on April 13, 1941.	2. Japan had conquered large areas of China and was pulling out ten crack divisions to invade Malaya, Singapore, and the Dutch East Indies.
3. Germany invaded Russia on June 22, 1941.	3. Japan invaded French Indochina (now Vietnam) on July 24, 1941, giving her air bases for offensive operations against China, Thailand, Malaya, and Burma.
4. The American Trade Embargo of July 26, 1941, cut off Japan's oil supply, leaving her with oil reserves to last eighteen months.	4. Japan had air bases on Formosa and Hainan within easy striking distance of American air bases in the Philippines.
5. There were vast supplies of oil and rubber in the Dutch East Indies and Malaya to replace the materials Japan could no longer purchase from America.	5. If war broke out in the Pacific or Southeast Asia with Japan, the ABCD Nations—America, Britain, China, and the Dutch—would join together to fight Japan.
6. Japanese military leaders believed that destruction of the American Pacific fleet would lead to a negotiated peace between Japan and America.	6. Airfields in Eastern China would place B-17 Flying Fortress and Lockheed Hudson bombers within striking distance of Japan.

APPENDIX 5

Timeline—The Road to War

• **September 18, 1931:** A bomb blew up a section of Japanese railroad near Mukden. Japan used the "Mukden Incident" as an excuse to annex Manchuria.[1]

• **July 7, 1937:** Claiming they were searching for a missing soldier, Japanese troops entered Yuanping County. Chinese resistance led to the outbreak of the Sino-Japanese War.[2]

• **December 7, 1937:** Nanking, the capital of China, fell to the Japanese. The Japanese army embarked on a massacre in which approximately 300,000 Chinese were brutally slaughtered. This incident is remembered as "The Rape of Nanking."[3]

• **December 12, 1937:** The USS *Panay* is attacked and sunk by Japanese aircraft, killing several Americans, despite the fact that the American flag was prominently displayed.

• **January 17, 1940:** Bruce Leighton (Lieutenant Commander USNR, ret.), a business associate of William Pawley's, visited the United States Navy Department, Office of Chief of Naval Operations (CNO). Leighton advocated the formation, as a commercial venture, of an efficient guerrilla air corps in China under the auspices of Intercontinent Corporation, an American firm selling aircraft to China.[4]

• **March 30, 1940:** Japan set up a puppet government in Nanking.[5]

• **July 16, 1940:** The French closed the Yunnan Railway under pressure by Japan. Immediately after it was closed, America placed an embargo on the sale of aviation fuel to Japan.[6]

• **August 2, 1940:** Japan demanded transit rights for its troops and use of airfields in French Indochina.[7]

• **August 18, 1940:** The Burma Road was closed for a short period because the British were concerned about retaliation by Japan.[8]

---

[1] See *Mukden Incident*, discussed at http://www.fact index.com/m/mu/mukden_incident.html.
[2] See *The War Breaks Out!!*, discussed at http://www.hkuhist2.hku.hk/studentprojects/japan /1997b/jap6.htm.
[3] See Iris Chang, *The Rape of Nanking—The Forgotten Holocaust of World War II*, New York: Penguin Books, 1998 ("Chang"), p. 38.
[4] See Exhibits 5, 6, and 7 identified in Appendix 3 to this text.
[5] See *The Encyclopedia of World History*, displayed at http://www.bartleby.com/67/2624.html confirming Japan supported the establishment of a puppet government under Wang Ching-wei on March 30, 1940.
[6] Christopher Shores and Brian Cull with Yasuho Izawa, *Bloody Shambles, Volume I—The Drift to War to the Fall of Singapore*, London: Grub Street, 1992 ("Bloody Shambles, Volume I"), p. 24.
[7] *Ibid.*
[8] *Ibid.*, p. 25. Also, see secret memorandum from British General Headquarters in the Far East to General Douglas MacArthur, September 19, 1941, discussed *infra*.

• **August 30, 1940:** Japan recognized French sovereignty over Indochina in return for economic and military concessions.[9]

• **September 27, 1940:** The Tripartite Pact was signed by Japan, Germany, and Italy.[10]

• **September 1940:** The United States placed an embargo on the sale of scrap iron to Japan.[11]

• **October 1940:** Japan coerced the Dutch government into an agreement whereby 75 to 100 percent of the exports from the Dutch East Indies would be sold to Japan, especially oil.[12]

• **November 1940:** America imposed an embargo on the sale of tin and steel to Japan.[13]

• **December 12, 1940:** Chiang Kai-shek sent a telegram to President Roosevelt thanking the United States for a "substantial loan to China," at a time when America was ostensibly neutral in the Sino-Japanese War.[14]

• **December 21, 1940:** Captain Claire Chennault presented his plan for preemptive strikes on Japan to Henry Morgenthau, secretary of the Treasury.[15]

• **December 23, 1940:** The Roosevelt administration authorized the diversion of one hundred Curtiss Tomahawk fighter planes previously allocated to Britain for sale to China.[16]

• **February 2, 1941:** Commander Minoru Genda was ordered to develop plans for a surprise attack on Pearl Harbor.[17]

• **February 3, 1941:** William Pawley and Captain Claire Chennault reached an agreement with Curtiss-Wright Aircraft Company to purchase one hundred Curtiss Tomahawk fighter planes for export to China.[18]

• **April 13, 1941:** A non-aggression pact was signed between Japan and Russia.[19]

• **April 14, 1941:** Captain Frank Beatty, aide to Navy Secretary Frank Knox, wrote letters of introduction for Claire Chennault and Rutledge Irvine to visit naval air stations and recruit pilots and technicians for service in China.[20]

---

[9] *Ibid.*, p. 24.
[10] *Ibid.*, p. 27.
[11] *Ibid.*, p. 27.
[12] *Bloody Shambles, Volume I*, p. 30.
[13] *Ibid.*
[14] See Exhibit 13 identified in Appendix 1 to this text.
[15] See Exhibit 18 identified in Appendix 1 to this text.
[16] See Exhibits 17, 18, and 19 identified in Appendix 1 to this text. Also see Ford, p. 48, and Craig Nelson, *The First Heroes—The Extraordinary Story of the Doolittle Raid—America's First World War II Victory*, New York: Penguin Books, 2003 ("Nelson"), p. 105.
[17] See Chapter 13, Section 2 of this text.
[18] See Exhibit 2 identified in Appendix 2 to this text.
[19] See World War Two and the Soviet Union, discussed at http://www.worldwarhistory.info/in/USSR.html.
[20] See Exhibits 3 and 4 identified in Appendix 2 to this text.

• **June 22, 1941:** Germany invaded Russia.[21]

• **June 23, 1941:** Indochina was proclaimed a joint Franco-Japanese protectorate by Japan and the Vichy French government.[22]

• **July 8, 1941:** Before departing San Francisco, Chennault received a telegram from Lauchlin Currie, aide to President Roosevelt, indicating America would be providing China with a Second American Volunteer Group, including bombers, one hundred pilots, and 181 gunners and radiomen by November 1941.[23]

• **July 9, 1941:** A United Press correspondent in San Francisco filed this dispatch:

"Thirty United States airplane mechanics and maintenance men arrived here today from New York, and will go to Rangoon next week en route to [China], where they will aid the Chinese Air Force. It was understood that a number of American planes of various types already have arrived at Rangoon and that more were en route there."[24]

• **July 10, 1941:** Members of the First American Volunteer Group sailed from San Francisco aboard the Dutch ship *Jagersfontein*. West of Hawaii, the ship was escorted by two United States cruisers, *Salt Lake City* and *Northampton*. En route, a Japanese radio announcer declared that the ship would not reach its destination, but would be sunk.[25]

• **July 23, 1941:** President Roosevelt endorsed Joint [Army/Navy] Board 355, Serial 691 providing for a Second American Volunteer Group, including Lockheed Hudson and Douglas DB-7 Bombers.[26] On the same day, Dr. Lauchlin Currie sent a telegram to the American Embassy in Chungking for delivery to Madame Chiang, declaring China would receive sixty-six bombers during 1941, with twenty-four being delivered immediately.[27]

• **July 24, 1941:** Japan invaded French Indochina.[28]

• **July 26, 1941:** The United States froze all Japanese assets in America.[29] Chennault inspected Kyedaw Airfield, a Royal Air Force facility in Burma, a British colony, where the First American Volunteer Group could engage in flight training.[30]

---

[21] *Bloody Shambles, Volume I*, p. 31.
[22] *Ibid.*
[23] Claire Lee Chennault, *Way of a Fighter*, New York: G.P. Putnam's Sons, 1949 ("Fighter"), p. 104.
[24] Ford, p. 64.
[25] *Fighter*, p. 104. The author personally verified that the *Jagersfontein* sailed from San Francisco on July 10, 1941. See the document entitled: "Jagersfontein DU M/S 1941 R.J.R. Brauwer 6164" a copy of which was obtained by the author from the San Francisco Maritime Museum.
[26] See Exhibits 44 and 45 identified in Appendix 3 to this text.
[27] Telegram from Dr. Lauchlin Currie to the American Embassy in Chungking, July 23, 1941.
[28] See *The Second World War Chronology*, adapted from Olivier Zunz appearing at http://astro.temple.edu/~kilsdouk/wwii.htm.
[29] See *Bloody Shambles, Volume I*, p. 31, where it is reported the United States froze all Japanese assets on July 25, 1941.
[30] See Ford, p. 69, regarding Chennault's inspection of Kyedaw Airfield on July 26, 1941.

• **July 28, 1941:** Japanese troops arrived in Saigon, French Indochina.[31]

• **August 1, 1941:** A total trade embargo on Japan was imposed by America, supported by the British and the Dutch.[32] Also, Generalissimo Chiang Kai-shek issued Order Number 5987, declaring:

1) The First American Volunteer Group is constituted this date.

2) Colonel Chennault will organize this Group with the American Volunteers now arriving in China to participate in the war. Additional personnel required to complete the organization of this group shall be supplied by the commission.[33]

• **September 6, 1941:** There was an imperial conference among key figures in the Japanese government who resolved that America must relent in its economic embargos, or Japan would go to war with America. The presence of an American military mission, along with the American Volunteer Group, was submitted to be proof of an alliance between China and the United States against Japan.[34]

• **September 12–13, 1941:** Chart maneuvers of the Combined Fleet were conducted at the Naval Staff College in Japan. These maneuvers related to the surprise attack on Pearl Harbor.[35]

• **September 19, 1941:** A secret memorandum entitled "The Problem of Defeating Japan—Review of the Situation" was provided by British General Headquarters in the Far East to American general Douglas MacArthur in the Philippines, advocating air and submarine attacks against Japanese forces and the positioning of "mobile forces as near Japan as practicable." The memorandum confirmed air bases in China were being prepared and stocked.[36]

• **September 30, 1941:** President Roosevelt sent a secret memorandum to Navy Secretary Knox and Secretary of War Stimson, advising that in addition to the 100 Curtiss P-40 fighters already provided to China, America would be delivering in the next few months 269 pursuit planes and 66 bombers.[37]

• **October 1, 1941:** Genda was summoned to the flagship headquarters of Admiral Nagumo.[38]

---

[31] *Bloody Shambles, Volume I*, p. 31.
[32] *Ibid.*
[33] *Ibid.*, p. 72.
[34] *Ibid.*, p. 87. Also see p. 31 discussing the Imperial Conference. The Imperial Conference is also discussed in other texts, to wit: Layton, p. 152.
[35] See Chapter 13, Section 2 of this text.
[36] Memorandum from British General Headquarters in the Far East to General Douglas MacArthur, September 19, 1941.
[37] See Exhibit 15 identified in Appendix 2 to this text.
[38] See Chapter 13, Section 2 of this text.

• **October 3, 1941:** Chart maneuvers of the Combined Fleet of the Japanese navy were conducted aboard the *Nagato*.[39]

• **October 24, 1941:** Three squadron leaders in the First American Volunteer Group flew from Kyedaw Airfield in Burma to Chiang Mai, Thailand, scouting for Japanese aircraft.[40]

• **October 26, 1941:** A Japanese reconnaissance aircraft flew over the First AVG's training base at Kyedaw Airfield. Five P-40 Tomahawks were dispatched to intercept it, but failed.[41]

• **October 27, 1941:** Eriksen Shilling, a pilot in the Second Squadron of the First AVG, observed five silver aircraft. Chennault assumed they were Japanese intruders, since all allied aircraft had camouflage paint schemes. The Japanese aircraft had flown from Hanoi, French Indochina, to scout the First AVG training base.[42]

• **October 31, 1941:** The *United States News* published a story entitled BOMBER LANES TO JAPAN, which included a graphic illustration depicting a circle around Tokyo. Bomber routes with flying times were illustrated, among others, with flying times from Hong Kong and Chungking.[43]

• **November 2, 1941:** The task force that would attack Pearl Harbor assembled at Ariake Bay, where maneuvers were carried out against Saeki and Sukumo as targets simulating Pearl Harbor.[44]

• **November 14, 1941:** General Marshall declared to a group of reporters that America was preparing for an offensive war against Japan. The weapons would be America's B-17 Flying Fortresses. The bombers would set Japanese cities on fire.[45]

• **November 17, 1941:** Imperial Japanese Navy Task Force Order Number One was printed and distributed prior to the departure of the task force from Saeki Bay.[46]

• **November 17, 1941:** Imperial Japanese navy ships left Saeki Bay at intervals in scattered groups and assembled at Hitokappu Bay on November 22, 1941.[47]

• **November 19, 1941:** The *New York Times* published an article by Arthur Krock entitled PHILIPPINES AS A FORTRESS. This article featured an illustration

---

[39] *Ibid.*
[40] Ford, p. 83.
[41] *Ibid.*
[42] *Ibid.*
[43] See *The United States News, October 31, 1941*, pp. 18–19, the article entitled BOMBER LANES TO JAPAN—FLYING TIME FROM STRATEGIC POINTS.
[44] See Chapter 13, Section 2 of this text.
[45] Ford, p. 93. The date of this event has also been reported as November 5, 1941. See Nelson, p. 81.
[46] See Chapter 13, Section 2 of this text.
[47] *Ibid.*

with Tokyo in the center, along with the distances from bases where attacks by American bombers could be launched. The article included the following language:

"Before Mr. Kurusu (the Japanese ambassador) leaves Washington, he may have been officially acquainted with these circumstances of war-making in the Far Pacific area, for official transmission to his government, which is considering the grave question of peace or war."[48]

• **November 21, 1941:** A secret memorandum for the American Secretary of War concerning an "Air Offensive against Japan" was issued. It concerned a request from G-2 in the Philippines (where two heavy bombardment groups of American bombers were stationed) for bombing objectives in Japan.

Also, members of the Second American Volunteer Group sailed from San Francisco, California, aboard the *Noordam* and *Bloemfontein*. The Central Aircraft Manufacturing Company (CAMCO) owned by William Pawley and H. H. Kung (Chiang Kai-shek's brother) had hired 82 pilots and 359 technicians for the Second AVG. Thirty-three DB-7 Bostons were being shipped, or would be shipped, to Africa, where they would be assembled and flown to Burma. Thirty-three Lockheed Hudsons were to have long-range fuel tanks installed and be flown across the Pacific to serve under the command of Claire Chennault. Vultee Vanguard fighter planes to be operated by a Third AVG were being allocated for provision to China.[49]

• **November 24, 1941:** Task Force Order Number Three, which was the plan of attack on Pearl Harbor, was completed and distributed to all other ships, together with Order Number One.[50]

• **November 26, 1941:** Japanese Task Force sailed from Hitokappu Bay for the attack on Pearl Harbor.[51]

• **December 7, 1941, 7:53 A.M. (in Hawaii):** The Japanese carried out their surprise attack on Pearl Harbor. One half hour before the attack, Churchill had drafted a telegram to Roosevelt seeking confirmation that America would support Britain if Britain made a preemptive strike on the Japanese.[52]

• **December 7, 1941: 2:05 P.M.:** Japanese ambassadors Saburo Kurusu and [Admiral] Kichisaburō Nomura delivered a message to Secretary of State Cordell Hull severing diplomatic relations with the United States.[53]

---

[48] See the *New York Times*, November 18, 1941, and the article PHILIPPINES AS A FORTRESS—NEW AIR POWER GIVES ISLANDS OFFENSIVE STRENGTH, CHANGING STRATEGY IN THE PACIFIC, by Arthur Krock.
[49] See Chapter 11, Sections 1 and 4 and Chapter 12, Section 4 of this text.
[50] See Chapter 13, Section 2 of this text.
[51] *Ibid.*
[52] See Layton, p. 311. A copy of Churchill's "draft" of a telegram to Lord Halifax is the seventh appendix to Layton.
[53] See Prange, p. 554.

ENDNOTES

1. Henry Morgenthau Jr. Diary 342A, China Bombers, December 3–22, 1940 ("Morgenthau Diary").

2. Martha Byrd, *Chennault: Giving Wings to the Tiger*, Tuscaloosa: University of Alabama Press, 1987 ("Byrd"), p. 60.

3. Claire Lee Chennault, *Way of a Fighter*, New York: G. P. Putnam's Sons, 1949 (*"Fighter"*) p. 29; Byrd, p. 60; and Daniel Ford, *Flying Tigers—Claire Chennault and the American Volunteer Group*, Washington: Smithsonian Institution Press, 1991 (hereinafter "Ford"), p. 17. While *Fighter* relates the farewell performance was in 1936 at the Pan-American Air Maneuvers, the evidence suggests it was on December 11–14, 1935. See Byrd and also e-mail from Daniel Ford to the author of May 7, 2004.

4. Telephone interview of Rosemary Chennault Simrall by the author, June 22, 2004.

5. Chester G. Hearn, *The Illustrated Directory of the United States Navy*, London: Salamander Books, Ltd., 2003 ("Hearn"), p. 174.

6. *Ibid.*

7. *Ibid.*

8. Byrd, p. 60.

9. "The Role of Defensive Pursuit," Air Force Historical Research Agency (AFHRA), Document Number 248.282.4 (hereinafter "Defensive Pursuit").

10. Byrd, p. 60.

11. *Ibid.*

12. *Ibid.*, p. 61.

13. *Ibid.*, p. 62.

14. *Ibid.*

15. *Ibid.*, p. 63.

16. *Ibid.*, p. 64.

17. *Ibid.*

18. *Ibid.*, p. 65.

19. Ford, p. 19.

20. *Ibid.*

21. See Barbara Tuchman, *Stilwell and the American Experience in China*, New York: McMillan, 1970 ("Tuchman").

22. See Patrick Laureau, *Condor: The Luftwaffe in Spain 1936–1939*, East Yorkshire: Hikoki Publications, Ltd., 2000 ("Laureau").

23. Ford, p. 23.

24. *Ibid.*

25. *Ibid.*

26. *Ibid.*, p. 25.

27. *Ibid.*

28. Warren M. Bodie, *The Lockheed P-38 Lightning*, Hayesville, NC: Widewing Publications, 1991 (hereinafter *"Lightning"*).

29. *Ibid.*

30. Report of interview with Commander Bruce G. Leighton, USNR, by Major Rodney A. Boone, USMC, January 17, 1940 ("Boone Report"), p. 2.

31. Henry Stimson was Secretary of War during the time in question. However, the Joint Board's recommendation to President Roosevelt of July 18, 1941, was signed by Acting Secretary of War Robert Patterson and Navy Secretary Frank Knox. See Exhibit 45 to Appendix 3, Joint Board Papers.

32. Byrd, p.107.

33. *Fighter*, p. 96.

34. Anderson would be in command of the battleships anchored at Pearl Harbor on December 7, 1941.

35. Boone Report, p. 1.

36. Apparently, Leighton referred to activities of CAMCO, Intercontinent's subsidiary, as those of Intercontinent.

37. *Ibid.* Clearly, "Lowning" was meant to be Loiwing.

38. *Ibid.*

39. *Ibid.*

40. *Ibid.*

41. This is most likely a reference to the Vultee A-19 attack plane which never served in great numbers in the Army Air Corps. It was a single-engine, three seat [pilot, bombardier/navigator, gunner] powered by an in-line engine that carried a bomb load of approximately 1,000 pounds. It was exported to, among other countries, China.

42. This was a reference to the export version, the Curtiss-Hawk Model H75 derivative of the Army Air Corps P-36 aircraft.

43. This is a reference to a low-wing monoplane designed by Curtiss-Wright known as the CW-21. Lightweight in construction and powered by an engine developing approximately 1000 horsepower, these aircraft enjoyed dramatic climb performance. They were, however, lacking in self-sealing fuel tanks or protection for the pilot. They were operated by the air forces of China and the Netherlands East Indies.

44. Boone Report.

45. *Ibid.*

46. *Ibid.*

47. Major Rodney A. Boone served in the Office of Naval Intelligence (ONI), Far Eastern Section under Lieutenant Commander Arthur McCollum.

48. Boone Report.

49. *Ibid.*

50. *Ibid.*

51. *Ibid.*

52. *Ibid.*

53. *Ibid.*

54. *Ibid.*

55. Confidential Memorandum for the Chief of Naval Operations, January 17, 1940, from Admiral W. S. Anderson (the "Anderson Memorandum"), Joint Board Papers.

56. Admiral James O. Richardson, who had preceded Kimmel as the commander of the American Pacific fleet, wrote the orders relieving Stark of his duties as chief of naval operations.

57. Anderson Memorandum.

58. See the one-page document marked "Confidential" in the folder of Joint Board 355 immediately after the Anderson Memorandum (the "Leighton Memorandum").

59. Leighton Memorandum.

60. *Ibid.*

61. *Ibid.*, emphasis added.

62. Robert B. Stinnett, *Day of Deceit—The Truth About FDR and Pearl Harbor*, New York: Simon & Schuster, 2000 (hereinafter, "Stinnett"), p. 7.

63. *Ibid.*

64. *Ibid.*, Appendix A, p. 275.

65. *Fighter*, p. 91.

66. Letter from William D. Pawley to Claire Chennault, January 31, 1939; Richard L. Dunn, monograph, "Curtiss-Wright CW-21 Interceptor."

67. Lauchlin Currie was Canadian by birth, studied economics at the London School of Economics, and obtained his doctorate from Harvard.

68. See Herbert Rowerstein and Eric Breindel, *The Venona Secrets—Exposing Soviet Espionage and America's Traitors*, Washington: Regnery Publishing, Inc., 2001.

69. *Ibid.*

70. See Memorandum of Secretary of the Treasury Henry Morgenthau (Morgenthau), December 8, 1940, Henry Morgenthau Jr. Diary Book 342A—China Bombers: December 3–22, 1940 ("Morgenthau Diary") identified as Exhibit 4 in Appendix 1.

71. See Secret Memorandum from the Chinese Government, November 30, 1940, Morgenthau Diary ("China's Secret Memorandum, November 30, 1940"), identified as Exhibit 5 in Appendix 1.

72. *Ibid.*

73. *Fighter*, p. 92.

74. See Iris Chang. *The Rape of Nanking—The Forgotten Holocaust of World War II*, New York: Penguin Books, 1998 (hereinafter "Chang"), p.38.

75. See James Bradley, *Flyboys*, New York: Little, Brown and Company, 2003 (hereinafter "Bradley"), pp. 52–62.

76. *Ibid.*

77. *Ibid.*

78. Morgenthau Memorandum, December 8, 1940, Morgenthau Diary, identified as Exhibit 4 in Appendix 1. Two memoranda appear on Exhibit 4 in Appendix 1, the first dated December 7, 1940, and the second dated December 8, 1940.

79. See Secret Memorandum from the Chinese Government, November 30, 1940, identified as Exhibit 5 in Appendix 1 (hereinafter "China's Secret Memorandum").

80. *Ibid.*

81. Richard L. Dunn, "The Vultee P-66 in Chinese Service," Monograph, http://www.warbirdforum.com/dunnp66 htm, October 5, 2005.

82. *Ibid.*

83. China's Secret Memorandum.

84. *Ibid.*

85. *Ibid.*

86. *Ibid.*, emphasis added.

87. Handwritten letter from Dr. T. V. Soong to Morgenthau, dated December 9, 1940, (hereinafter the "Soong Letter"), Morgenthau Diary, identified as Exhibit 6 in Appendix 1.

88. *Ibid.*

89. *Ibid.*

90. Morgenthau Memorandum of December 10, 1940 (hereinafter the "Hull/Morgenthau Conference Memorandum") identified as Exhibit 9 in Appendix 1.

91. *Ibid.*

92. *Ibid.*

93. *Ibid.*

94. See Linda R. Robertson, *The Dream of Civilized Warfare—World War I Flying Aces and the American Imagination*, Minneapolis: University of Minnesota Press, 2003.

95. Memorandum of Morgenthau, December 3, 1940, confirming a meeting with Ambassador Lothian "yesterday" (the "Lothian/Morgenthau Memorandum"), identified as Exhibit 3 in Appendix 1.

96. *Ibid.*

97. Morgenthau's Memoranda, December 7 and 8, 1940, identified as Exhibit 4 in Appendix 1.

98. *Ibid.*

99. For a more complete discussion of the Battle of Britain, see: Peter Townsend, *Duel of Eagles*, Edison: Castle Books, 2003 ("Townsend"); Lynne Olson and Stanley Cloud, *A Question of Honor: The Kosciuszko Squadron—Forgotten Heroes of World War II*, New York: Alfred A. Knopf, 2003 ("Olson and Cloud"); Philip Kaplan and Richard Collier, *The Few—Summer 1940, The Battle of Britain*, London: Orion Publishing Group, 2002 ("Kaplan and Collier"); Norman Franks, *Battle of Britain*, New York: Gallery Books, 1981 ("Franks"); John Ray, *The Battle of Britain*, London: Cassell & Co., 1994, ("Ray"); Leonard Mosley, *The Battle of Britain*, Morristown: Time-Life Books, Inc., 1977 ("Mosley").

100. The Lothian/Morgenthau Memorandum, December 3, 1940, identified as Exhibit 3 in Appendix 1.

101. A. Scott Berg, *Lindbergh*, New York: G. P. Putnam's Sons, 1998 (hereinafter "Berg"), p. 387.

102. *Ibid.*, p. 357.

103. *Ibid.*, p. 386.

104. *Ibid.*, p. 387.

105. *Ibid.*

106. *Ibid.*

107. *Ibid.*, p. 388.

108. *Ibid.*, p. 389.

109. *Ibid.*, p. 393.

110. Von Hardesty, *Lindbergh—Flight's Enigmatic Hero*, San Diego: Tehabi Books, Inc., 2002 ("Hardesty"), p. 133.

111. Berg, p. 396.

112. *Ibid.*

113. *Ibid.*, pp. 396–97.

114. *Ibid.*, p. 397. Lindbergh, who had been awarded medals from nations throughout the world, was awarded the Service Cross of the German Eagle by Hermann Göring during a diplomatic dinner at the American embassy in Berlin on October 18, 1938. Hardesty, p. 132.

115. *Ibid.*

116. *Ibid.*, pp. 397–98.

117. *Ibid.*, p. 398.

118. Presidential address, September 21, 1939, "Recommending a Revision of the Neutrality Law" ("Presidential Address").

119. Berg, p. 399.

120. Hardesty, p. 133.

121. The United Kingdom spent £6,685,500,000 on non-munitions imports and £2,555,800 on munitions imports between 1940 and 1945. John Keegan, *Atlas of the Second World War*, Ann Arbor: Borders Press, 2003 ("Keegan").

122. Translation of Chinese telegram dated December 12, 1940, from General Chiang Kai-shek to President Roosevelt (the "Chiang Kai-shek Telegram"), RPL identified as Exhibit 13 in Appendix 1.

123. *Ibid.*

124. *Ibid.*

125. Translation of Chinese telegram from General Chiang Kai-shek to Secretary Morgenthau, dated Chungking, December 16, 1940 (the "Second Chiang Kai-shek Telegram"), identified as Exhibit 14 in Appendix 1.

126. *Ibid.*

127. See Note of Morgenthau, December 19, 1940, reciting: "After Cabinet, the Secretary gave Mr. Hull a copy of each of the two letters from General Chiang Kai-shek (the "Hull Note") identified as Exhibit 15 in Appendix 1 and Morgenthau's Memorandum of December 20, 1940, confirming a meeting with Dr. Soong, a Mr.

Young, and a Mrs. Klotz (the "Soong Meeting Memorandum") identified as Exhibit 16 in Appendix 1.

128. Morgenthau's memorandum of a phone conversation with President Roosevelt, December 18, 1940 (the "Roosevelt Phone Memorandum"), identified as Exhibit 10 in Appendix 1.

129. *Ibid.*

130. *Ibid.*

131. *Ibid.*

132. *Ibid.*

133. *Ibid.*

134. *Ibid.*

135. Memorandum of Morgenthau, December 18, 1940, concerning a phone conversation with Dr. Soong (the "First Soong Memorandum"), identified as Exhibit 11 in Appendix 1.

136. *Ibid.*

137. Morgenthau's memorandum of a second conversation with Dr. Soong on December 18, 1940 (the "Second Soong Memorandum"), identified as Exhibit 12 in Appendix 1.

138. *Ibid.*

139. Confidential oral statement appended to letter from the Division of Far Eastern Affairs of the Office of Secretary of State to Secretary Hull, December 3, 1940 ("The Oral Statement").

140. *Ibid.*

141. *Ibid.*

142. *Fighter*, p. 92.

143. The Soong Meeting Memorandum, identified as Exhibit 16 in Appendix 1.

144. This is believed to be a reference to the Consolidated Aircraft Corporation's Coronado four-engine patrol bomber.

145. The Soong Meeting Memorandum identified as Exhibit 16 in Appendix 1.

146. John Toland, *The Flying Tigers*, New York: Random House, 1963 (hereinafter, "Toland"), p. 4.

147. Byrd, p. 68

148. *Ibid.*, pp. 68–69.

149. See Robert Somerville, editor, with other contributors, *Century of Flight*, Richmond: Time Life Books, 1999, ("Somerville"), p. 108.

150. Transcript of telephone conversation between Frank Knox and Henry Morgenthau, December 20, 1940, 5:13 P.M. found at pages 20–23 of the Morgenthau Diary ("The Knox/Morgenthau phone conversation") identified as Exhibit 17 in Appendix 1.

151. Notes on conference at home of the secretary, 5:00 P.M., Saturday, December 21, 1940 (the "Bombing Mission Memorandum"), identified as Exhibit 18 in Appendix 1.

152. *Ibid.*

153. *Ibid.*

154. *Ibid.*

155. *Ibid.*

156. *Ibid.*

157. *Ibid.*

158. *Ibid.*

159. *Ibid.*

160. *Ibid.*

161. *Ibid.*

162. *Ibid.*

163. *Ibid.*

164. *Ibid.*

165. *Ibid.*

166. *Ibid.*

167. Morgenthau memorandum of meeting at Stimson's home, December 22, 1940 ("The Stimson Meeting"), identified as Exhibit 19 in Appendix 1.

168. *Ibid.*

169. Ford, pp. 47–48

170. The Stimson Meeting.

171. *Ibid.*

172. See Confidential Memorandum from Mr. Young to the Secretary, December 22, 1940, pages 29–31 of the Morgenthau Diary ("The Young Memorandum"), identified as Exhibit 20 in Appendix 1.

173. Berg, p. 413.

174. *Ibid.*, p. 412.

175. *Ibid.*, pp. 414–15.

176. *Ibid.*, p. 418.

177. *Ibid.*

178. *Ibid.*, p. 419.

179. *Ibid.*, p. 420.

180. *Ibid.* Further discussion of the conflict between Roosevelt and Lindbergh is found in Joseph E. Persico, *Roosevelt's Secret War—FDR and World War II Espionage*, New York: Random House, 2001 ("Persico"), pp. 39, 129.

181. Edwin P. Hoyt, *Japan's War—The Great Pacific Conflict*, New York, Cooper Square Press, 2001 ("Hoyt"), pp. 214, 475, fn. 8, Chapter 20.

182. Dan Van der Vat, *Pearl Harbor, The Day of Infamy: An Illustrated History*, Toronto: Basic Books, 2001 ("Van der Vat"), p. 19.

183. *Ibid.*, p. 20.

184. *Ibid.*

185. Affidavit of Minoru Genda, March 15, 1948. The text of Commander Genda's affidavit is published in *The Pearl Harbor Papers—Inside the Japanese Plans*, edited by Donald M. Goldstein and Catherine D. Dillon. Dulles, Virginia: Brassey's, 1993 (the *"Pearl Harbor Papers"*), p. 13.

186. *Ibid.*

187. Stinnett, p. 31.

188. Secret Memorandum from Navy Secretary Frank Knox to Secretary of War Stimson, January 24, 1941 (the "Knox Warning Memorandum").

189. *The Pearl Harbor Papers*, pp. 18–19.

190. *Ibid.*

191. *Ibid.*, p. 19.

192. *Ibid.*

193. Telegram to U.S. Department of State from Major James M. McHugh, February 10, 1941 ("McHugh Telegram").

194. *Ibid.*

195. McQuillen Report, p. 2.

196. See report of Major F. J. McQuillen, USMC, assistant naval attaché for air, circa early June 1941, and e-mail to author from Richard Dunn, Esq., December 16, 2005 ("McQuillen Report").

197. *Ibid.*, p. 4.

198. Ford, p. 350.

199. *Ibid.*

200. *Ibid.*

201 See Craig Nelson, *The First Heroes-The Extraordinary Story of the Doolittle Raid—America's First World War II Victory*, New York: Penguin Books, 2003 (hereinafter "Nelson"), p. 77.

202 Van der Vat, p. 26.

203. Nelson, p. 77.

204. Minutes of meeting of Steering Committee of the Expert Control Commodity Division of the U.S. Department of Commerce, dated April 22, 1941 ("Steering Committee Minutes"), National Archives, FEA. Administrator of Export Control, Box 698, Entry 88.

205. *Ibid.*

206. Hoyt, p. 194.

207. Secret Memorandum for President Roosevelt, the Commander-in-Chief, from Captain W. R. Purnell, U.S. Navy Chief of Staff, United States Asiatic Fleet, USS *Houston*, May 13, 1941, regarding "Certain Strategic Considerations in Connection with Orange War—Rainbow III" ("Orange War—Rainbow III"), Franklin D. Roosevelt Library: Small Collections: FDR Library: Misc.: Joint Board 355 ("Joint Board Papers") (hereinafter, the "Purnell Memorandum").

208. *Ibid.*

209 *Ibid.*

210. *Ibid.*

211. *Ibid.*

212. *Ibid.*

213. *Ibid.*

214. *Ibid.*

215. *Ibid.*

216. *Ibid.*

217. *Ibid.*

218. *Ibid.*

219. *Ibid.*

220. *Ibid.*

221. *Ibid.*

222. *Ibid.*

223. *Ibid.*

224. *Ibid.*

225. *Ibid.*

226. *Ibid.*

227. Alan Schom, *The Eagle and the Rising Sun*, New York: W. W. Norton & Company, 2004 ("Schom"), p.107.

228. The Purnell Memorandum.

229. *Ibid.*

230. *Ibid.*

231. *Ibid.*

232. *Ibid.*

233. *Ibid.*

234. *Ibid.*

235. *Ibid.*

236. *Ibid.*

237. *Ibid.*

238. *Ibid.*

239. *Ibid.*

240. *Ibid.*

241. *Ibid.*

242. *Ibid.*, italics supplied.

243. *Fighter*, p. 93.

244. *Ibid.*

245. *Ibid.*, p. 94.

246. *Ibid.*

247. *Ibid.*

248. *Ibid.*

249. Charles F. Romanus and Riley Sunderland, *China-Burma-India Theater: Stilwell's Mission to China (United States Army in World War II)*, Washington, D.C., Office of the Chief of Military History, Department of the Army, 1953 ("Romanus and Sunderland"), p. 12.

250. See Bert Kinzey, "P-40 Warhawk in Detail," Volume 61," Peachtree City: Detail & Scale, Inc., 1999, p. 61, for the performance figures on the P-40B Tomahawk exported by Curtiss as the Model H81-A2 and designated by the RAF as the Tomahawk II and Tomahawk IIA (hereinafter "Kinzey/Warhawk").

251. The checklist procedures were derived from: 1) Royal Air Force. Pilot's Notes-Tomahawk I. Publication 2013A, n.d.; 2) Pilot Flight Manual for the Curtiss P-40 Warhawk, distributed by Aviation Publications of Appleton, Wisconsin, ISBN No. 0-87994-018-2; and 3) the U.S. Army Air Force training film entitled *Ways of the War Hawk* [sic], distributed by Historic Aviation, New Brighton, Minnesota.

252. *Fighter*, p. 102.

253. *Ibid.*

254. Daniel Whitney, *Vee's for Victory!: The Story of the Allison V-1710 Aircraft Engine, 1929–1948*. Atglen, Pa.: Shiffer Military History, 1998 ("Whitney").

255. *Ibid.*

256. Telephone interview of General David Lee "Tex" Hill by the author, January 7, 2003, (the "Hill Interview").

257. *Ibid.*

258. *Ibid.*

259. *Ibid.*

260. *Ibid.*

261. *Ibid.*

262. *Ibid.*

263. Charles Bond and Terry Anderson, *A Flying Tiger's Diary*, College Station: Texas A&M University Press, 1984 (hereinafter "Bond").

264. See Gregory Boyington, *Baa, Baa, Black Sheep*, New York: Putnam, 1958, (hereinafter "Boyington"); Bruce Gamble, *Black Sheep One—The Life of Gregory "Pappy" Boyington*, Novato: Presidio Press, Inc., 2000 (hereinafter "Gamble").

265. Michael Schaller, *The U.S. Crusade in China, 1938–1945*, New York: Columbia University Press, 1979 ("Schaller"), p. 84.

266. See U.S. Navy American Volunteer Group Papers, Record Group 4-9. Emil Buehler Naval Aviation Library, National Museum of Naval Aviation, Accession Number 1997.269 ("the Pensacola Papers").

267. See Statement of Commander Bruce Leighton, circa 1941 ("Leighton's Statement"), U.S. Navy American Volunteer Group Papers, Record Group 4.9, Emil Buehler Naval Aviation Library, National Museum of Naval Aviation, Accession Number 1997.269 ("the Pensacola Papers") described more fully as Exhibit 1 to Appendix 2 to this text.

268. *Ibid.*

269. *Ibid.*

270. *Ibid.*

271. *Ibid.*

272. *Ibid.* This is a reference to the repair facility of CAMCO at Loiwing.

273. *Ibid.*

274. *Ibid.*

275. While Leighton's Statement makes reference to the "formal agreement" as an appendix to his statement, the Pensacola Papers available to the author did not include a copy of that agreement.

276. See Exhibit 2 discussed in Appendix 2, the Pensacola Papers, Chennault's memorandum of introduction issued by Captain Beatty, April 14, 1941.

277. See Exhibit 3 discussed in Appendix 2, the Pensacola Papers, Irvine's memorandum of introduction issued by Captain Beatty, April 14, 1941.

278. See Leighton's Statement, Exhibit 1 to Appendix 2 of this text, the Pensacola Papers. According to Commander Leighton's Statement, the letters of introduction to Air Corps bases came from the "Office of Chief of the Air Corps."

279. *Ibid.*

280. *Ibid.*

281. *Ibid.* Leighton's Statement (Exhibit 1 discussed in Appendix 2, the Pensacola Papers) is in conflict with the Secret Memorandum from Admiral Nimitz to Navy Secretary Frank Knox dated August 15, 1941 (Exhibit 12 summarized in Appendix 2), which was issued when Admiral Nimitz took over the China Project from Captain Beatty. While Commander Leighton related that navy personnel would enjoy the *same* seniority as their contemporaries, Admiral Nimitz's view on this topic was that the volunteers would *not* accrue retirement benefits or seniority during the time they were members of the American Volunteer Group in China.

282. *Ibid.*

283. *Ibid.*

284. See Confidential Memorandum for the Secretary of the Navy from W. L. Keys, February 3, 1941, (the "Keys Memorandum") from the Pensacola Papers. See Exhibit 2 discussed in Appendix 2 to this text.

285. *Ibid.*, italics supplied.

286. *Ibid.*

287. *Ibid.*

288. *Ibid.*

289. *Ibid.*

290. Memorandum for the Commanding Officer, Naval Air Station Jacksonville from Captain Frank E. Beatty, aide to Secretary Knox, April 14, 1941 (the "Chennault Letter of Passage"), discussed as Exhibit 3 in Appendix 2, the Pensacola Papers.

291. Memorandum for the Commanding Officer, Jacksonville Naval Air Station from Captain Frank E. Beatty, aide to Secretary Knox, April 14, 1941 (the "Irvine Letter of Passage"), discussed as Exhibit 4 in Appendix 2, the Pensacola Papers.

292. *Fighter*, p. 102.

293. Duane Schultz, *The Maverick War: Chennault and the Flying Tigers*, New York: St. Martin's Press, 1987 (hereinafter "*The Maverick War*"), p. 10, italics supplied. Also see, Toland, p. 16: "On April 15, 1941, the President signed an unpublished executive order. It authorized reserve officers and enlisted men to resign from the Army Air Corps, the Naval and Marine services so they could join Chennault's American Volunteer Group."

294. Telephone interview with Robert Parks of The Roosevelt Presidential Library by Alan Armstrong on May 12, 2003.

295. Letter from Captain Beatty to Captain James Shoemaker, August 4, 1941 (the "Adair Introduction Letter"), summarized as Exhibit 5 in Appendix 2, the Pensacola Papers.

296. *Ibid.*, italics supplied.

297. "Chennault Is Sticking It Out In China," *Montgomery Advisor*, August 31, 1937.

298. See Secret Memorandum from Commander J. B. Lynch to Admiral Chester W. Nimitz, August 7, 1941 (the "Lynch Memorandum"), summarized as Exhibit 6 in Appendix 2, the Pensacola Papers.

299. *Ibid.*, italics supplied.

300. *Ibid.*, italics supplied.

301. *Ibid.*, italics supplied.

302. *Ibid.*

303. *Ibid.*

304. *Ibid.*

305. *Ibid.*

306. *Ibid.*

307. *Ibid.*, italics supplied.

308. Letter from Aubrey W. Fitch, Commander Carrier Division I, USS *Saratoga*, to the Chief of the Bureau of the Aeronautics, August 7, 1941 (the "Fitch Letter"), summarized as Exhibit 7 to Appendix 2, the Pensacola Papers.

309. *Ibid.*

310. *Ibid.*

311. Secret Memorandum from Captain H. N. Briggs to the Chief of the Bureau of Navigation of the United States Navy, August 8, 1941 (the "Briggs Memorandum"), summarized as Exhibit 8 in Appendix 2, the Pensacola Papers.

312. *Ibid.*

313. *Ibid.*

314. *Ibid.*

315. *Ibid.*

316. *Ibid.*

317. *Ibid.*

318. See Memorandum for the Admiral, August 14, 1941, from H. G. Hopwood, August 14, 1941 with a handwritten inscription on the margin of the document which reads: "Admiral Dunfield, AVN, Harry M. Geselbracht, No. 83389, Secret Memo dated 8/15/41, personal safe of the Chief of BuNav" (the "Hopwood Memorandum"), summarized as Exhibit 9 in Appendix 2, the Pensacola Papers.

319. Confidential Memorandum from Captain Frank E. Beatty to Secretary Frank Knox, August 15, 1941, regarding "Release of Naval Personnel for Ultimate Employment by the Chinese Government" (the "Beatty Memorandum"), Exhibit 10 in Appendix 2, the Pensacola Papers.

320. *Ibid.*

321. *Ibid.*

322. *Ibid.*

323. *Ibid.*

324. *Ibid.*, italics supplied.

325. *Ibid.*, italics supplied.

326. Handwritten note by C. W. Nimitz, August 18, 1941 (the "Nimitz Note"), identified as Exhibit 11 in Appendix 2, the Pensacola Papers.

327. *Ibid.*

328. *Ibid.*

329. *Ibid.*

330. *Ibid.*

331. Memorandum for Admiral Nimitz from Commander J. B. Lynch, August 19, 1941, regarding "Releases and Resignations to Accept Employment with Central Aircraft Manufacturing Co." (the "Lynch Memorandum"), discussed as Exhibit 13 in Appendix 2, the Pensacola Papers.

332. *Ibid.*

333. Secret Memorandum for the Secretary of the Navy from Admiral C. W. Nimitz, August 15, 1941, regarding "Release of Naval Personnel for Ultimate Employment by the Chinese Government" (the "Nimitz Memorandum"), discussed as Exhibit 12 in Appendix 2, the Pensacola Papers.

334. *Ibid.*

335. Leighton Statement, italics supplied.

336. Nimitz Memorandum, italics supplied.

337. Lynch Memorandum to Nimitz, August 7, 1941, italics supplied.

338. Nimitz Memorandum.

339. *Ibid.*

340. *Ibid.*

341. *Ibid.*

342. *Ibid.*

343. *Ibid.*

344. See Secret Memorandum from Franklin D. Roosevelt to Navy Secretary Frank Knox, September 30, 1941 (the "Roosevelt Secret Memorandum"), discussed as Exhibit 15 in Appendix 2, the Pensacola Papers.

345. *Ibid.*, italics supplied.

346. Letter from Harry Claiborne to Admiral C. W. Nimitz, Chief of Bureau of Navigation, October 4, 1941 (the "Claiborne Letter") discussed as Exhibit 16 in Appendix 2, the Pensacola Papers.

347. *Ibid.*

348. Letter from Richard Aldworth to Dr. Laughlin [sic] Currie, October 4, 1941, cc: Admiral Chester Nimitz (the "Weekly Progress Letter"), discussed as Exhibit 17 in Appendix 2, the Pensacola Papers.

349. *Ibid.*

350. Confidential Memorandum for Admiral Nimitz, Captain V. D. Chapline, October 18, 1941, concerning pilots required and available—January through March, 1941 (the "Chapline Memorandum"), discussed as Exhibit 18 in Appendix 2, the Pensacola Papers.

351. *Ibid.*

352. Letter from Navy Secretary Frank Knox to Dr. Lauchlin Currie, Executive Office of the President, November 7, 1941 (the "Knox Letter"), discussed as Exhibit 19 in Appendix 2, the Pensacola Papers.

353. *Ibid.*

354. Letter from Lauchlin Currie, administrative assistant to the president, to Honorable Frank Knox, Secretary of the Navy, November 8, 1941, (the "Currie Letter"), discussed as Exhibit 20 in Appendix 2, the Pensacola Papers.

355. *Ibid.*

356. Memorandum for Admiral Nimitz from Navy Secretary Frank Knox, November 10, 1941, bearing notations at the bottom indicating: "1) Tower says OK to him, 2) it is OK with me, 3) I will prepare reply—CWN" (the "Knox Memorandum to Nimitz"), discussed as Exhibit 21 in Appendix 2, the Pensacola Papers.

357. Letter from Lauchlin Currie, administrative assistant to the president, to Rear Admiral C. W. Nimitz, chief of Bureau of Navigation, Navy Department, December 4, 1941 (the "Currie AVG Letter"), discussed as Exhibit 22 to Appendix 2, the Pensacola Papers.

358. Robert Smith Thompson, *A Time for War: Franklin D. Roosevelt and the Path to Pearl Harbor*, New York: Prentice Hall, 1991 ("Thompson"), p. 322.

359. During the Cold War, Dr. Lauchlin Currie fled the United States, took up residence in Columbia, and had his American citizenship revoked in 1956.

360. Currie's memorandum to Roosevelt of May 9, 1941, was published in the Pearl Harbor Hearings as Part 19, pages 3489–3495. RPL, President's Secretary's File, Diplomatic Correspondence, China: 1941, Box 27.

361. Letter from Dr. Lauchlin Currie to General George C. Marshall, May 12, 1941, identified as Exhibit 13 in Appendix 3 (the "Currie to Marshall Letter").

362. Memorandum from Lieutenant Colonel E. E. MacMorland of the Office of the War Department to Colonel Orlando Ward, secretary to the General Staff, May 12, 1941 (the "MacMorland Memorandum"), Joint Board Papers.

363. Documents consisting of four pages, beginning with the inscription "Strategic Estimate" following the MacMorland Memorandum (the "Strategic Estimate"), italics supplied, Joint Board Papers.

364. *Ibid.*, italics supplied.

365. *Ibid.*, italics supplied.

366. *Ibid.*

367. Letter from President Roosevelt to Dr. Lauchlin Currie, May 15, 1941 (the "Roosevelt Letter").

368. Memorandum for Mr. Lovett from Major General H. H. Arnold, deputy chief of staff for Air, June 11, 1941, regarding "Status of Chinese Requests for Aid" [sic], (the "Arnold Memorandum"), Joint Board Papers.

369. Strategic Estimate, Joint Board 355.

370. *Ibid.*

371. *Ibid.*

372. *Ibid.*

373. *Ibid.*

374. *Ibid.*

375. *Ibid.*

376. *Ibid.*

377. *Ibid.*

378. Japan and Russia signed a Neutrality Pact on April 13, 1941.

379. Strategic Estimate, Joint Board 355.

380. *Ibid.*

381. See Letter from Lauchlin Currie, administrative assistant to the president to Honorable Frank Knox, Secretary to the Navy, May 28, 1941 (the "Currie Letter"), Joint Board Papers, identified as Exhibit 33 in Appendix 3 to this text.

382. See documents entitled "Short-Term Aircraft Program for China," dated May 29, 1941 (one day after Dr. Currie's letter), ("A Short-term Aircraft Program for China"), Joint Board Papers, identified as Exhibit 32 in Appendix 3 to this text.

383. See President Roosevelt's Secret Memorandum, September 30, 1941, addressed to Secretary Frank Knox. A memorandum with identical text was dispatched to Secretary of War Henry Stimson, as discussed in Chapter Seven.

384. President Roosevelt's Secret Memorandum of September 30, 1941, as well as the Strategic Estimate included in Joint Board 355 (Serial 691) mention one hundred P-40s, either in China or en route to China. As discussed earlier, one P-40 fuselage was dropped into New York Harbor, leaving ninety-nine serviceable Tomahawks provided to China's Special Air Unit.

385. A Short-Term Aircraft Program for China.

386. *Ibid.*

387. *Ibid.*

388. *Ibid.*

389. *Ibid.*

390. *Ibid.*

391. *Ibid.*

392. *Way of a Fighter*, p. 107: "I recruited the rest of the staff from whatever American civilians happened to be available in India and China during the summer."

393. Arnold Memorandum, italics supplied.

394. Secret Memorandum for Chief of Staff regarding airplanes for China from Brigadier General L. D. Gerow, May 29, 1941 (the "Gerow Secret Memorandum"), Joint Board Papers, identified as Exhibit 17 in Appendix 3 to this text.

395. *Ibid.*

396. *Ibid.*

397. See Secret Radiogram No. 1135, June 14, 1941, 10:00 P.M. from Lieutenant General George Grunert in Manila to the War Department ("Grunert Radiogram"), Joint Board Papers, Exhibit 18, Appendix 3; Secret Memorandum from Brigadier General L. T. Gerow, Acting Assistant Chief of Staff for the War Department, June 1941 (the exact date is missing), (the "Gerow/Philippines Training Memorandum"), Joint Board Papers, Exhibit 19, Appendix 3.

398. Letter from W. L. Bond to Lauchlin Currie, June 6, 1941 (the "Bond Letter"), Joint Board Papers, Exhibit 21, Appendix 3.

399. Letter from Lauchlin Currie, assistant to the president, to Honorable Henry L. Stimson, Secretary of War, June 7, 1941 (the "China National Airways Letter"), Joint Board Papers, Exhibit 22, Appendix 3.

400. Confidential Memorandum of Kendall Perkins, chairman, Joint Aircraft Committee, Subcommittee on the Allocation of Deliveries, June 3, 1941, concerning Case No. 704, Addendum 1, PHR No. (none), 125 Republic P-43 aircraft for China (the "Perkins Memorandum"), Joint Board Papers, Exhibit 26, Appendix 3.

401. See letter of Lauchlin Currie, administrative assistant to the president, to Honorable Frank Knox, May 28, 1941, together with attachment "A Short-Term Aircraft Program for China, May 28, 1941" (the "Revised Request"), Joint Board Papers, Exhibit 33, Appendix 3.

402. Revised Short-Term Aircraft Program, Joint Board Papers, Exhibit 32, Appendix 3.

403. *Ibid.*

404. The Arnold Memorandum.

405. *Ibid.*

406. See report from the Joint Planning Committee of the Joint Board to the Joint Board, dated July 9, 1941, concerning Aircraft Requirements for the Chinese Government (the "Joint Planning Committee Report"), Joint Board Papers, Exhibit 43, Appendix 3.

407. See Secret Memorandum from Admiral Harold R. Stark, Chief of Naval Operations ("CNO") to Secretary of War Stimson, July 14, 1941 (the "Stark Memorandum"), Joint Board Papers, Exhibit 44, Appendix 3.

408. See Secret Letter from Acting Secretary of War Robert P. Patterson and Navy Secretary Frank Knox to President Roosevelt, July 18, 1941 (the "Patterson/Knox Letter"), Joint Board Papers, Exhibit 45, Appendix 3.

409. *Ibid.*

410. See Secret Memorandum from Lieutenant Colonel W. P. Scobey to the Chief of Naval Operations, July 23, 1941, concerning aircraft requirements to the Chinese government, and also Secret Memorandum from Lieutenant Colonel W. P. Scobey to the Chief of Staff, July 23, 1941, concerning aircraft requirements for the Chinese government ("Correctively, the Joint Board Authorization Memoranda"), Joint Board Papers, Exhibits 53 and 54, Appendix 3.

411. See Confidential Memorandum for Admiral Kelly Turner from Lieutenant Colonel W. P. Scobey, August 28, 1941, concerning J.B. No. 355 (serial 691)—Aircraft Requirements for the Chinese Government (the "Scobey Memorandum to Turner"), Joint Board Papers, Exhibit 55, Appendix 3.

412. *Ibid.*

413. *Ibid.*

414. Memorandum of Major James M. McHugh, USMC, June 9, 1941, concerning conference of Claggett air mission with the generalissimo (the "First McHugh Memorandum").

415. *Ibid.*

416. *Ibid.*, pp. 5, 9.

417. *Ibid.*

418. *Ibid.*

419. *Ibid.*

420. *Ibid.*

421. *Ibid.*, p. 3.

422. *Ibid.*

423. Memorandum of Major James M. McHugh, USMC, June 10, 1941, concerning the conference of the Claggett air mission and the generalissimo (the "Second McHugh Memorandum").

424. McQuillen Report.

425. *Ibid.*, p. 1.

426. *Ibid.*

427. *Ibid.*

428. *Ibid.*

429. *Ibid.*, p. 3.

430. *Ibid.*

431. *Ibid.*, p. 5.

432. *Ibid.*, p. 9.

433. *Ibid.*

434. *Ibid.*

435. Gordon W. Prange, *At Dawn We Slept—The Untold Story of Pearl Harbor*, New York: Penguin Books, 1982 ("Prange"), p.17.

436. Tokyo Circular No. 1139, May 29, 1941, to Japanese offices in Nanking, Shanghai, Peking, and Canton concerning message number 267 from Hong Kong on May 28, 1941 (the "First Tokyo Message").

437. Circular Number 1209 from Tokyo to Nanking, Shanghai, Canton, and Peking, June 6, 1941 (the "Second Tokyo Message").

438. Tokyo Circular Number 1437 of July 5, 1941, concerning message number 322 from Hong Kong, dispatched to Japanese offices in Nanking, Shanghai, Canton, and Peking (the "Third Tokyo Message").

439. *The Pearl Harbor Papers*, p. 19.

440. *Ibid.*, p. 19.

441. *Ibid.*, p. 21.

442. *Ibid.*

443. *Ibid.*

444. *Ibid.*, p. 24.

445. Van der Vat, p. 26.

446. *The Pearl Harbor Papers*, p. 33.

447. *Ibid.*

448. *Ibid.*, p. 34.

449. *Ibid.*

450. *Ibid.*

451. *Ibid.*, p. 35.

452. *Ibid.*, p. 36.

453. *Ibid.*

454. *Ibid.*

455. Memorandum from General Clayton Bissell to General Joseph Stilwell, June 26, 1942 ("Bissell Memorandum").

456. *Fighter*, p. 97

457. See Japanese Radio Circular Number 2176, October 14, 1941, from Tokyo to the "Net," regarding "Message from Hong Kong #500 on the 14th" (the "Fourth Tokyo Message").

458. *Ibid.*

459. *Ibid.*

460. *Fighter*, p. 104.

461. *Ibid.*

462. *American Aviation Daily*, July 15, 1941, p. 14, and the story captioned: "British Veto Conversion Suggestion; Hudsons Suddenly Moved Up to Canada—*American Aviation Daily* Queries British Quarters on Trans-Canada and Slow Bomber Movement Gets Quick Results."

463. *Ibid.*

464. *Maverick War*, p. 14.

465. *Ibid.*

466. Telegram from Dr. Lauchlin Currie of the United States Department of State to the American Embassy in Chungking, for Madame Chiang, July 23, 1941 (the "Currie Telegram").

467. *Fighter*, p. 105.

468. Christopher Shores and Brian Cull with Yasuho Izawa, *Bloody Shambles, Volume II—The Defense of Sumatra to the Fall of Rangoon*, London, Grub Street, 1993 (hereinafter, "*Bloody Shambles, Volume II*") at Appendix V.

469. *Bloody Shambles, Volume II*, at Appendix V.

470. *Fighter*, p. 113.

471. *Ibid.*, p. 112.

472. *Ibid.*, p. 113.

473. Ford, p. 83.

474. *Ibid.*

475. *Ibid.*

476. Jack Samson, *The Flying Tiger—The True Story of General Claire Chennault and the U.S. 14th Air Force in China*, Guilford: The Lyons Press, 1987 ("Samson").

477. Telegram from Lauchlin Currie to the American consulate in Rangoon, November 12, 1941 ("Currie's Larger Duties Telegram").

478. Memorandum for the President, November 17, 1941, from Lauchlin Currie, forwarding Churchill's message to Chiang Kai-shek, Franklin D. Roosevelt Library: President's Secretary's File, Diplomatic File, China (hereinafter "China Diplomatic File").

479. See Memorandum for the President from Dr. Lauchlin Currie, May 1, 1941, with attached statement to the press regarding publicity in connection with air mission to China (hereinafter the "Air Mission Press Release"), italics supplied, China Diplomatic File.

480. Cable to Lauchlin Currie from Madame Chiang Kai-shek, Chungking, July 22, 1941 (the "Madame Chiang Telegram"), China Diplomatic File.

481. *Ibid.*, italics supplied.

482. Memorandum for the President from Lauchlin Currie, regarding hiring of pilots for China, October 3, 1941, China Diplomatic File.

483. *Ibid.*

484. Memorandum for the President from Lauchlin Currie, regarding pilots for China, September 18, 1941 (the "Pilots for China Memorandum"), China Diplomatic File.

485. *Ibid.*

486. Roosevelt Secret Memorandum.

487. Memorandum for the President from Harry L. Hopkins, September 30, 1941 (the "Hopkins Memorandum"), China Diplomatic File.

488. *Ibid.*

489. Ford, pp. 93–94. Note: The Douglas Boston had an export designation of DB-7 and an Army Air Corps designation of A-20.

490. Ford, p. 94.

491. *Ibid.*

492. *Ibid.* Also see the documentary film *Call to Glory*, produced and directed by Joy Fahnley and William Loeffler, which aired on the Discovery Channel and won the Blue Ribbon at the American Film and Video Festival, 1991.

493. Ford, p. 94.

494. See "A Short-Term Aircraft Program for China," Joint Board Papers, Exhibit 32, Appendix 3.

495. Ford, p. 94.

496. Chennault's plans to have bombers flown to China from America are discussed more fully in Chapter 14 of this text.

497. Chennault's base in Burma was across the International Date Line. Accordingly, the date of the Japanese preemptive strike was December 8, 1941, in Southeast Asia.

498. Schultz, pp. 11–12.

499. Thompson, p. 375.

500. *Ibid.*

501. George C. Marshall Foundation; Hanson Baldwin Papers, Box 8, Folder 20.

502. *The United States News*, October 31, 1941, pp. 18–19.

503. *Ibid.*

504. *Ibid.*

505. *The New York Times*, November 18, 1941, p. 10.

506 *Ibid.*

507. *Ibid.*

508. *Time*, November 17, 1941.

509. *Ibid.*, pp. 32–33.

510. *Ibid.*

511. *Ibid.*

512. "The Problem of Defeating Japan—Review of the Situation," secret memorandum from British General Headquarters in the Far East, September 19, 1941, General Douglas MacArthur Foundation; Rec. Grp. 2, Box 1, MacArthur Personal Folder, "26 July 1941–12 September 1941."

513. Rear Admiral Edwin T. Layton, USN (Ret.), with Captain Roger Pineau, USNR (Ret.) and John Costello, *"And I Was There" Pearl Harbor and Midway—Breaking the Secrets*, New York: William Morrow and Company, Inc., 1985 ("Layton"), p. 273.

514. Draft telegram from British Prime Minister Churchill to Lord Halifax in Washington, December 7, 1941.

515. See the Second Appendix in Layton, Secret Memorandum for the Secretary and General Staff, November 21, 1941, regarding air offensive against Japan (the "Bombing Offensive Memorandum").

516. *Ibid.*

517. *Ibid.*

518. *Ibid.*

519. *Ibid.*

520. *Ibid.*

521. *Ibid.*

522. See the Third Appendix in Layton, a map of the Western Pacific depicting the radii of action of the B-17, the B-24, and the B-18 from various potential air bases in that region.

523. Lewis H. Brereton, *The Brereton Diaries*, New York: William Morrow and Company, 1946 (*"The Brereton Diaries"*), p. 22.

524. John Costello, *The Pacific War 1941–1945*, New York: Harper Collins Publishers, Inc., 1981 (*"Costello"*), p. 638.

525. *The Brereton Diaries*, p. 36.

526. William H. Bartsch, *December 8, 1941—MacArthur's Pearl Harbor*, College Station: Texas A&M University Press, 2003 ("Bartsch"), p. 243.

527. *Ibid.*, pp. 142–43.

528. *Ibid.*

529. *Ibid.*

530. *Ibid.*

531. Costello, p. vii.

532. Telegram from Lauchlin Currie to Madame Chiang, August 6, 1941 ("the Currie Hurricane Telegram").

533. *Ibid.*

534. Telegram from Lauchlin Currie to Madame Chiang, August 26, 1941 ("the Second Currie Hurricane Telegram").

535. Radiogram from General John Magruder to the Secretary of War of Chief of Staff, November 8, 1941, at 8:27 A.M. (the "First Magruder Radiogram").

536. *Ibid.*

537. *Ibid.*

538. *Ibid.*

539. *Ibid.*

540. *Ibid.*, p. 2.

541. Radiogram from General John Magruder from Chungking to AMMISCA, November 9, 1941, 3:33 P.M. (the "Second Magruder Radiogram").

542. Letter of Claire Chennault to Dr. T. V. Soong, September 4, 1941 (the "First Chennault-Soong Letter"), Hoover Institution Archives, Collection Title, Claire Chennault, Box 2, Folder I.D., Number 6.

543. Letter from Claire Chennault to Dr. T. V. Soong, September 23, 1941 (the "Second Chennault-Soong Letter"), Hoover Institution Archives, Collection Title, Claire Chennault, Box 2, Folder I.D., Number 26.

544. *Ibid.*

545. Telegram from Claire Chennault to Lauchlin Currie, October 22, 1941, Hoover Institution Archives, Collection Title, Claire Chennault, Box 2, Folder I.D., Number 26.

546. Letter of Lauchlin Currie to Claire Chennault, November 22, 1941 (the "Currie Supply Letter"), Hoover Institution Archives, Collection Title, Claire Chennault, Box Number 2, Folder I.D., Number 26.

547. *Ibid.*

548. *Ibid.*

549. Note on meeting between C.A., Org. 2, Org. 5, and Mr. W. Pawley, president, CAMCO, 20 November 1941 ("the British Special Air Unit Note"), Hoover Institution Archives, Claire Chennault Collection, Box 4, Folder I.D., Number 11.

550. *Ibid.*

551. *Ibid.*

552. *Ibid.*

553. *Ibid.*

554. Carl von Clausewitz, *On War*, Princeton: Princeton University Press, 1976, p. 198.

555. Van der Vat, p. 27.

556. See: Susan Wells, *December 7, 1941—Pearl Harbor, America's Darkest Day*, San Diego: Tehabi Books, 2001 ("America's Darkest Day"); Dan Van der Vat, *Pearl Harbor, The Day of Infamy: An Illustrated History*, Toronto: Basic Books, 2001 ("Van der Vat"); Gordon W. Prange, *At Dawn We Slept—The Untold Story of Pearl Harbor*, New York: Penguin Books, 1982 ("Prange"); Rear Admiral Edwin T. Layton, USN (Ret.), with Captain Roger Pineau, USNR (Ret.), and John Costello, *"And I Was There"—Pearl Harbor and Midway—Breaking the Secrets*, New York: Morrow and Company, Inc., 1985 ("And I Was There"); Craig Nelson, *The First Heroes—The Extraordinary Story of the Doolittle Raid—America's First World War II Victory*, New York: Penguin Group, 2002 ("Nelson"); Carl Smith, *Pearl Harbor: Day of Infamy*, Oxford: Osprey Publishing, 1999 ("Pearl Harbor"); and Bert Kinzey, *Pearl Harbor—Awakening the Sleeping Giant*, Peachtree City: Detail and Scale, Inc., 2001 ("Awakening").

557. Christopher Shores, Brian Cull, and Yasuho Izawa, *Bloody Shambles, Volume I—The Drift to War to the Fall of Singapore*. London: Grub Street, 1992, pp. 97–98 ("*Bloody Shambles, Volume I*").

558. *Ibid.*

559. *Ibid.*, pp. 108–27.

560. *The New Webster Encyclopedic Dictionary of the English Language*, Chicago: Consolidated Book Publishers, p. 800.

561. *Ibid.*, p. 33.

562. Address of President Franklin D. Roosevelt to a Joint Session of Congress, December 8, 1941.

563. Congressional Declaration of War on Japan, approved, December 8, 1941, 4:10 P.M., EST.

564. Congressional Declaration of War on Germany, approved December 11, 1941.

565. Berg, pp. 431–32.

566. Nelson, p. 111.

567. Robert L. Scott, *God is My Co-Pilot*, New York: Charles Scribner's Sons, 1943 ("Scott"), p. 50.

568. Nelson, pp. 119–30.

569. *Ibid.*, p. xii.

570. Schaller, p. 83.

571. See page 9 of the Strategic Estimate in the Joint Board Plan supplied by Dr. Currie to Colonel E. E. MacMorland, referenced in MacMorland's memorandum of May 12, 1941, to Colonel Orlando Ward, concerning Chinese aircraft requirements.

572. *American Aviation Daily* magazine, August 1, 1941, p. 18. Also see e-mail to author from Richard Dunn, December 18, 2005, at 10:00 P.M.

573. E-mail to author from Richard Dunn, November 14, 2005, at 11:01 A.M.

574. *Ibid.*

575. *Ibid.*

576. *Ibid.*

577. *Ibid.*

578. Romanus and Sunderland, p. 12.

579. Japanese Monograph Number 76, "Air Operations in the Chinese Area," (prepared under the auspices of the Chief of History, U.S. Army).

580. *Ibid.*

581. *Ibid.*

582. Romanus and Sunderland, pp. 12–13.

583. Richard Dunn's e-mail to author, October 9, 2005.

584. E-mail from aviation historian Bert Kinzey, July 16, 2004, indicating there had been 13 Y1B-17s, 1 B-17A, 39 B-17 Bs, 38 B-17 Cs, 42 B-17 Ds, and 102 B-17 Es delivered by the end of 1941.

585. Richard L. Dunn, "The Vultee P-66 in Chinese Service." October 5, 2005. http://www.warbirdforum.com/dunnp66.htm.

586. *Ibid.*

587. Richard L. Dunn, "Republic P-43 Lancer in China Service." October 5, 2005. http://www.warbirdforum.com/richdunn.htm.

588. Richard L. Dunn, "Chennault and the Flying Tigers—Heroes, But Were They Legal?" October 5, 2005, http://www.warbirdforum.com/legal.htm.

589. General Brereton, in *The Brereton Diaries*, p. 11, relates his departure from Washington was October 17, 1941, while William H. Bartsch in *December 8, 1941—MacArthur's Pearl Harbor*, relates that Brereton was briefed in Washington on October 18, 1941, and that General Brereton was confused about the date, since *The Brereton Diaries* were written by the general sometime after the events actually took place.

BIBLIOGRAPHY

American Aviation Daily. July 15, 1941, p. 14: "British Veto Conversion Suggestion; Hudsons Suddenly Moved Up to Canada—American Aviation Daily Queries British Quarters on Trans-Canada and Slow Bomber Movement Gets Quick Results" (story includes photograph of 155 Lockheed Hudsons at the Lockheed Air Terminal in Burbank, California).

———. August 1, 1941, p. 18: "1,000th Lockheed Hudson Received by Britain."

American Volunteer Group. "Group War Diary, 1941–1942." AFHRC 863.305.

———. "Official War Diary" (December 17, 1941–July 19, 1942), Hoover Institution, Sanford, California.

Baisden, Chuck. *Flying Tiger to Air Commando*. Atglen, PA: Schiffer Publishing, Ltd., 1999.

Bartsch, William H. *December 8, 1941—MacArthur's Pearl Harbor*. College Station: Texas A&M University Press, 2003.

Berg, A. Scott. *Lindbergh*. New York: G. P. Putnam's Sons, 1998.

Bergerud, Eric M. *Fire in the Sky—The Air War in the South Pacific*. Boulder: Westview Press, 2000.

Bishop, Lewis Sherman, and Shiela Irwin Bishop. *Escape From Hell—An AVG Flying Tiger's Journey*. Bloomington: Tiger Eye Press, 2004.

Bix, Herbert P. *Hirohito and the Making of Modern Japan*. New York: Harper Collins Publishers, Inc., 2000.

Bodie, Warren M. *The Lockheed P-38 Lightning*. Hayesville: Widewing Publications, 1991.

Bond, Charles, and Terry Anderson. *A Flying Tiger's Diary*. College Station: Texas A&M University Press, 1984.

Boyington, Gregory. *Baa, Baa, Black Sheep*. New York: Putnam, 1958.

Bradley, James. *Flyboys*. New York: Little, Brown and Company, 2003.

Brereton, Louis H. *The Brereton Diaries*. New York: William Morrow and Co., 1946.

Britain, Royal Air Force. "Pilot's Notes: Tomahawk I." Publication 2013A, n.d.

————. "Pilot's Notes for Fortress GR.IIA, GR.II & III, BII & BIII—Four Cyclone R.1820-65 or R.1820-97 Engines," Air Publication 2099B, C, D, E, & F (May 1944), superseding Pilot's Notes (December, 1942).

Byrd, Martha. *Chennault: Giving Wings to the Tigers*. Tuscaloosa: University of Alabama Press, 1987.

Call to Glory, videocassette. Directed by Joy Fahnley and William Loeffler (Discovery Channel, 1991).

Chang, Iris. *The Rape of Nanking—The Forgotten Holocaust of World War II*. New York: Penguin Books, 1998.

Chennault, Anna. *A Thousand Springs*. New York: Ericksson, 1962.

Chennault, Claire Lee. *Way of a Fighter*. New York: G. P. Putnam's Sons, 1949.

————. "The Role of Defensive Pursuit." Department of the Air Force, Air Force Historical Research Agency. Historical document number 248.282-4.

"Chennault is Sticking it Out in China." *Montgomery Advisor*, August 31, 1937.

Cohen, Stan. *East Wind Rain—A Pictorial History of the Pearl Harbor Attack*. Missoula: Pictorial Histories Publishing Company, 1981.

Collier, Basil. *Japanese Aircraft of World War II*. New York: Mayflower Books, 1979.

Costello, John. *The Pacific War, 1941–1945*. New York: Harper Collins Publishers, Inc., 1981.

Dower, John W. *Embracing Defeat—Japan in the Wake of World War II*. New York: W. W. Norton and Co., Inc., 1999.

Dunn, Richard L. "Chennault and the Flying Tigers—Heroes, But Were They Legal?" October 5, 2005. http://www.warbirdforum.com/legal.htm.

————. "Curtiss-Wright CW-21 Interceptor." October 5, 2005. http://www.warbirdforum.com/cw21.htm.

————. "Nakajima Type 1 Army (Ki43-1) Armament—A Reassessment." 2004.- October 6, 2005. http://www.warbirdforum.com/rdunn43.htm.

————. "Republic P-43 Lancer in Chinese Service." October 5, 2005. http://www.warbirdforum.com/richdunn.htm.

———. "The Vultee P-66 in Chinese Service." n.d. October 5, 2005. http://www.warbirdforum.com/dunnp66.htm.

———. E-mail to author. October 3, 2005.

———. E-mail to author. October 9, 2005.

———. E-mail to author. December 22, 2005, 7:37 P.M.

———. E-mail to author. December 23, 2005, 1:16 P.M.

———. E-mail to author. December 23, 2005, 3:43 P.M.

———. E-mail to author. December 23, 2005, 4:34 P.M.

———. E-mail to author. January 4, 2006, 10:21 P.M.

———. E-mail to author. January 9, 2006, 10:41 P.M.

———. E-mail to author. January 10, 2006, 9:07 A.M.

Feis, Herbert. *The Road to Pearl Harbor*. Princeton: Princeton University Press, 1950.

Fischer, Daniel. Telephone interview. October 25, 2004.

Ford, Daniel. *Flying Tigers—Claire Chennault and the American Volunteer Group*. Washington: Smithsonian Institution Press, 1991.

Franklin D. Roosevelt Library: Collections: FDR Library: Misc.: Joint Board 355.

———. Official File No. 4961, Pawley, William D.

———. PSF: Diplomatic Correspondence, China: 1941.

Franks, Norman. *Battle of Britain*. New York: Gallery Books, 1981.

Gallagher, O. *Action in the East*. New York: Doubleday, Doran and Co., Inc., 1942.

Gamble, Bruce. *Black Sheep One—The Life of Gregory "Pappy" Boyington*. Novato: Presidio Press, Inc., 2000.

Gannon, Michael. *Pearl Harbor Betrayed*. New York: Henry Holt and Company, 2001.

Goldstein, Donald M., and Catherine D. Dillon. *The Pearl Harbor Papers—Inside The Japanese Plans*. Dulles: Brassey's, 1993.

Greenlaw, Olga. *The Lady and the Tigers*. New York: Dutton, 1943.

Groom, Winston. *1942—The Year that Tried Men's Souls*. New York: Atlantic Monthly Press, 2005.

Gunston, Bill. *The Illustrated Directory of Fighting Aircraft of World War II*. London: Salamander Books, Ltd., 1988.

Hardesty, Von. *Lindbergh—Flight's Enigmatic Hero*. San Diego: Tehabi Books, Inc., 2002.

Hearn, Chester G. *The Illustrated Directory of the United States Navy*. London: Salamander Books, Ltd., 2003.

Hill, David Lee ("Tex"). Telephone interview. January 7, 2003.

Howard, James. *Roar of the Tiger*. New York: Orion Books, 1991.

Hoyt, Edwin P. *Japan's War—The Great Pacific Conflict*. New York: Cooper Square Press, 2001.

Japanese Radio Circular No. 1139, May 29, 1941, from Tokyo to Japanese offices in Nanking, Shanghai, and Canton, regarding "Message from Hong Kong #267 on the 28th," translated June 3, 1941.

Japanese Radio Circular No. 1209, June 6, 1941, from Tokyo to Japanese offices in Nanking, Shanghai, and Canton, regarding "Message from Hong Kong #267," translated July 17, 1941.

Japanese Radio Circular No. 1437, July 5, 1941, from Tokyo to Japanese offices in Nanking, Shanghai, and Canton, regarding "Message from Hong Kong #322," translated July 15, 1941.

Japanese Radio Circular No. 2176, October 15, 1941, from Tokyo to "Net" regarding "Message from Hong Kong #500," translated October 18, 1941.

Kaplan, Philip, and Richard Collier. *The Few—Summer 1940, The Battle of Britain*. London: Orion Publishing Group, 2002.

Keegan, John. *Atlas of the Second World War*. Ann Arbor: Borders Press, 2003.

Kimmel, Admiral Husband E. Letter to Hon. Clarence Cannon. June 3, 1958.

———. Letter to Hon. Clarence Cannon. July 7, 1958.

Kinzey, Bert. E-mail to author. April 4, 2004.

———. E-mail to author. July 16, 2004.

———. "P-40: Warhawk in Detail." Vol. 61. Peachtree City: Detail and Scale, Inc., 1999.

———. *Pearl Harbor—Awakening the Sleeping Giant*. Peachtree City: Detail and Scale, Inc., 2001.

Klinkowitz, Jerome. *With the Tigers over China, 1941–1942.* Lexington: University Press of Kentucky, 1999.

Krock, Arthur. "Philippines as a Fortress—New Air Power Gives Islands Offensive Strength, Changing Strategy in the Pacific." *The New York Times.* November 18, 1941.

Laureau, Patrick. *Condor: The Luftwaffe in Spain, 1936–1939.* East Yorkshire: Hikoki Publications, Ltd., 2000.

Layton, Edwin T., with Roger Pineau and John Costello. *"And I Was There"—Pearl Harbor and Midway—Breaking the Secrets.* New York: Morrow and Co., Inc., 1985.

Mikesh, Robert C. *Japanese Aircraft Code Names and Designations.* Atglen, PA: Schiffer Publishing Ltd., 1993.

Mitchell, William. *Winged Defense.* New York: G. P. Putnam's Sons, 1925.

Morgenthau, Henry, Jr. Diary 342A, China: Bombers, December 3–22, 1940.

Morris, James M. *America's Armed Forces—A History.* Englewood Cliffs: Prentice Hall, Inc., 1991.

Mosley, Leonard. *The Battle of Britain.* Morristown: Time-Life Books, Inc., 1977.

Nelson, Craig. *The First Heroes—The Extraordinary Story of the Doolittle Raid—America's First World War II Victory.* New York: Penguin Books, 2003.

Olson, Lynne, and Stanley Cloud. *A Question of Honor: The Kosciuszko Squadron—Forgotten Heroes of World War II.* New York: Alfred A. Knopf, 2003.

Olynyk, Frank. *Stars and Bars—A Tribute to the American Fighter Ace, 1920–1973.* London: Grub Street, 1995.

Ormsby, Robert, Jr. Telephone interview. July 16, 2004.

Persico, Joseph E. *Roosevelt's Secret War—FDR and World War II Espionage.* New York: Random House, 2001.

Prange, Gordon W. *At Dawn We Slept—The Untold Story of Pearl Harbor.* New York: Penguin Books, 1982.

Prange, Gordon W., Donald M. Goldstein, and Katherine V. Dillon. *God's Samurai: Lead Pilot at Pearl Harbor.* Washington: Brassey's, 1990.

Ray, John. *The Battle of Britain.* London: Cassell & Co., 1994.

Real Flying Tigers, The, videocassette. (The History Channel, 1996).

Robertson, Linda R. *The Dream of Civilized Warfare—World War I Flying Aces and the American Imagination*. Minneapolis: University of Minnesota Press, 2003.

Romanus, Charles F., and Riley Sunderland. *China-Burma-India Theater: Stilwell's Mission to China (United States Army in World War II)*. Washington, D.C.: Office of the Chief of Military History, Department of the Army, 1953.

Roosevelt, Franklin D. Congressional Address. Washington, D.C., September 21, 1939.

———. Address. Joint Congressional Session. Congress, Washington, D.C., December 8, 1941.

Ross, Walters. *The Last Hero: Charles A. Lindbergh*. New York: Harper & Row, 1964.

Samson, Jack. *The Flying Tiger—The True Story of General Claire Chennault and the U.S. 14th Air Force in China*. Guilford: The Lyons Press, 1987.

Schaffer, Ronald. *Wings of Judgment—American Bombing in World War Two*. New York: Oxford University Press, 1985.

Schaller, Michael. *The U.S. Crusade in China 1938–1945*. New York: Columbia University Press, 1979.

Schom, Alan. *The Eagle and the Rising Sun*. New York: W. W. Norton & Co., 2004.

Schultz, Duane. *The Maverick War: Chennault and the Flying Tigers*. New York: St. Martin's Press, 1987.

Scott, Robert L. *God is My Co-Pilot*. New York: Charles Scribner's Sons, 1943.

———. *Flying Tiger*. Garden City: Doubleday, 1959.

Seagrave, Gordon S. *Burma Surgeon*. New York: W. W. Norton & Company, Inc., 1943.

Shores, Christopher, Brian Cull, and Yasuho Izawa. *Bloody Shambles, Vol. I—The Drift to War to the Fall of Singapore*. London: Grub Street, 1992.

———. *Bloody Shambles, Vol. II—The Defense of Sumatra to the Fall of Burma*. London: Grub Street, 1993.

Simrall, Rosemary Chennault. Telephone interview. June 22, 2004.

Smith, Carl. *Pearl Harbor: Day of Infamy*. Oxford: Osprey Publishing, 1999.

Smith, Felix. *China Pilot—Flying for Chennault during the Cold War*. Washington: Smithsonian Institution Press, 1995.

Smith, R. T. *Tale of a Tiger*. Van Nuys: Tiger Originals, 1986.

Smith, Robert M. *With Chennault in China—A Flying Tiger's Diary*. Atglen, PA: Schiffer Military History, 1997.

Somerville, Robert, ed. *Century of Flight*. Richmond: Time-Life Books, 1999.

Stinnett, Robert B. *Day of Deceit—The Truth about FDR and Pearl Harbor*. New York:
Simon & Schuster, Inc., 2000.

Sugiyama, Katsumi. Monograph. *Fundamental Issues Underlying U.S.–Japan Alliance*.

Thompson, Robert Smith. *A Time for War: Franklin D. Roosevelt and the Path to Pearl
Harbor*. New York: Prentice Hall, 1991.

Toland, John. *The Flying Tigers*. New York: Random House, 1963.

Townsend, Peter. *Duel of Eagles*. Edison: Castle Books, 2003.

Tuchman, Barbara. *Stilwell and the American Experience in China*. New York: McMillan, 1970.

United States Army Air Forces. "Aircraft Flight Manual for Lockheed Hudson." n.d.

———. "Distribution of Air Material to the Allies, 1939–1944: Controls, Procedures,
and Policies," AFHRC (AAFRH-6).

———. "Erection and Maintenance Instructions for Army Model P-40E-1, British
Model Kittyhawk IA." Technical Order No. 01-25-CJ-2. Detroit: Evans-Winter-Hobb,
Inc., 1942.

———. "History of the Chinese Air Force," May 16, 1946, Project No. 2863.

———. "Hydraulic and Fuselage Tank Service Instructions, P-40 Series Airplanes."
Technical Order No. 01-25C02. Evansville: Keller-Crescent Company, n.d.

———. Memorandum from General Clayton Bissell, USAAF, to General Joseph
Stilwell, July 26, 1942.

———. "Parts Catalogue for Army Models P-40M and P-40N, British Models Kittyhawk III and IV Airplanes." AN-01-25C-4. Evansville: Keller-Crescent Company,
July 20, 1944.

———. "Pilot's Manual for Curtiss P-40 Warhawk." ISBN: 0-87994-018-2. Appel-
ton: Aviation Publications, n.d.

———. Secret Radiogram to War Department Message Center from General Magruder, November 9, 1941, at 3:33 P.M.

———. Secret Telegram to Secretary of War Henry Stimson and Chief of Staff of
George C. Marshall from General Magruder, November 8, 1941.

———. Status of Planes Allotted to China. April 1, 1942. AFHRC.

———. *Ways of the War Hawk*, videocassette. U.S. Army Air Force Training Film. Historic Aviation, n.d.

United States Congress. *Congressional Declaration of War on Japan*. December 8, 1941.

———. *Congressional Declaration of War on Germany*. December 11, 1941.

United States Department of State. Letter from the Division of Far Eastern Affairs to Secretary Cordell Hull with attached Oral Statement to Dr. T. V. Soong, December 3, 1940.

———. Telegram from Dr. Lauchlin Currie to Madame Chiang Kai-shek, July 23, 1941.

———. Telegram from Dr. Lauchlin Currie to Madame Chiang Kai-shek, August 6, 1941.

———. Telegram from Dr. Lauchlin Currie to Madame Chiang Kai-shek, August 26, 1941.

United States Navy. "American Volunteer Group Papers." Record Group 4.9, Emil Buehler Naval Aviation Library. National Museum of Naval Aviation. Accession Number 1997.269.

———. Naval Attaché, Tokyo, Report No. 161-40, September 30, 1940, Japan Cities and Towns—Coast Defenses—Air Defenses.

———. Naval Attaché, Tokyo, Report No. 180-40, October 30, 1940, Japanese Economic Activities in the South Seas Area.

———. Naval Attaché, Tokyo, Report No. 18-41, February 5, 1941, Japan Cities and Towns—Coast Defenses—Air Defenses

———. Naval Attaché and Naval Attaché for Air, Chungking, Major J. M. McHugh, USMC, strictly confidential telegram to U.S. State Department, February 10, 1941.

———. Naval Attaché and Naval Attaché for Air, Chungking, Major J. M. McHugh, USMC, "Conference of Claggett Air Mission with the Generalissimo," June 9, 1941.

———. Assistant Naval Attaché and Naval Attaché for Air, Chungking, Major F. J. Mc-Quillen, Chungking, USMC, "Present Status of the Chinese Air Force," June, 1941.

———. Naval Attaché and Naval Attaché for Air, Chungking, Major J. M. McHugh, USMC, "Conference of the Claggett Air Mission with the Generalissimo," June 10, 1941.

————. Kesaris, Paul. "OSS/State Department Intelligence and Research Reports." University Publications of America, Inc., Washington, 1977.

————. Nimitz Library, United States Naval Academy, Abstract N-2-83, Admiral Takahashi's Views on 1) Inevitable Defeat of Britain, 2) Mounting American-Japanese Friction, March 12, 1941.

————. Abstract N-2-84, Danger of War, March 12, 1941.

————. Abstract N-2-85, Possibility of Air Raids, March 12, 1941.

————. Abstract, American Reconstruction of Chinese Air Force, July, 1941.

————. Abstract, American-Japanese Relations, July, 1941.

————. Abstract, Extraordinary Session of Diet, July, 1941.

————. Abstract, Occupation of Indochina, July, 1941.

————. Abstract, Failure of Negotiations with Netherlands East Indies, July, 1941.

————. Abstract, Japanese Fleet Maneuvers and Preparations, July, 1941.

————. Abstract, Calling Up the Reserves, July, 1941.

United States News, The, "Bomber Lanes to Japan—Flying Time from Strategic Points." October 31, 1941: 18–19.

Van der Vat, Dan. *Pearl Harbor, The Day of Infamy: An Illustrated History*. Toronto: Basic Books, 2001.

Webster, Donovan. *The Burma Road*. New York: Farrar, Straus and Giroux, 2003.

Wells, Susan. *December 7, 1941—Pearl Harbor, America's Darkest Day*. San Diego: Tehibi Books, 2001.

White, Theodore H., and Annalee Jacoby. *Thunder Out of China*. New York: William Sloane Associates, Inc., 1946.

Whitney, Daniel. *Vee's for Victory!: The Story of the Allison V-1710 Aircraft Engine, 1929–1948*. Atglen, PA: Schiffer Military History, 1998.

Willmott, H. P. *Zero A6M*. London: Bison Books, Ltd., 1980.

PERMISSIONS

INDEX